The Advance on Caen

The Advance on Caen

From Sword Beach towards the City, 6–9 June 1944

Tim Saunders

Pen & Sword
MILITARY

First published in Great Britain in 2025 by
PEN & SWORD MILITARY
an imprint of Pen & Sword Books Ltd
Yorkshire – Philadelphia

ISBN 978-1-03610-443-6

A CIP catalogue record for this book is available from the British Library.

Typeset by Concept, Huddersfield, West Yorkshire, HD4 5JL.
Printed and bound in England by CPI Group (UK) Ltd, Croydon, CR0 4YY.

MIX
Paper | Supporting responsible forestry
FSC www.fsc.org
FSC® C013604

The Publisher's authorised representative in the EU for product safety is Authorised Rep Compliance Ltd, Ground Floor, 71 Lower Baggot Street, Dublin D02 P593, Ireland – www.arccompliance.com

For a complete list of Pen & Sword titles please contact
PEN & SWORD BOOKS LTD
47 Church Street, Barnsley, South Yorkshire, S70 2AS, England
E-mail: enquiries@pen-and-sword.co.uk
Website: www.pen-and-sword.co.uk
or
PEN & SWORD BOOKS
1950 Lawrence Rd, Havertown, PA 19083, USA
E-mail: uspen-and-sword@casematepublishers.com
Website: www.penandswordbooks.com

Contents

Acknowledgements

As usual, there is a long list of those who have helped me with this project, starting with Richard Hone and his encyclopaedic knowledge of the Second World War and the German Army, and his library of regimental histories. As ever, he generously came to my aid with information and clarification when needed. I am also most grateful for the assistance provided by the Lessons Exploitation Cell at the Land Warfare Centre and the staff of the Government Reading Room at the National Archives for their help in making documents available beyond the usual war diaries. Originally used for battlefield studies, insights from their pages have now found their way into this book.

I must extend my thanks to the museums of the regiments that fought with the 3rd Division. They are, of course, valued custodians of their battalions' wartime history. The time and help provided by their staff in offering opinions, information and photographs are hereby gratefully acknowledged. Finally, I would like to thank the members of various forums and the Guild of Battlefield Guides with whom discussion has done much to shape my ideas about the battles for Caen.

In quoting those who fought in the battles for Caen, I have followed my usual practice of using the rank that officers and soldiers held at the time of the fighting. Many, of course, were promoted later in the campaign or during post-war service. Although there are plenty of references and notes, to keep them to a reasonable number I have avoided repetition where the source is obvious.

Finally, I would like to thank Pen & Sword for allowing me to increase the scope of this project by splitting this book into two. This first volume covers D Day and the first battles for Caen; the second will focus on the fighting during June 1944 and the final fall of the city during Operation CHARNWOOD.

Introduction

This book covers the period that Brigadier Belchem, General Montgomery's senior Special Plans officer, described as 'the first phase of the invasion', but as far as the 3rd Infantry Division was concerned it was the first of their battles for Caen. The opening moves to capture the city begin, of course, with the division's assault landing on SWORD Beach, but that landing in the context of the battles for Caen was simply an 'enabling activity'. Therefore, the focus of the chapters that cover the opening phase of the invasion is tightly drawn on the fortunes of the units committed to the advance to the city and the reasons why they did not succeed on D Day. Similarly, the failure of the attacks over the following three days is constrained. The boundary to the west that I drew for myself is inclusive of Carpiquet, the village of Cambes and the farm complex of Galmanche. The fighting there against the leading regiment of the 12th *Hitlerjugend* Panzer Division is germane to the Germans' containment of I Corps' drive south.

Of the result of 3rd Division's D Day operations, a War Office report had this to say:

> The Division had failed to achieve the primary task which it was set, the capture of Caen. However, the wording of I Corps' order for the assault implies that this objective, though eminently desirable, could only be achieved under most favourable circumstances by 'bouncing' an enemy thoroughly unprepared, surprised and disorganised. Failure to capture it on D Day was not only anticipated but it was foreseen that thereafter probably a considerable period of build-up would be essential before a highly organised major operation could be launched on this key communication centre which the enemy would do everything possible to hold.[1]

This verdict has been regularly challenged since the end of the war, particularly by those who looked no further than the various operation orders and the date that Caen was eventually captured. This book seeks to discover whether the above 1947 judgement is valid. However, with expectations of early capture, written orders and the reality of enemy forces all being at variance, this book cannot be definitive.

The controversy over the failure to capture Caen on D Day was first ignited by Ingersoll's now largely discredited book *Top Secret*,[2] published immediately after the war, in which he was highly critical of virtually every Allied commander other than the two he served under as a junior staff officer. When Ingersoll's finger of blame was pointed at the 3rd Division, its brigades and units promptly resorted to counter-accusations of their own. The exchanges of blame based on slowness and mishandling of the battle were and still are numerous. Consequently, this book takes an objective view of what happened on the battlefields around Caen and why. Surprisingly often in this process, taking a wider view of neighbouring actions resolves most of the narrowly defined and hotly debated issues.

Following D Day and its immediate aftermath, with I Corps halted, the Second Army's main effort transferred to the west, where XXX Corps attempted to fight their way south towards Villers Bocage. The front north of Caen was, however, seldom quiet, and operations for the remainder of June into July will be the subject of a further volume.

Tim Saunders MBE
Warminster, 2025

Tim Saunders is an accredited member of the Guild of Battlefield Guides

Glossary of Terms

All wars produce their own lexicon. Therefore, it is no surprise that abbreviations abound in war diaries and accounts of the NWE (North-West Europe) campaign. The main ones are listed here, but in an army where combat training took priority over staff work, many non-standard and local variations were used. The following list will help:

2iC	Second in Command
A1 Echelon	Immediate replenishment of combat supplies
A2 Echelon	Further back planned replenishment of combat supplies
AA	Anti-aircraft
ACV	Armoured Command Vehicle
ADC	Aide de Camp
Adjt	Adjutant, unit commanding officer's staff officer
Admin	Administration
Adv	Advance
AGRA	Army Group Royal Artillery, a corps' artillery 'division', consisting of heavy, medium and field regiments plus anti-aircraft guns
AFV	Armoured Fighting Vehicle
Amn	Ammunition
AOP	Air/Armoured Observation Post
AP	Armour-piercing or anti-personnel
APCBC	Armour-piercing ballistic-capped
APC	Armoured Personnel Carrier
APDS	Armour Piercing Discarding Sabot, 6- and 17-pounder anti-tank ammunition
APIS	Air Photo Interpretation Section
Arty	Artillery
Assy Area	Assembly Area, where troops regroup (e.g., tanks, infantry and gunners) for an operation prior to moving to the FUP
Aslt	Assault
A/Tk	(+ variants) Anti-tank
ARV	Armoured Recovery Vehicle
AVRE	Armoured Vehicle Royal Engineer
Axis	The central direction of advance
BC	Battery Commander

B Echelon	The entry point of combat supplies into a unit's logistic infrastructure
BCR	Battle Casualty Replacement
Bde	Brigade (British) equivalent to a US or German regiment
BK	Battery Captain
BMA	Beach maintenance Area (logistic dumps)
Bn	Battalion
Br	Bridge
Bty	Battery
Cas	Casualties
Casevac	Casualty evacuation
CCP	Casualty Clearing Post
CCS	Casualty Clearing Station
Cdn	Canadian
Centre Line	Axis of Advance
C in C	Commander-in-Chief
Civ	Civilian
CL	Centre Line or axis of advance
CO	Commanding Officer*
Co-ax	Coaxial machine gun mounted in tanks alongside the main armament
Coln	Column
Conc	Concentrate, also Conc Area, where units assigned to an operation gather before moving forward to the assy area
Comd	Command
Coord	Coordinate
Coy	Company
CP	Command Post
Cpl	Corporal
CPO	Command Post Officer (artillery)
CS	Close Support
CSM	Company Sergeant Major
D Day	The day on which an operation begins
Dem	Demolition
Dets	Detachments
DF	Defensive fire, pre-planned artillery, mortar or medium machine gun target areas on likely enemy approaches, etc.
DGNS	Dragons
Div	Division
DP	Distribution Point, logistic
DR	Dispatch rider, also 'Don R' or 'Don Romeo'

*Today the distinction between CO and OC is well-defined, with the former commanding a unit such as a battalion and the latter a sub-unit such as a company, but in many British Second World War memoirs and documents they are transposed or used inconsistently.

DZ	Drop Zone
Ech	Echelon, normally referring to fighting echelon and logistic echelons of a unit
Fmn	Formation, i.e. brigade, division, etc.
En	Enemy
Enfilade	Fire from a flank
Fd Regt	Field Regiment RA
FMC	Field Maintenance Centre
FOB	Forward Officer Bombardment (naval gunfire)
FOO	Forward Observation Officer (artillery)
FUP	Forming Up Place
Fwd	Forward
Gd	Guard, typically advanced, flank or rear guard
GOC	General Officer Commanding
GPO	Gun Position Officer
Gr	Grenadier
H Hour	The hour (time) at which an operation starts
HE	High Explosive
Hy	Heavy
Inf	Infantry
Int	Intelligence
I Sec	Intelligence Section
JNCO	Junior Non-Commissioned Officer
KIA	Killed in action
KO	Knocked out
LAA	Light Anti-Aircraft
LAD	Light Aid Detachment
LCA	Landing Craft Assault
L Cpl	Lance Corporal
LCT	Landing Craft Tank
Ldr	Leader
Line	Field telephone wire
LZ	Landing Zone
MG	Machine Gun
MIA	Missing in Action
MMG	Medium Machine Gun
MSR	Main Supply Route
O Group	Orders group, assembly of subordinate commanders for the issue of orders
OC	Officer Commanding
OP	Observation Post
P Hour	Time of a parachute drop
PIAT	Projector Infantry Anti-Tank
Pl	Platoon

Posn	Position
Pt	Point
Pte	Private (rank)
PW	Prisoner of War
Pz	Panzer
QM	Quartermaster
RAP	Regimental Aid Post
Rd	Road
Regt *or* Rgt	Regiment
REME	Royal Electrical and Mechanical Engineers
RHA	Royal Horse Artillery
RHU	Reinforcement Holding Unit
RMO	Regimental Medical Officer
RPM	Rounds per minute
RSM	Regimental Sergeant Major
RSO	Regimental Signals Officer
RV	Rendezvous point
SA	Small Arms
SB	Stretcher bearer
Sec *or* Sect	Section
Shelldrake	Appointment title for artillery
Shellrep	Report of enemy shelling, used to locate enemy batteries
Sgt	Sergeant
Sitrep	Situation Report
Sjt	Serjeant, the old form of Sergeant still used by some regiments
SL	Start Line
Smk	Smoke
SNCO	Senior Non-Commissioned Officer
SP	Self-Propelled or support
Sta	Station
Stand-to	'Stand to arms', fully man defensive positions. Also routine at dawn and dusk
Sub-unit	Company-, squadron- or battery-sized unit
Sunray	Commander of any sized unit or formation
Sups	Supplies
Sqn	Squadron
Svy	Survey
Tac	Tactical, usually used in context of a tactical headquarters
Tac/R	Tactical reconnaissance by aircraft
Target	All guns within range when an '*xxxxx* target' was called: Mike (regiment), Uncle (division), Victor (corps), York (army)
Tgt	Target
Tk	Tank
Tp	Troop

Tpt	Transport
Unit	An infantry battalion or a British artillery or armoured regiment
Wef	With effect
WIA	Wounded in Action
X Rds	Crossroads
Yd(s)	Yards
Yeo	Yeomanry

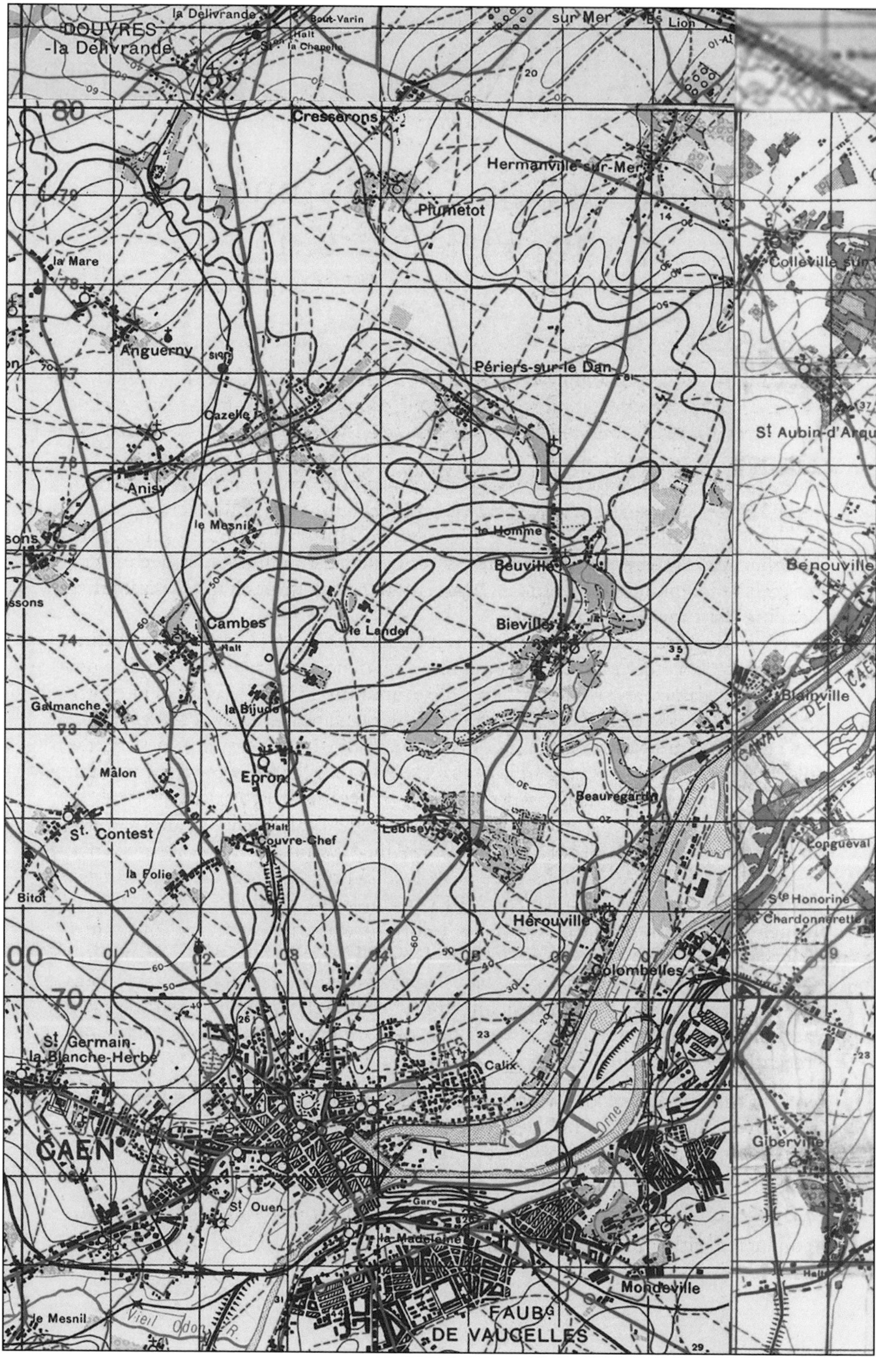
DOUVRES
-la Délivrande
la Delivrande
Bout-Varin
la Chapelle
Sur Mer
Lion
Cresserons
Hermanville-sur-Mer
Plumetot
Colleville sur
la Mare
Anguerny
Périers-sur-le Dan
St Aubin-d'Arqu
Cazelle
Anisy
le Mesnil
le Homme
Beuville
Bénouville
Cambes
le Landel
Bieville
Galmanche
la Bijude
Blainville
CANAL DE CAEN
Mâlon
Epron
Beauregard
St. Contest
Couvre-Chef
Lebisey
Longueval
la Folie
Bitot
Ste Honorine
le Chardonnerette
Hérouville
Colombelles
St Germain-
la Blanche-Herbe
Calix
Orne
CAEN
Giberville
St Ouen
Gare
la Madeleine
Mondeville
le Mesnil
Vieil Odon R.
FAUBG
DE VAUCELLES

Chapter One

Caen and the Development of the 'Master Plan'

It could be said that planning for the North-West European Campaign began on 4 June 1940, when Combined Operations Command was formed by Prime Minister Winston Churchill, with one of its tasks being to 'study the problems associated with a return to Europe'. This was at a time when such a return seemed extremely unlikely, and much of its work appeared to be entirely theoretical. Nonetheless, maps, charts and postcards, for example, were collected to form the basis of a detailed analysis of the northern coastline of mainland Europe. In another area of the work, the Royal Navy designed and built or converted a series of craft for amphibious operations, from landing ships through to the diminutive landing craft for assault infantry.

With the American entry into the war in late 1941, 1942 saw the theoretical starting to become actual, with practical experience of large-scale amphibious operations gained as a result of the Anglo-American TORCH landings in North Africa. In January 1943 the Allies met at the Casablanca Conference (SYMBOL) to chart the future course of the war. Churchill got his way in opening the Mediterranean and knocking Italy out of the Axis, but his feet were firmly held to the fire over a commitment to the invasion of North-West Europe in 1944.

To start the planning process, Lieutenant General Sir Frederick Morgan was promptly appointed Chief of Staff Supreme Allied Commander (Designate), soon rendered as 'COSSAC'. He had been involved in preparing various operations in the Mediterranean as commander of I Corps under General Eisenhower, during which he had impressed Ike with his ability to work alongside the Americans. Morgan established his headquarters at Norfolk House in St James's Square. In a meeting with Churchill's chief of staff General Ismay in the Cabinet War Rooms on his appointment, Morgan was introduced to 'the mountain of paper that had accumulated over the years', the work of Combined Operations and more recently the Combined Chiefs of Staff. He later wrote:

> I was made free of this vast bibliography and invited to produce for the British Chiefs of Staff my idea for a plan of what should be done next. The request to me was rounded off with the typical phrase: 'No hurry, old boy, tomorrow will do'.[1]

Meanwhile, for the build-up of US forces in the UK (Operation BOLERO) to be conducted without unacceptable losses, the Allied navies had to win the Battle of

Lieutenant General Sir Fredrick Morgan.

the Atlantic. At the time the decision was made to invade North-West Europe, the naval situation did not look favourable, with German U-boats having sunk 240,000 tons of shipping over the winter of 1942/43. However, technical developments in submarine hunting and killing, along with longer-range aircraft bridging the Mid-Atlantic Gap, and above all the code-breakers at Bletchley Park cracking the four-rotor Kriegsmarine Enigma, changed the situation. U-boats and their supply ships were hunted down, and in 'Black May' 1943 forty-nine were sunk, with total German losses in that year being 258 submarines. Without delivering this essential victory over the U-boat wolf packs in the Atlantic, there could have been no BOLERO and no D Day.

Orders for another essential shaping operation were issued in the POINT-BLANK directive of July 1943, which instructed RAF Bomber Command and the Eighth US Air Force to prioritize the targeting of German aircraft production. As a result, for instance, costly deep penetration raids were mounted by US bombers against the ball bearing factories at Schweinfurt and the Messerschmitt fighter assembly plants around Regensburg in Bavaria. These raids forced the Germans to commit resources to the defence of the Reich and brought the Luftwaffe into battle, where they suffered irreplaceably heavy losses, so much so that the prerequisite of Allied air supremacy over northern France was more than met during the spring of 1944. This, as we will see, proved to be an important factor in forming Field Marshal Montgomery's 'Master Plan' for 21st Army Group's campaign in Normandy and the battles for Caen.

The COSSAC Framework

The directive given to General Morgan by the Combined Chiefs of Staff was to produce an outline plan that would enable the Allies

> to mount and carry out an operation, with forces and equipment established in the United Kingdom and with target date 1 May 1944, to secure a lodgement on the Continent from which further offensive operations could be developed. The lodgement area must contain sufficient port facilities to maintain a force of some twenty-six to thirty divisions and enable that force to be augmented by follow-up shipments from the United States or elsewhere of additional divisions and supporting units at the rate of three to five divisions per month.

The choice of landing area on the northern coast of France and the Low Countries was in practice restricted by the range of single-seater fighter and fighter-bomber aircraft operating from airfields in the UK. Most of the options had merits that appealed to one or more of the services, but they also presented problems, normally as a result of waterways or the terrain. Consequently, recommending a location for the invasion was General Morgan's first task, with the short sea route across from Dover being the obvious candidate. However, the COSSAC planners argued:

> The Pas de Calais has many obvious advantages such as that good air support and quick turn-around for our shipping can be achieved. On the other hand, it is a focal point of the enemy fighters disposed for defence and the maximum air activity can be brought to bear over this area with the

The effective range of British fighter cover. The landing options considered were for a variety of reasons reduced to Lower Normandy.

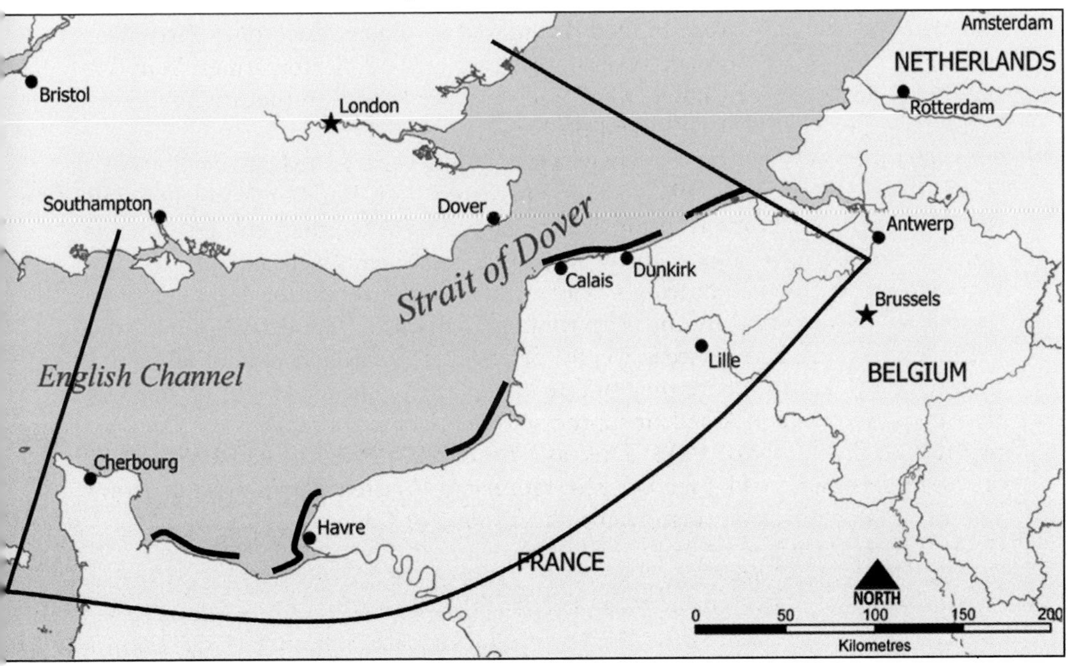

> minimum movement of his Air Forces. Moreover, the Pas de Calais is the most strongly defended area of the whole French coast . . . Further, this area does not offer good opportunities for expansion. It would be necessary to develop the bridgehead to include either the Belgian ports as far as Antwerp, or the Channel ports westward to include Le Havre and Rouen.[2]

It was also an area that German commanders from Hitler downwards regarded as the most obvious route to Germany's military industrial heartland, the Ruhr. Consequently, defences were being rapidly built up in the Pas de Calais, and it was soon to be viewed by COSSAC as being far too heavily defended to contemplate. The Anglo-American planning staff eventually selected Lower Normandy, noting that at the time:

> The Caen sector is weakly held; the defences are relatively light and the beaches are of high capacity and sheltered from the prevailing winds. Inland the terrain is suitable for airfield development and for the consolidation of the initial bridgehead; and much of it is unfavourable for counter-attacks by panzer divisions. Maximum enemy air opposition can only be brought to bear at the expense of the air defence screen covering the approaches to Germany; and the limited number of enemy airfields within range of the Caen area facilitates the local neutralisation of the German fighter force. The sector suffers from the disadvantage that considerable efforts will be required to provide adequate air support for our assault forces and sometime must elapse before the capture of a major port.[3]

A pre-war postcard collected by Combined Ops, showing the cleft at Berneval. This was used when briefing commandos during the Dieppe Raid of August 1942.

As General Morgan recalled, getting the selection of Lower Normandy agreed by OVERLORD's largely British critics was by no means straightforward.

> One by one the points on which the British Chiefs of Staff required more information were amplified, and those on which their criticism centred were discussed and ironed out. One gathered that a state of affairs was eventually reached at which they felt themselves prepared to take the next step. They were not demonstratively enthusiastic.[4]

In August 1943 the framework and the reasons for the selection of Lower Normandy were presented to the Allied Chiefs of Staff and political leadership at the First Quebec Conference (QUADRANT). The COSSAC presenters noted that again, 'Our plans were examined from every conceivable and subject to the minutest scrutiny' before being approved.

The work so far, as Morgan stressed, was very much a skeleton for development into an operational plan by those who would command the invasion, but one of the intractable issues was the envisaged scale. The resources that the COSSAC staff were allocated to work with were slim. General Morgan wrote: 'All doubts and there were many, stemmed from the meagre resources allotted to us of landing craft and shipping.' This led to an initial assault force that amounted to just three infantry divisions and a pair of small armoured brigades, plus an airborne division and commandos. This was all that the Combined Chiefs of Staff thought would be available and, equally importantly, were the resources that those with vested single-service interest were willing to commit to a project that some had little faith in. The overall lack of resources was a major factor in the decision to launch the assault on the less well defended Normandy coast, as stated by Morgan in a memorandum to the British chiefs of staff in London:

> I have come to the conclusion that, in view of the limitation in resources imposed by my directive, we may be assured of a reasonable chance of success on 1st May 1944, only if we concentrate our efforts on an assault across the Norman beaches about Bayeux.

Only once attention had switched from the Mediterranean and Italy was the issue of a 25 per cent uplift in size proposed by Churchill at Quebec and properly confronted by the politicians.

Once the location of the invasion had been settled, General Morgan considered 'Caen to be the key' to the battle that was to be fought in Normandy:

> The first object of the foremost troops on landing must be to capture and prepare to defend an area enclosed by the rough line from Grandcamp to Bayeux to Caen and so back to the sea about Ouistreham. Above and beyond everything it was evident from the first moment that the objective of supreme importance was the town of Caen with its command of communications.

As such, the COSSAC plan called for the city and the Caen Canal/River Orne to be captured by the airborne division at the opening of the invasion. Given the

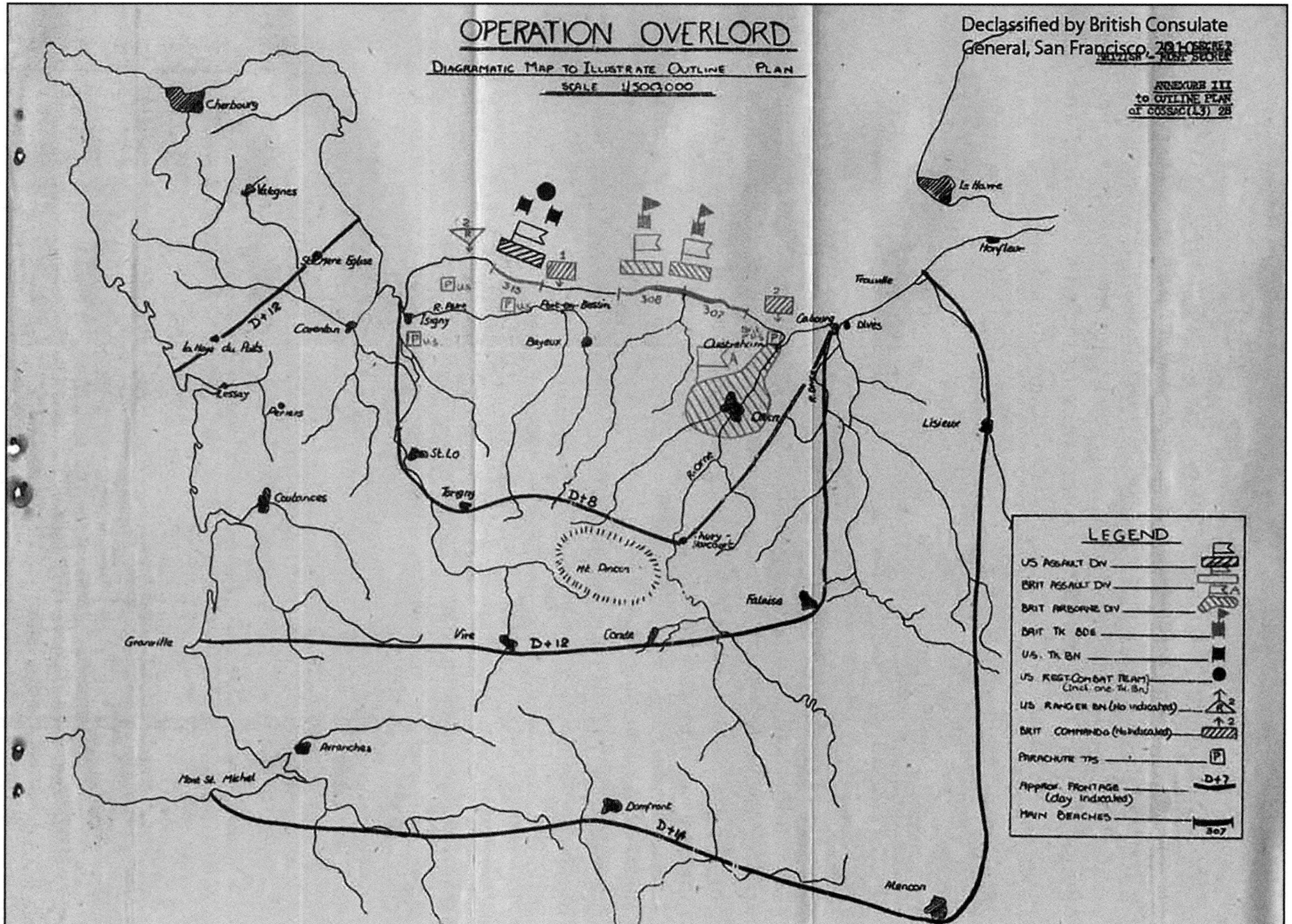

The outline COSSAC plan for the assault before Montgomery's addition of UTAH Beach and the insertion of another division in what would become the British sector that would land on SWORD Beach. The map also has the first set of what were to be a series of controversial phase lines drawn up against the 1943 level of anticipated opposition.

defences and the number of German divisions in the west at the time, these were entirely plausible objectives.

Montgomery Takes Command

With General Eisenhower appointed as Supreme Allied Commander and Montgomery to the command of 21st Army Group, there was to be no command for General Morgan. Instead, remaining at Norfolk House, he became one of Eisenhower's deputy chiefs of staff in SHAEF (Supreme Headquarters Allied Expeditionary Force). Eisenhower paid tribute to the work of the COSSAC staff who were dispersed to join SHAEF and 21st Army Group, writing:

> The great contribution of the COSSAC staff to OVERLORD was not that they devised a final or even a feasible plan for invasion, but that they determined the basic considerations which would govern success and overcame most of the practical difficulties which had seemed insurmountable to earlier planners.

Having handed over command of the Eighth Army in Italy, General Montgomery was summoned to meet Churchill, who was convalescing from pneumonia in Marrakesh. Here, on 31 December, he and Eisenhower, who was on his way to the US, were shown the COSSAC plan by the Prime Minister. The teetotal Montgomery avoided a late-night session with Churchill by retiring to bed

General Montgomery and the King during a visit to the troops.

with the plan, and by morning he had drafted his first impressions. These were typed up and taken to the Prime Minister, who was breakfasting in bed, the following morning. Montgomery's key criticism in a long document was that 'The initial landing is on too narrow a front and is confined to too small an area.'[5] Other key sections of his critique were:

3. From the purely Army point of view the following points are essential:
   (a) The initial landings must be made on the widest possible front.
   (b) Corps must be able to develop their operations from their own beaches, and other corps must NOT land *through* those beaches.
   (c) British and American areas of landing must be kept separate. The provisions of (a) above must apply in each case.
   (d) After the initial landings, the operation must be developed in such a way that a good port is secured quickly for the British and for American forces. Each should have its own port or group of ports.
4. The type of plan required is on the following lines:
   (a) One British army to land on a front of two, or possibly three, corps. One American army similarly.
   (b) Follow-up divisions to come into the corps already on shore.
   (c) The available assault craft to be used for the landing troops. Successive flights to follow rapidly in any type of un-armoured craft, and to be poured in.
   (d) The air battle must be won before the operation is launched. We must then aim at success in the land battle by the speed and violence of our operations.

Montgomery's reservations were not unique to him and were shared by others, including General Paget, C-in-C Home Forces, who expressed his concerns in November. and by General Eisenhower, who had seen a copy of the plan on his appointment as Supreme Commander, expressed the view that the plan as it stood was 'risky'.

Arriving in west London during the first week of January, General Montgomery shook up the Headquarters of 21st Army Group, based in St Paul's School, which had been for the previous four years GHQ Home Forces. A number of senior officers were posted out and the overall size of the staff was reduced. The new Commander-in-Chief also brought back with him trusted members of his Eighth Army headquarters 'who knew my ways and would get on with the job without bellyaching.' He later commented that 'Army Group headquarters now look like the Eighth Army.'[6]

During the first two weeks of January Montgomery's staff worked on revising the plan. The Chief of Staff, Major General Freddie de Guingand, briefly flirted with Brittany as an alternative, until they realized there were simple factors, such as air support, which had ruled it out for the COSSAC planners. Once briefed by the COSSAC staff, 'based on lessons learned from the stern school of active fighting', they concentrated on addressing their master's concerns over the Normandy option:[7]

- *First* – It is essential to relate what is strategically desirable to what is tactically possible with the forces at your disposal.
- *Second* – To this end it is necessary to decide the development of operations before the initial blow is delivered. There must be a direct relationship between the two.
- *Third* – If your flanks and rear are secure, you are well placed for battle.
- *Fourth* – Simplicity is vital in the planning of operations. Once complications are allowed to creep in, the outcome is in danger.

West of OMAHA Beach to assist with the capture of the port of Cherbourg, UTAH Beach was inserted at the base of the Cotentin Peninsula, and in accordance with his third lesson above, a fifth beach was also added, SWORD Beach.

SWORD, originally Beach 306, had been identified during the work conducted by Combined Operations as practicable, but had not been selected by COSSAC as it had a frontage between areas of rock of less than 1,000 yards. Beaches 307 and 308, JUNO and GOLD, respectively, were far more suitable given the limited scale of the invasion.[8]

Another change in the revised plan was that the British airborne brigades were no longer to simply secure the line of the River Orne and the Canal de Caen from Ouistreham into the city, but were now to act as a buffer between the Orne and the inundated valley of the Dives in order to protect the left flank of the beachhead. The reason for this was concern over the likely intervention of 'the enemy reserve division from Liseux'; rightly so, since this was the 12th *Hitlerjugend* SS Panzer Division. Therefore, Caen was no longer the concern of the airborne troops but was the objective of the division that was to land on SWORD Beach.[9]

General Morgan and others argued that without airborne forces capturing Caen and its Orne bridges on D Day, the city, being 10 miles inland, could not be taken on the first day of the invasion. Morgan went so far as to say that Montgomery failed to appreciate the significance of Caen and only paid 'lip service' to its early capture.

On his return from the US, Eisenhower, along with his deputy, Air Marshal Leigh Mallory, approved Montgomery's changes to the COSSAC plan on 21 January. Rather than a single corps conducting the landing, command of the up-scaled Operation OVERLORD would be split between the First US and Second British Armies, each with two corps headquarters overseeing the assault landings across five beaches. Of these corps, Lieutenant General Crocker's I Corps would command the airborne insertion east of the Orne, along with the amphibious landings on SWORD and JUNO beaches.[10]

The significant increase in the size of OVERLORD delayed the target date by a month to the end of May, in order to provide more time for redeployment and production of additional air and landing craft, plus the training of their crews.

A meeting between Eisenhower and his senior commanders was held at Norfolk House, London, 1 February 1944.

Single-service interests continued to stand in the way, requiring presidential and prime ministerial intervention. Eisenhower wrote in frustration in his personal diary: 'The war would be won more easily if someone were to shoot King.' Admiral King had been prepared to release just 2,493 landing craft from his Pacific Fleet's holding of 31,123. On this subject the President was reluctant to intervene, but Churchill had no hesitation in giving direction to the heads of the British services.[11]

Caen's Place in the 'Master Plan'

The campaign plan that Montgomery produced was based on an analysis of numerous factors, chief amongst which were his strategic directive from the Combined Chiefs, resources available, ground and intelligence. His key point was that the overall framework should be adhered to and not repeatedly knocked off course.[12] The resulting outline plan was for British Second Army to draw the enemy and fix them on the left, while the Americans broke out on the right, which when executed, ultimately resulted in the envelopment of the Seventh German Army between Falaise and Chambois. This scheme of manoeuvre was endorsed and adopted by Eisenhower and was used by the Allied Armies from the assault landings up to reaching the line of the Seine, where Montgomery handed overall command to SHAEF. Final agreement on the detail was only reached on 8 May and was briefed to senior commanders at the final presentation of plans at St Paul's School on 15 May 1944.[13]

With the role of the left flank in what Montgomery called his master plan, Caen and its immediate environs were at the heart of his intent, and he shared Morgan's view of the significance of the city. Brigadier David Belchem,

Brigadier David Belchem.

Montgomery's Brigadier General Staff (Special Plans), described the significance of the area on the left flank of the beachhead:[14]

> It was the centre at which the main road and rail communications from the east and southeast converged, and thence led to the Cherbourg Peninsula and to Brittany. Moreover, reserves sent south from Fifteenth German Army, by whatever route they followed (assuming that there would be no bridges usable over the Seine west of Paris), would reach the combat zone through Caen, and the same applied to reinforcements brought up from farther afield, for the rail and road bridges over the Loire were also to be destroyed.[15]

Belchem concluded:

> From consideration of the immense strategic importance of Caen, Montgomery anticipated that the Germans would react violently, at the expense of the rest of the bridgehead, to any major offensive by the Allies in the area of the town.

In answer to Morgan's criticism, Montgomery explained that he intended to draw and fix German forces *around* Caen through a sustained major threat, utilising the fact that the Germans would be bound to fight hard to retain or to regain possession of the city. He stated that he aimed to capture Caen 'on D Day or shortly afterwards', which Morgan dismissed as an 'exhortatory phrase'.

Forming a front against the expected arrival of German divisions from the Pas de Calais and fixing and fighting them around Caen were intended to assist the First US Army. This was crucial while the Americans were facing in two directions as VII Corps advanced to capture Cherbourg, and then when the First US Army was fighting its way south through the bocage country to a point from which they could break out. To Montgomery it was clear that whether he held Caen and the ground to the south or not, the threat of the Second British Army making progress into the more open country towards Falaise meant that area was bound to be the focus of fighting on the left flank. This fact was reiterated in virtually all of Montgomery's directives written during the campaign.

Once ashore, and the beachhead protected by what was known during OVERLORD's planning phase as the 'covering position', there was the issue of the army groups' wheel to the east. Where the Second Army would pivot and begin its advance to the east emerged as a problem, or 'the horns of a dilemma', in gaining detailed agreement for Montgomery's strategy. His expectations of fighting around Caen were at variance with the air forces' need for extensive tracts of open ground for temporary airfields south of the city. This would have required an advance as far south as Falaise to take airfields in the Bourgébus and Verrières area out of range of enemy artillery.

Despite his earlier agreement, the delay into May of approving the detailed campaign plan was due to Leigh Mallory's refusal to accept the proposal for the Second Army to pivot on Caen. Therefore, Montgomery and his chief planner drew up illustrative maps that placed the pivot well to the south in the Falaise/Argentan area. Brigadier Belchem, while believing Montgomery was 'sincere in his statements ... thought that short of a miracle – such as a complete German collapse – there was little hope of the British Second Army reaching Argentan, or even Falaise, in the early stage of the Battle of Normandy.'

Montgomery repeatedly stressed that the enemy's likely reaction would heavily influence the progress of the battle, and he also questioned whether resources for such an extensive drive south in the time frame demanded by the air forces was possible. It was only once Montgomery had confirmed that he would endeavour to deliver the ground demanded by Leigh Mallory that the detailed master plan was agreed.[16] It should be noted that by this stage 21st Army Group's planners were well aware of the success of Operation POINTBLANK in establishing air supremacy in Western Europe, and if the airmen had to wait a little longer for their temporary airfields, so be it.

The issue of airfields was at the heart of the criticism of Montgomery's conduct of the campaign, which ironically grew to a crescendo just as the 'master plan' came to fruition in the middle of August. Montgomery later wrote that General Morgan, without a command and with his plan 'discarded', 'lost no opportunity of trying to persuade Eisenhower that I was defensively minded and unlikely to breakout anywhere!' – and the frustrated airmen 'were only too glad to be able to suggest that something had gone wrong.'

Linked to getting inland to establish airfields was the issue of not becoming bogged down in a beachhead stalemate. The results of Churchill's accusations of a lack of drive at both Salerno and Anzio, particularly the latter, of which he

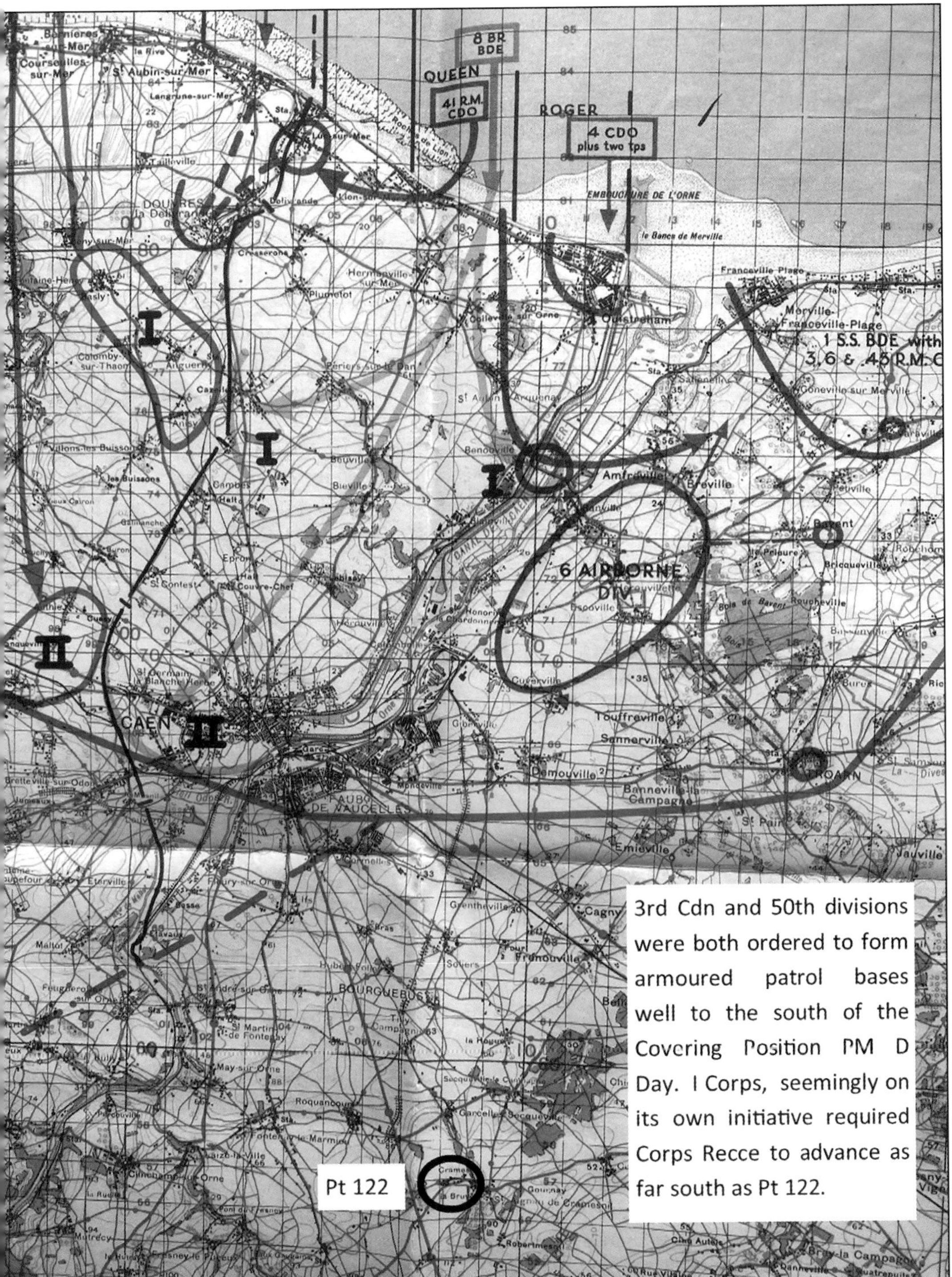

An extract of the Second Army map showing I Corps' D Day objectives and covering position and I Corps' advance patrol base south of Caen.

Patrol Bases

An important feature of the 'master plan' was the throwing forward of patrols of various size, as explained by I Corps in its report.[1]

> 4. Action after the Covering Position had been secured.
>
> (a) After making good the line Putot-en-Bessin – Caen – R. Orne to the sea, it was considered essential to retain the initiative by vigorous patrolling and by pushing forward strong offensive elements, including armour, to facilitate the further advance by gaining control of the area over which it was to be made; and to interfere with enemy developments whereby time would be gained for the proper organization of the cowering position.
>
> (b) The strength of these offensive elements and their role would depend on the situation existing at the time, the ground and the general Army plan. They would range from a squadron of tanks with a company of Infantry to a complete armoured brigade group. The role of the smaller column was reconnaissance, the denying of reconnaissance to the enemy, and, generally, the control of 'no-man's-land' until the enemy deployed such strong forces that it was compelled to withdraw. On the other hand, the role of the complete brigade group was to secure some piece of ground which was vital to the enemy if he was to develop his operation; and in such strength that the enemy would not be able to ignore it. Thus, the task of the brigade group was to force the enemy to deploy and fight. The group could only withdraw when absolutely forced to do so and then it would repeat the process further back. By these tactics we should retain the initiative and, as our own build-up developed, the advance would be resumed against a weakened and improperly organised enemy.

Field Marshal Montgomery wrote in *High Command in War*: 'It is necessary to gain quickly, and to keep, the initiative. Only in this way will the enemy be made to dance to your tune and to react to your thrusts.'

The I Corps' patrol bases were to be established at Evrecy with 2 Canadian Armoured Brigade, and by 3rd Division on the high ground 5 miles south of Caen where the Falaise road crosses it at Point 122. The divisional patrol base force was planned to consist of the following, under command OC Sqn, Staffs Yeo:

One squadron Staffs Yeo with reconnaissance elements
SP Tps: 41 and 45 A/Tk Btys
One company 2 Warwick (on bicycles if possible)
One platoon 1 Norfolks (on bicycles if possible)
Two sections carrier platoon 2 Warwick
Two sections carrier platoon 2 KSLI

said, 'I had hoped we were hurling a wildcat into the shore, but all we got was a stranded whale,' are to be found everywhere one looks in orders and memoirs. For instance, Major Illing, a company commander in 2 Warwicks, wrote that he had been warned to expect an advance on bicycles some 40 miles inland during the first few days of the invasion.[17] However, by the time 3rd Division was briefed at the end of May, it was well known by senior commanders that with the German reinforcement of Normandy, unless the enemy collapsed this was vanishingly unlikely. These expectations fostered during briefings were most likely to have been aimed at generating an offensive mindset.

Second Army

General Dempsey's Headquarters Second Army, along with representatives from subordinate corps headquarters, naval and air planners, opened in central London on 26 January.

> The work at ASHLEY GARDENS was essentially joint naval, military and air force planning. It centred round the allotment of craft to assault formations and established the plan for a rapid build-up. The co-ordination of all available fire support for the assault was fixed.
>
> The operation for the concentration of the forces prior to embarkation was drawn up and the administration of the venture was developed concurrently upon principles appropriate to the tactical plan.
>
> A suitable plan was developed to overcome the beach obstacles and a sound system of communications for the first few days of the battle was established.[18]

It sounds straightforward, but every query and change of plan required calculation and recalculation. It was an intense four and a half months of detailed work.

Despite Montgomery's reservations, the requirement to capture Caen and ground to the south was headlined in Second Army's Operation Order No. 1, issued before a German reinforcement was fully apparent:

> Mission – Second Army will:
> (a) Assault between PORT EN BESSIN [*sic*] 7587 and THE R. ORNE.
> (b) Secure and develop a bridgehead South of the Line CAUMONT 7059 – CAEN 0368 and SE of CAEN in order to secure airfield sites and to protect the flank of First US Army while the latter capture CHERBOURG and the BRITTANY Ports.[19]

With the invasion imminent, General Dempsey and his main headquarters of Second Army joined the redeployment of commanders from London to Embarkation Area A, in their case to the old Palmerston Fort Southwick, overlooking Portsmouth.

Mapping the Defences

Lance Corporal Hiscocks, a Royal Engineer, was a clerk in a Drawing Section working on producing maps of enemy defences.

> We commenced [Operation] 'BENSON' which was to be the foundation for the invasion of Europe, comprising maps at 1:25,000 made from photographs taken by the RAF.[1] Many were the doubts regarding these maps, few believed

A photograph of German defensive preparations at WN-20 Objective COD and on SWORD Beach, taken by PRU aircraft prior to D Day.

that they would ever be used, but we plodded along, the sameness of the work constituting a good reason for 'moaning'.

Military training was now all for assault, landings, in short for our invasion. So BENSON continued until the early months of 1944. In February of that year, I became part of a detachment at 2nd Army HQ in Ashley Gardens London and helped with maps [the 'Defences overprint series'] from which models of the French coast were made, and on special task maps that showed the state of the ground near rivers, marshes etc. [going maps]. Wall maps for the brass hats to lecture upon. In May we moved to Purbrook near Cosham, Portsmouth. All men who had anything at all to do with the planning were 'BIGOT' men, that is, their past record and antecedents were looked into. All the work was 'Top Secret' and 'NEPTUNE'.

On the day I arrived in Pompey I went by truck to Fort Southwick, taking the top road on the side of the Downs, which road had only known me, and many others when we were all pleasure bent, cycling, motoring, in the charabanc, but now the tracks streamed with military traffic of all kinds, from trucks to tanks. Glorious weather, Portsmouth down below, barrage balloons above her, and on her waters many barges of all types. Hosts of RAF planes flew low over us on their pre-invasion shoot-ups, tying up the German communications . . .

So into the fort itself after much checking of AB64 [ID Card] and special [BIGOT] passes. Down into the many steps of the subway into a secret room well below the ground to prepare wall maps for the 83 Group [RAF], of [Temporary] landing strips D1 to D+7 and so on, and so now I knew exactly

A grey-painted photo recce Spitfire Mk II, with invasion stripes painted on fuselage and wings.

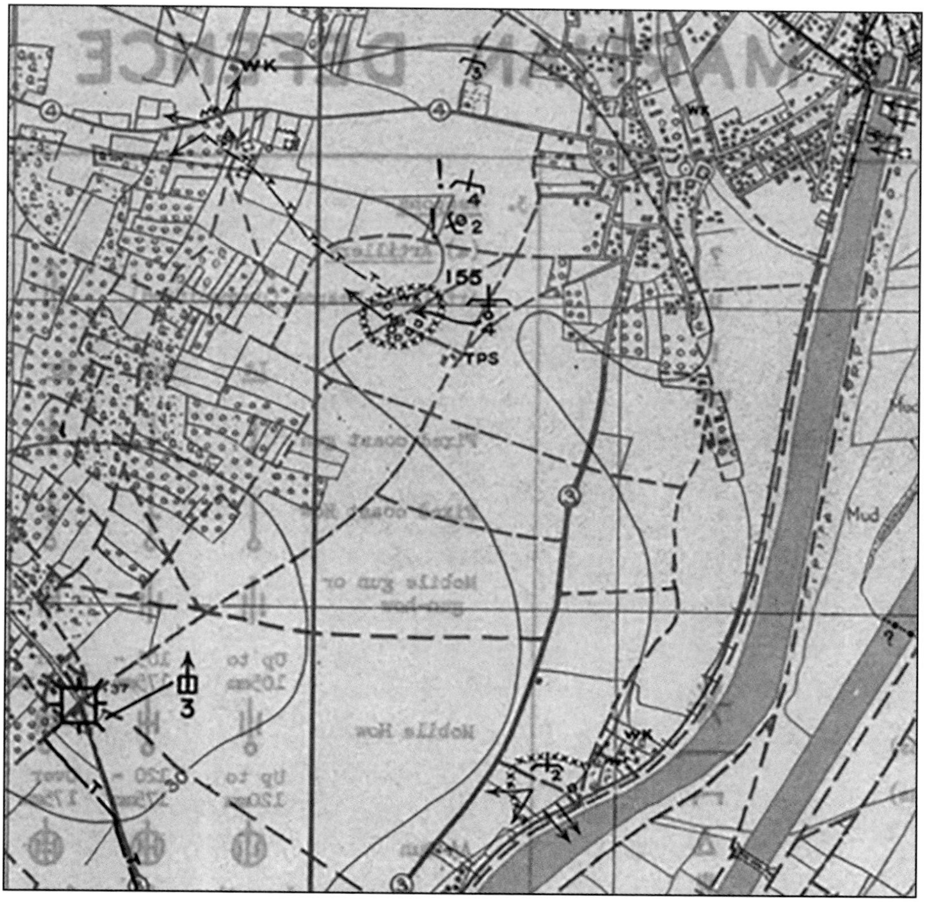

(**Above & opposite**) Extracts of the same grid squares of two 1:25,000 Defences overprint maps of the type that Sapper Hiscocks worked on. They show the development of the coastal gun battery WN-12 in the SWORD area, nicknamed DAIMLER, and other defences. These editions were published on 19 December 1943 and 20 May 1944, which was the final STOP PRESS edition. The guns were originally in vulnerable open gun pits to the west of Ouistreham (Objective BEER) but were moved in the days before D Day to the newly commissioned DAIMLER casemates.

where the landings would be. BENSON maps were largely used in all the planning as was one of these was the first map I handled in London. At night the Hun sent over aeroplanes, I had experienced my first London raid in February but under canvas in Portsmouth it was rather different, because of the danger of flak coming into the tents. Sometimes I could get home to Southampton for the night, and I found all the roadsides full of equipment, including the roads near, and outside my home, all waiting for D Day. I had guessed that the 8th June would be the day. I was 'duty clerk' during the night of Sunday the 4th and I had an unusual message 'MT 12 leaving Victoria Docks tomorrow at 7am 13 units with no maps aboard' so I knew that the time was getting close.

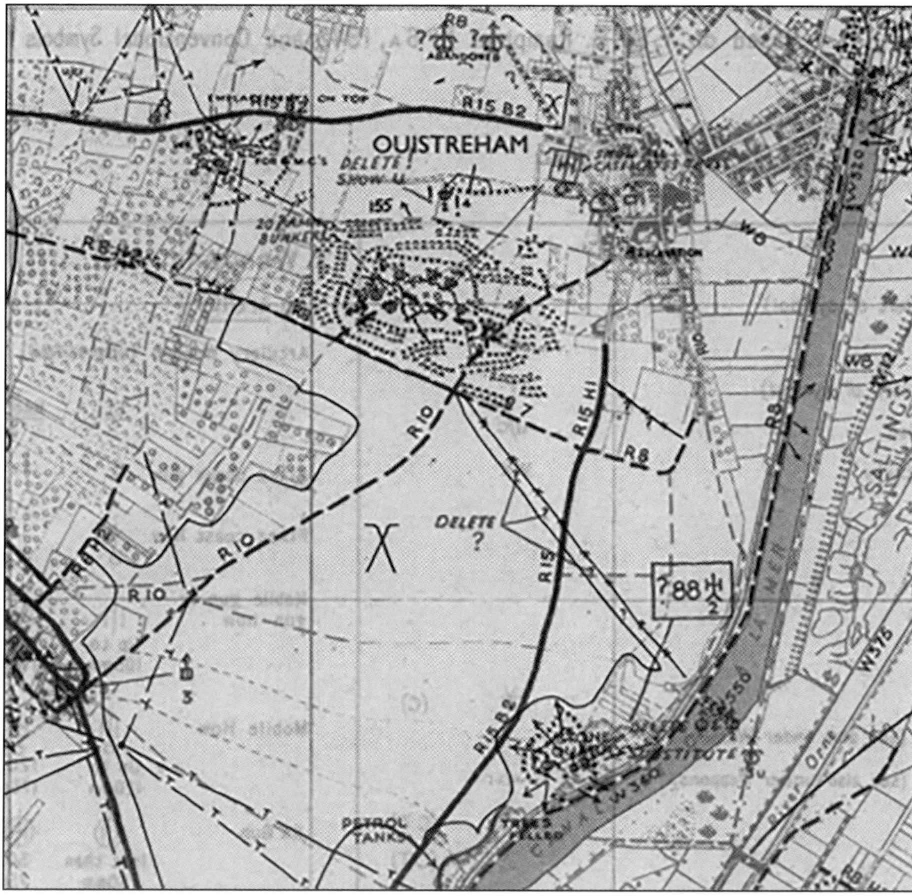

I Corps

In the corps' Op O General Crocker gave his two divisions instructions for conduct of the advance to the covering position:

> The task of the assaulting divs is to break through the coastal defences and advance some 10 miles inland on D Day.
>
> Great speed and boldness will be required to achieve this. It will be necessary to forestall the action of the enemy's local reserves quickly, to overcome minor resistance met with during the advance, to get set before the arrival of reserve formations, and be ready to meet the enemy's first counter attacks, which must be expected to develop by the evening of D Day.
>
> As soon as the beach defences have been penetrated therefore, not a moment must be lost in beginning the advance inland. Armour should be used boldly from the start. Such action will forestall the enemy's reaction, confuse him, magnify his fears and enable ground to be made quickly.
>
> All available artillery must be ready to support the advance. If opposition is met which cannot be overcome by these strong advance guards, simple

General Crocker, the commander of I Corps.

> plans embodying the full resources of artillery and armour must be employed to dislodge the enemy quickly and certainly. Hastily staged, ill supported infantry attacks are unlikely to succeed and are likely to be slow and costly in the long run.[20]

Clearly, it was considered possible that bold and decisive action on D Day would, with the help of the air forces, slow enemy reaction and might deliver Caen into the hands of I Corps. If, however, the enemy were quickly able to bring strong forces into action against the corps, and the city remained in German hands, an advance south around it would not be possible. It was considered that the rate of build-up would not permit a further general advance before D+3 or D+4. During the interval it was anticipated that the enemy would mount his major initial counter-attacks.

> If the enemy were still holding Caen at this stage, it might be necessary, as a preliminary to any further advance on I Corps' front, to capture and clear the town. This operation might be carried out by 3 Brit Div developing a converging attack on both sides of the River Orne and the Canal, or as a Corps attack employing 51 (H) Div as well as 3 Brit Div. In the latter case the operation could not take place before D+5 or D+6.[21]

As will be seen in the next chapter, information on reinforced German defences was working its way into I Corps' plans.

3rd Division

The role of Major General Rennie's heavily reinforced divisional group that was to land on SWORD Beach was equally explicit: 'The 3rd British Infantry Division will land on QUEEN RED and WHITE beaches and capture CAEN, and a bridgehead SOUTH of the R ORNE at that place.'

SWORD Beach was narrow, being hemmed in by the low cliffs and rocks towards Lion-sur-Mer to the west and more rocks and, most importantly, the strong defences around the port of Ouistreham to the east. Despite the depth of the objective of seizing a bridgehead in a city some 10 miles inland, the 3rd Division would, unlike the other assault divisions, land on a single brigade frontage. The upscaling of the invasion and the reluctance of Admiral King to release landing craft from the Pacific also had a bearing on the adoption of a narrow front. In short, General Rennie had to concentrate on the drive to Caen at the expense of objectives to the flanks of his main thrust, especially those beyond the coastal defences.

The initial assault landing was to be undertaken by 8 Infantry Brigade Group. The two leading battalions were to overcome the beach defences and take the coastal settlements, while the brigade's third battalion was to punch through the centre, clearing Colleville and enemy batteries (MORRIS and HILLMAN) before securing the high ground around Point 61. This represented a penetration of some 2½ miles from the beach. The remaining 7 miles to the bridges in Caen were to be covered by the Intermediate Brigade, 185 Brigade, with the 'speed and boldness' demanded in orders from Second Army downwards. 9 Brigade was to land in reserve and had a list of contingencies to prepare. Extracts from 3rd Infantry Division's Op O No. 1 detailing the brigades' tasks are at Appendix I.

3rd Division's plan for the advance from SWORD Beach and the capture of Caen.

Chapter Two

The Defenders of Caen

> It is on the beaches that the fate of the invasion will be decided and, what is more, in the first 24 hours. [*Generalfeldmarschall* Erwin Rommel]

In 1941 Hitler issued *Führerbefehl* No. 40, the first orders for construction of what became known as the Atlantic Wall; but such were the demands of the Eastern Front for men and resources that little was achieved. Most of the defences built in 1942 and 1943 were concentrated around the Channel and Atlantic ports, the calculation being that the Allies would need a port big enough to sustain the sizeable force required to engage with the Wehrmacht in North-West Europe. Such defences as there were in between the more heavily defended areas amounted to little more than a thin screen.

The Saint-Nazaire and Dieppe raids in 1942 had amply demonstrated to the Germans the efficacy of concrete and steel defences, but had also encouraged the British to develop equipment and tactics to breach coastal defences and to avoid the most strongly defended areas. The Atlantic Wall at this stage in its development was characterized by *Generafeldmarschall* von Rundstedt as 'a propaganda illusion'. However, with the tide of war turning against Germany in 1943 following a string of disasters at Stalingrad, 'Tunisgrad', Kursk, Sicily and finally the Allied landing on the European mainland in southern Italy, action in the west was required. In October 1943 von Rundstedt, Commander-in-Chief West, wrote a memorandum to Berlin drawing attention to the inadequacies of both the defenders and defences of the west. Days later, Hitler's response was to issue *Führerbefehl* No. 51:

> For the past two and one-half years the bitter and costly struggle against Bolshevism has made the utmost demands upon the bulk of our military resources and energies. This commitment was in keeping with the seriousness of the danger, and the overall situation. The situation has since changed. The threat from the East remains, but an even greater danger looms in the West: the Anglo-American landing! In the East, the vastness of the space will, as a last resort, permit a loss of territory even on a major scale, without suffering a mortal blow to Germany's chance for survival.
>
> Not so in the West! If the enemy here succeeds in penetrating our defences on a wide front, consequences of staggering proportions will follow within a short time. All signs point to an offensive against the Western Front of Europe no later than spring, and possibly earlier.

Graffiti in the concrete of one of the open gun pits of the Merville Battery, whose 100mm Skoda guns were sited in range of SWORD Beach.

> For that reason, I can no longer justify the further weakening of the West in favour of other theatres of war. I have therefore decided to strengthen the defences in the West, particularly at places from which we shall launch our long-range war against England. For those are the very points at which the enemy must and will attack; there – unless all indications are misleading – will be fought the decisive invasion battle.

To add drive to construction, Rommel was moved from northern Italy to take command of Army Group B on the north coast of France and Belgium, with a simultaneous appointment as Inspector General of the Atlantic Wall. Under his supervision, 17 million cubic metres of concrete was poured, 1.2 million tons of steel erected and 5 million land mines laid. The effect of this huge amount of material was, however, dissipated by the Allied deception measures, which painted threats from Norway to the Atlantic coast of France. When this was reported to Hitler, he gave in response instruction after instruction for defences to be built up and down the 1,700 miles of coast from northern Norway to the Pyrenees, until he was finally overwhelmed by their sheer volume. Despite this, the Fifteenth Army in the Pas de Calais continued to add significant strength to its defences.

For most of its length away from the Pas de Calais, the Atlantic Wall remained a crust of concrete with little depth, despite the resources and effort put into its construction. However, in the five months prior to the Allied landings in Normandy, the location of which had been partly selected for its relatively weak defences, the coastal fortifications and the number of troops manning them multiplied in the Baie de Seine area.

By the spring of 1944 von Rundstedt had some fifty-eight divisions under his command split between two army groups. Rommel's Army Group B consisted of a single corps on the Dutch coast, *Generaloberst* von Salmuth's Fifteenth Army manning defences on the coast between the rivers Scheldt and the Seine, and *Generaloberst* Dollmann's Seventh Army deployed westwards from the Seine around Brittany to the Loire, in what was to become the invasion area. The two armies of *Generaloberst* Blaskowitz's Army Group G covered much of the rest of

Operation BODYGUARD and its component deception plans.

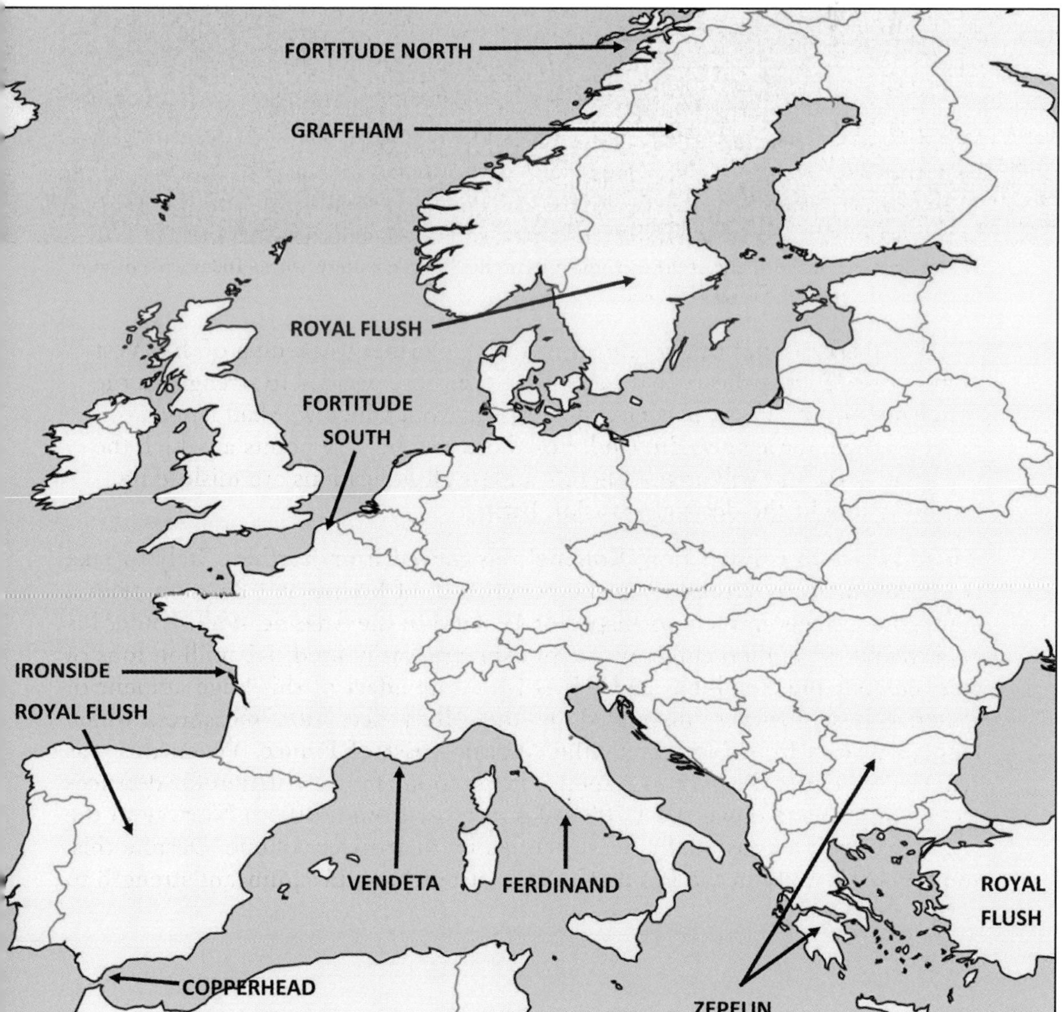

occupied France down to the Mediterranean. One veteran *Fallschirmjäger* (paratroop) soldier noted that this straightforward ground deployment was not supported by an equally simple chain of command to Luftwaffe assets. *Reichsmarschall* Göring, in common with other air commanders, wished to assert the independence of the Luftwaffe.

> Von Rundstedt had to rely for air support upon *Generafeldmarschall* Hugo Sperrle's 3rd Air Fleet. This was directly under Göring's control and not under operational command of the C-in-C West. It was a typical example of the muddled and overlapping command structure which Hitler loved to create and which, when added to his own tendency to interfere personally in the tactical detail of every battle, made it almost impossible for his senior commanders in the field to coordinate their operations. Furthermore, it denied them the freedom of action, which was so essential if they were to use such tactical mobility as the forces under their command possessed.[1]

The complications were not confined to the Luftwaffe but extended to command and employment of the *Panzerwaffe*. With the appointment of Rommel came experience of fighting in North Africa under the lash of growing Allied air power. No doubt influenced by the near success in defeating the landing of 36th Texas Division at Salerno, he argued for a 'string of pearls', or panzers within immediate striking distance of the beaches. It was on the beaches, while the Allies were at their most vulnerable, that Rommel believed they could be defeated. He used his experience of fighting in North Africa and the Mediterranean to justify his belief that panzers moving to attack from the hinterland of France would suffer significant attrition from fighter-bombers and be unlikely to arrive in time.

In contrast, von Rundstedt and General Geyr von Schweppenburg believed that the Allies would in all circumstances be able to form a beachhead, and thus maintain the traditional approach of keeping the panzer divisions in hand until the main Allied attack had been positively identified. Only then would Schweppenburg's *Panzergruppe* West, beyond the range of naval gunfire, launch an all-out counter-attack against the Allied beachhead. Thanks to ULTRA, the Allies were able to monitor the progress of much of this argument for command of the panzer divisions, along with Berlin's response.

The result of the argument was one of Hitler's typical compromises that satisfied neither party. Of the six Wehrmacht panzer divisions and the four SS panzer/*panzergrenadier* divisions in the west on D Day, six were divided between the two army groups and four held as a central reserve. Those allocated to Rommel, including 21st Panzer Division, came with so many restrictions imposed by Berlin that neither his 'string of pearls' strategy nor Schweppenburg's plan to mass armour could effectively be met.

Coastal Defence

Most of the troops manning the forward defences of the Atlantic Wall were formed into *bodenständig* or static divisions of a lower manpower establishment

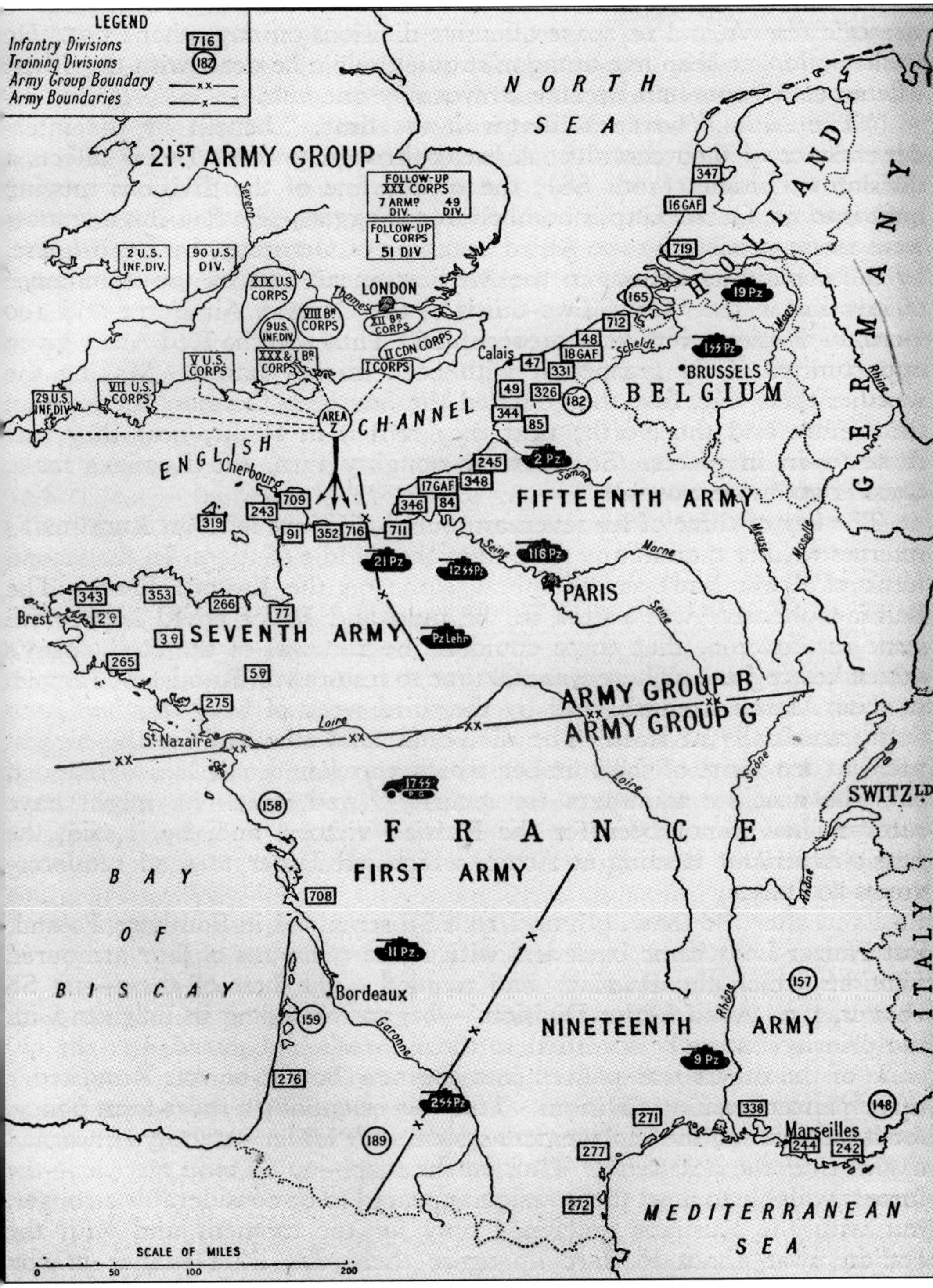

German divisions in the west at the time of the invasion.

with fewer support weapons, many of the latter, particularly artillery and anti-tank guns, having been captured and taken into use, or obsolescent. Being 'static', these divisions had very little transport. Such as they had was, in common with most of the Wehrmacht infantry, horse-drawn. Not only were the numbers of soldiers reduced, but their quality was also low. By 1944 most of the younger soldiers had been replaced by older men, those partly incapacitated by wounds and soldiers not otherwise fit for service in field grade divisions. All of these were, however, deemed suitable for manning coastal defences. In addition, there were significant numbers in Atlantic Wall divisions of *Beutedeutscher* ('booty' Germans) from the eastern parts of Greater Germany, plus prisoners of war that had 'volunteered' to serve with the Wehrmacht. In I Corps' sector, these were mainly in 439 and 642 *Ost* battalions, but sundry other '*Hiwi*' troops (an abbreviation of *Hilfswilliger*, auxiliary volunteers) were to be found across divisions in various administrative roles. One of the few bright spots was that after the issue of *Führerbefehl* No. 51, experienced officers and NCOs were posted into the static divisions to boost their combat effectiveness.

Generalleutenant Willhelm Richter's 716th Infantry Division was raised in Bielefeld during May 1941 and had been occupying the Lower Normandy coast between Franceville to the east and the River Vire in the west since June 1942. Strung out on a 45-mile frontage, it had a density of just a few hundred defenders per mile, but once Hitler's attention had switched from dealing with the Soviet offensive on the Eastern Front and the Allied attacks at Monte Cassino, he ordered a reinforcement of Lower Normandy.

During April, the field grade 352nd Infantry Division that had been training around Saint-Lô was brought forward to the coast, halving 716th's frontage to 25 miles.

In the Orne Sector that covered SWORD Beach, the defenders manning coastal defences were from *Oberst* Krug's 736 Grenadier Regiment. Astride the mouth of the River Orne in the port town of Ouistreham there was a *Stützpunkt* (STP) or support point, and further west four *Wieserstandneste* (WN) or resistance nets covering the beaches. Most of the divisional artillery and headquarters were 1 to 2 miles inland. A 21st Army Group report on the coastal defences reads:

> 12. All ports, even minor ones such as PORT EN BESSIN, and OUISTREHAM were heavily defended. Elsewhere, there was a chain of inf strong points along the coast at approximately 1,000 yards intervals and extending inland to a depth of some 200 yards. These were roughly of platoon strength, the largest concentrated at likely exits from suitable beaches which were blocked by anti-tank walls, roadblocks, minefields and ditches. They were well supplied with support weapons, medium machine guns, mortars and anti-tank guns, and sometimes included a French 75 mm gun or a German light howitzer.
>
> Gaps between strongpoints were mined, wired and covered by fire and where the gaps were too wide, they were flooded if the ground permitted.

Inland from SWORD, casemates at WN-16, known to the 3rd Division as Objective MORRIS, under construction, replacing open pits for four 100mm leFH 14/19 (t) guns with R669 casemates.

> Wire was used profusely to protect defensive positions. Use was also made of static flame throwers and demolition vehicles such as Goliaths.[2]

Rather than training for battle, the soldiers of 736 Grenadier Regiment laboured hard on construction of defences, concrete bunkers and shelters, plus trenches to link them. Also on shore there were miles of wire obstacles and tens of thousands of mines to be laid, while on the beach Rommel had ordered the construction of a 'devil's garden of obstacles'.

> 10. All beaches were obstructed with underwater obstacles. In February 1944, the enemy began his policy of obstructing beaches with underwater obstacles starting at high water mark and working towards low water mark, thickening up the obstacles in depth as the months went by. Many obstacles were mined with *Tellermines* or had shells fixed on to them, and there were *Tellermines* attached to floating rafts. Many of these obstacles were totally submerged at high tide.

The appearance of these obstacles during February 1944 effectively ended the debate in Allied circles over the advantages of landing under cover of night, but

A sketch reputedly by Rommel himself showing his 'devil's garden of obstacles'.

added to the engineers' task of clearing the beach of obstacles for subsequent waves of landing craft.

21st Panzer Division was also moved from Britanny during April to reinforce the Caen area. *General der Artillerie* Marcks, commander of LXXXIV Corps, came to the same conclusion as COSSAC, that the city was the key terrain, and most of 21st Panzer, less its panzer regiment, was deployed astride the River Orne to the north of Caen, where anti-tank ditches were dug in a more or less continuous arc around the city. Thus, inland from SWORD the 3rd Division would face not only the coastal crust but a Panzer division deployed in depth and a significant quantity of armour with which the Germans would surely counter-attack.

Hitler's Intuition

Believing in his own ability, Hitler's practice of intervening in operations, often down to the tactical level, has been referred to above; and, through the sheer number of times he did so, he was bound to be correct on occasions. True to his past record, even though overwhelmed by contradictory intelligence, Hitler had firm views on the likely location of the invasion. So successful was the deception of FORTITUDE SOUTH and its convincing proximity to the Reich, that German commanders believed the invasion would fall on the Pas de Calais or astride the mouth of the Somme. However, FORTITUDE was possibly too successful! After reports by agents such as Garbo on the scale of the build-up in the UK, the creation of General Patton's fictitious First US Army Group (FUSAG), and so on, Hitler and his commanders were increasingly convinced that there would be a subsidiary landing designed to draw their reserves away from the main assault. It was the sheer number of Allied troops appearing on the intelligence maps, rather than 'Hitler's intuition', that prompted the redeployment of forces to Lower Normandy. While he certainly supported the move of divisions to the Seventh Army, the art of persuading Hitler to take a particular course of action, from von Manstein's 'Sickle-Cut' of 1940 onwards, was to let him believe it was his idea! The staff of OB West certainly contributed to this process, even inventing additional Allied divisions.

Amidst the general reinforcement of the right flank of Seventh Army, the move forward to the coast of 352nd Infantry Division and the consequent shortening of 716th Division's front has already been mentioned. Of crucial importance to the capture of Caen, however, was the redeployment of 21st Panzer Division to the areas north and south of the city. On this one point Rommel had largely got his way, with the panzers being just two hours' drive from the coast. The division's tasks as issued by Headquarters *Panzergruppe* West were:

1. The division is to stand in readiness for: (a) Destruction of airborne enemy in its new billeting area. (b) Engagement in the battle at the coast during the first hours of an enemy landing. (c) Rapid movement for commitment within the *Heeresgruppe B* sector.
2. *OB Heeresgruppe B* has ordered that the *21.Panzer Division* is to consider its assembly area as a strongpoint, in which the division is to be ready, with its weapons dug in, to totally destroy even tenfold superior enemy forces, day or night. Accordingly, hills are to be occupied, built-up areas avoided. Numerous dug-in tank positions and field-fortified positions are to be prepared against enemy airborne landings.

In being expected to fight as a strongpoint in the event of a landing in Lower Normandy, Rommel was accepting that 21st Panzer would not fight as a formed division but in a series of unit actions. Many of the field fortification encountered by the 3rd Division as it advanced on Caen were pre-prepared in accordance with the above orders.

Confirmed and suspected intelligence regarding the increasing numbers of German formations in the invasion area had only gradually come through during April and into May. The reinforcement had initially been revealed thanks to ULTRA intercepts, but this was only passed to the highest level of Allied command thanks to rules designed to secure this vital source of intelligence. Only oblique references and tentative suggestions found their way into INTSUMS issued down the chain of command, such as 'It should not surprise us to find that 352nd Division had come forward to the coast.' Even though little explicit intelligence could be shared down the chain of command, increased opposition was indicated by the Resistance, SOE reports and air photographs. The latter, showing additional construction and an increasing number of tank tracks in air photography, naturally concerned the Allies in case their plans had been compromised, as the balance of forces on the invasion coast during the landing and build-up phase was narrowing significantly. The Allies correctly concluded that Rommel was planning to fight in the coastal area in order to defeat them on the beaches, rather than inland, but Brigadier Williams, Montgomery's chief of

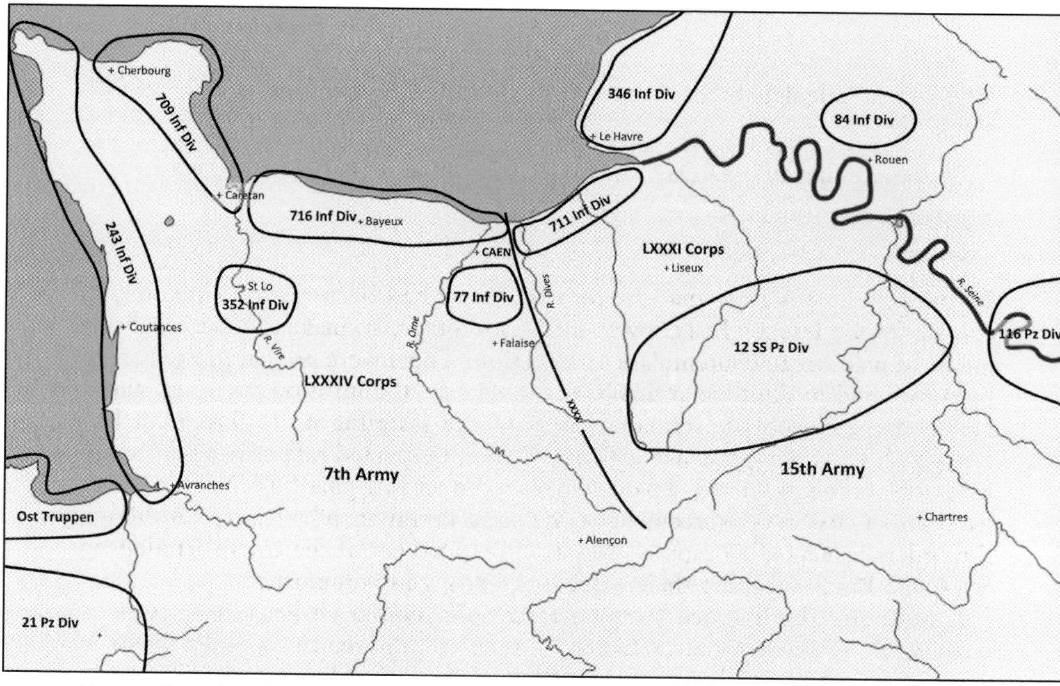

German formations in Normandy prior to the April redeployment.

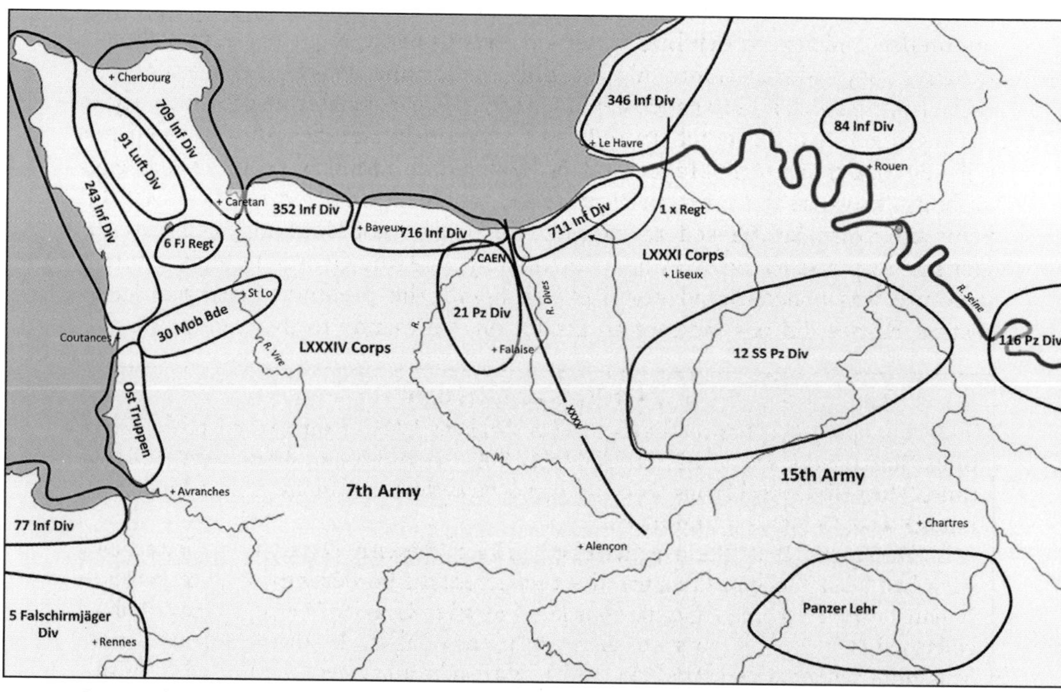

German formations in Normandy on D Day.

intelligence, calculated that in the worst case the respective build-up of divisions would be:

By the evening of	D Day	D+1	D+3	D+7	D+10
Allied	8	10	13	16	18
German	8	12	15	22	27

By the time it was clear that the Seventh Army had been reinforced it was, of course, far too late for Eisenhower and Montgomery to make significant adjustments to plans or to contemplate cancellation. There were no more resources to be committed in the time available; consequently, the invasion had to go ahead facing greater levels of German force than the planning up to that point had envisaged. Inevitably, this had an impact on the expected rate of progress south from the beaches, and with a panzer division effectively guarding Caen, nowhere would the German reinforcement be felt more keenly than by I Corps. Although the orders remained to capture the city, the prospect of the troops landing on SWORD Beach reaching their objectives was greatly diminished.

If defeating the in-place German forces was now a challenge, the issue of delaying the German build-up had also grown in importance and was a factor in ensuring that Eisenhower's priority of the air forces' sealing off the Normandy battlefield was met. The bomber barons were, of course, reluctant to 'prematurely' divert aircraft from their independent task of 'bombing Germany into impotence' and argued that hitting railways was difficult, requiring 'extraordinary accuracy' beyond that commonly available at the time. Having been ordered to strike rolling stock maintenance depots, which were invariably and fortuitously at railway junctions, the bombers and fighter-bombers significantly disrupted the rail network in eastern France and Belgium, thus reducing German strategic mobility. Only as the invasion approached would bridges, principally over the Seine and Loire, be attacked, to complete the isolation of Normandy and slow the German response to the invasion.[3] Fortunately, as Army Group B's logistic infrastructure was concentrated north of the Seine, the preliminary air attacks in eastern France did not indicate an assault on Normandy to the enemy.

21st Panzer Division

The origins of 21st Panzer Division date back to 1941, a time when Hitler was preparing to launch Operation BARBAROSSA, the invasion of Russia. At the same time, Mussolini's ambitions to carve out a new Roman Empire in the Mediterranean were beginning to unravel.

In December 1940 the overstretched British Western Desert Force launched what had been conceived as a five-day raid across the border into Libya to bat the Italians away from the Egyptian border. But after Graziani's army unexpectedly collapsed, the British pursued them deep into Libya. In these circumstances Mussolini accepted German help, and Wehrmacht units were nominated to form what was initially termed as a 'blocking force'.

The panzer grenadier officer wears the sun-bleached field cap beloved by *Afrikakorps* veterans when the 21st Panzer Division was re-formed in France.

In early February 1941, Rommel and the first units of what was to become the *Deutsches Afrikakorps* started to arrive in Tripoli. Those that were to become 21st Panzer Division principally came from 3rd Panzer Division, with others from across the Army making up a scratch formation, known as 5th Motorized Light Division.

The British were well aware of the arrival of the *Afrikakorps* but believed that they would not be ready for offensive operations until mid-April or even May. Rommel, however, had other ideas. Following an ostentatious parade through Tripoli by the first units to arrive, his blocking force was sent straight to the front and were in action on 20 February. By mid-March, with more of the division arriving, they started to push the British back in what was to become a see-saw campaign.

In August 1941, 5th Motorized Light Division, although it had never reached even the slim establishment of a light armoured division, started to be built up to the strength of a full panzer division, and in doing so was allocated the next available panzer division number, the 21st.

Over the next two years 21st Panzer Division fought in all the *Afrikakorps*' major battles – the long list includes: Tobruk, Sodum, El Agheila, Alam Halfa, Gazala, El Alamein, and Tobruk (again).

By early 1943 the Axis forces were driven back to Tunisia, with, following the Anglo-American TORCH landings, the First Army closing in from the west and the Eighth Army from the east. Most of the remnants of the renowned 21st Panzer Division eventually surrendered on 13 May after fighting desperate rear-guard actions, and the division ceased to exist for the time being. However, a number of experienced officers and NCOs, thanks to absence as a result of wounds, courses

Rommel with Major Becker (left) and *Generalmajor* Feuchtinger (right). The latter was known as a bohemian character who made the most of the opportunities offered by occupied France.

and leave, were no longer in Tunisia and thus available to forma a cadre when the time came to re-form the division and to embody its traditions.

By 1943 the Germans had been exploiting captured 1940-vintage British and French armour for some time. Various AFVs were cleaned up and used as they were, while others were converted to become weapon platforms for the latest German-manufactured weapons. Both were to be found in 21st Panzer Division. The leading exponent of wholesale conversion of captured armour was Major Becker, a reserve artillery officer, engineer and industrialist. He had produced conversions on the Eastern Front and had been ordered back to Berlin to demonstrate one of his vehicles to Hitler. The possibilities were obvious at a time of increasing

The badges of the *Afrikakorps* and 21st Panzer Division in Normandy.

shortages. Consequently, when the 'New' 21st Panzer was raised in May 1943, as the manpower and equipment crisis of that year bit, OKH instructed:

> Equipment (aside from communication kit) and vehicles are not allotted. It is expressly forbidden to requisition material for 21. Panzer Division in any way. The necessary equipment and motor vehicles are to be secured exclusively from French booty of from OB-West.

Becker eventually produced a total of 447 AFVs in the *Baukommando* Becker (Construction Staff)[4] works near Paris, first for *Schnelle* Brigade West[5] and then in August 1943, when the brigade became 21st Panzer Division, under the command of the newly promoted *Generalmajor* Feuchtinger.[6] The division's panzers were initially all French Somua vehicles, but these were steadily replaced with Panzer IVs and a few Panzer III command variants, so that by the beginning of June only 32 out of 130 tanks were Somuas. The rest of the division's vehicles were re-engineered, with all the difficulties typical of those that beset German war production between 1943 and 1945.[7]

French UNIC P107 Half-Tracks equipped two of the division's four infantry battalions.

At the time of the invasion 21st Panzer Division was nearly 700 men short of its 16,925-strong establishment. In common with other formations in the west, the division had been required to provide drafts of trained replacements to other theatres, while those joining the division, for example panzer drivers, arrived with eight weeks military training but little actual driving experience. Perennial shortages of fuel, ammunition and replacement tyres limited individual and collective training, as did the daily provision of labour details. Men were most frequently required to dig the anti-tank ditches and holes in which to erect anti-glider poles, known as *Rommel Spargel* (asparagus) in open areas around Caen.

With most of Army Group B labouring hard on coastal defences and attempts to develop some depth in defence, Rommel spent the majority of his time away from his headquarters, driving on construction, assessing the quality of units and adjusting their deployment, as this account of a visit to 21st Panzer Division exemplifies:

> With no advance notice, arriving from western Normandy, Rommel appeared at the command post of *Panzerregiment* 22 in Aubigny, north of Falaise, at approximately 0800 hours on 11 May 1944. The *Feldmarschall* was displeased because the regimental command post was not yet ready for operation and the commander of *Panzerregiment* 22, *Oberst* von Oppeln-Bronikowski, arrived late. 'You are a lazy slob! When do you start work?' His mood improved after he was shown the multiple-rocket launchers that had been built within the division by the inventive *Baustab* Becker. The multiple-rocket launchers impressed him. After viewing these weapons, he repeated his conceptions of defence during a noonday meal in Saint Pierre-sur-Dives.
>
> In the course of his talk, Rommel pointed out the significance of the city of Caen as a transportation hub. Because he was not satisfied with the existing state of defences in this area, he ordered additional measures that finally led to the transfer of *Panzerjäger Abteilung* 200 to the Martragny, Camilly and Basly area, west of Périers-sur-le-Dan, and the reinforced 7.*Kompanie*, *Panzergrenadier Regiment* 192 into field-positions north of Périers. He finally

The *Raketen Vielfachwerfer auf Fargestell Somua MCL* self-propelled launcher which fired a rocket that was a copy of the Soviet Katyusha. One is seen here during Rommel's inspection of 21st Panzer Division described above.

> attended an exercise of *Panzer-Aufklärungs-Abteilung* 21 and noted in his diary: 'The commander and men of the 21.*Panzer Division* made a good impression.'
>
> The 21st Panzer Division, with elements ordered to positions north of Caen and on both sides of the Orne River, was now split.[8]

Even though 21st Panzer Division was under Rommel's command, there were restrictions imposed by OKW on its release to Army Group B. Those concerning action in the event of an airborne landing were to be the cause of some confusion on D Day. Due to the known threat of Allied airborne landings, the 'General Instructions' dating back to Hitler's *Führerbefehl* No. 40 ordered that, in the event of an airborne assault, all divisions and units in the area of the attack were to

An extract from a German minefield map showing the defended areas in the Orne Sector.

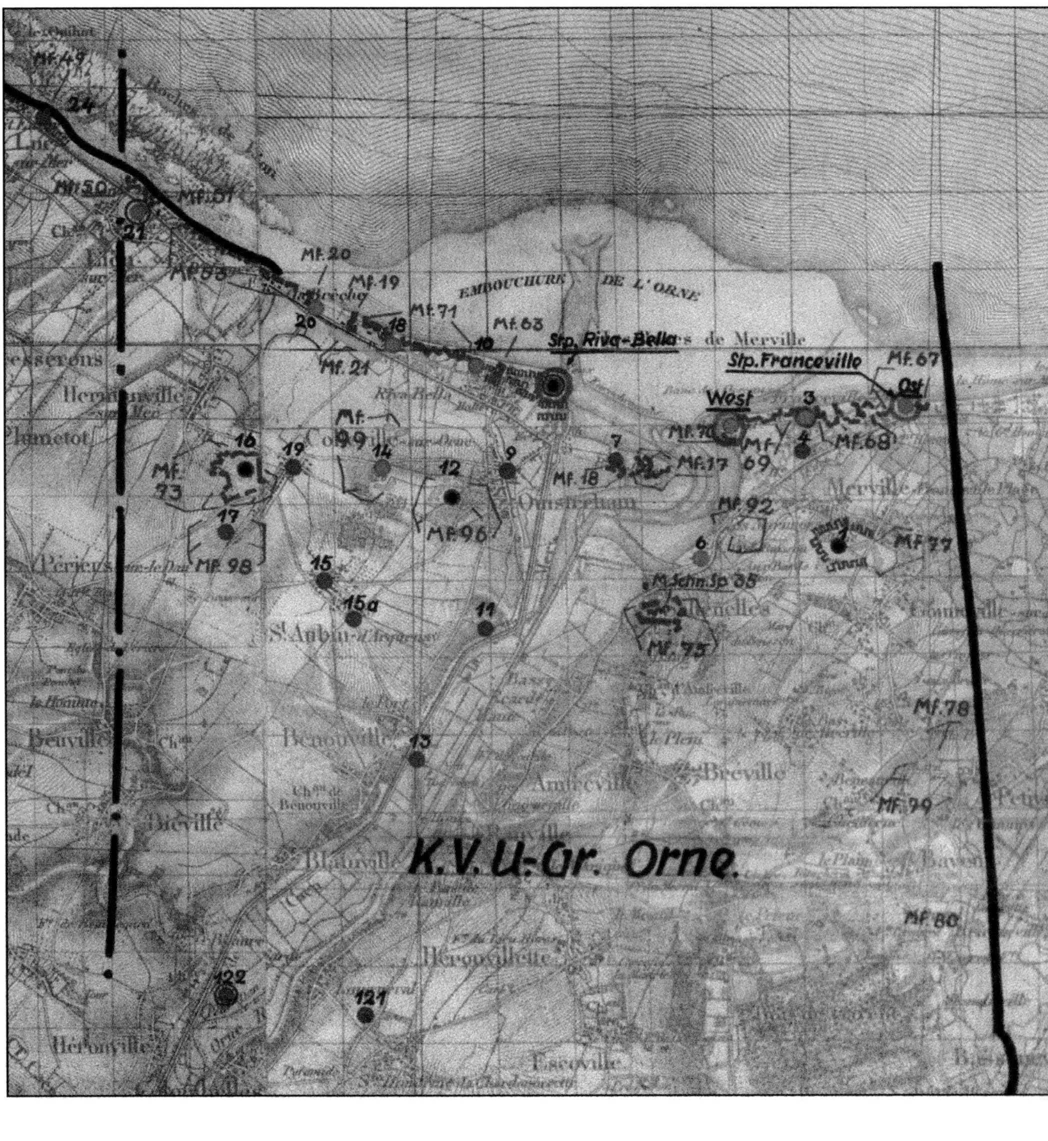

immediately counter-attack from their positions in order to destroy the enemy. To facilitate this, all troops in the area of the airborne assault were to be automatically attached to the division in whose area of responsibility the landings had occurred. Consequently, the units of the 21st Panzer Division stationed around Caen would be covered by this 'General Instruction'. In all other circumstances the division was not to go into action until it received orders from OKW, via Army Group B, to come under command of either Seventh or Fifteenth Army. This latter provision of course covered Feuchtinger's panzer regiment, as it was south of Caen around Falaise.

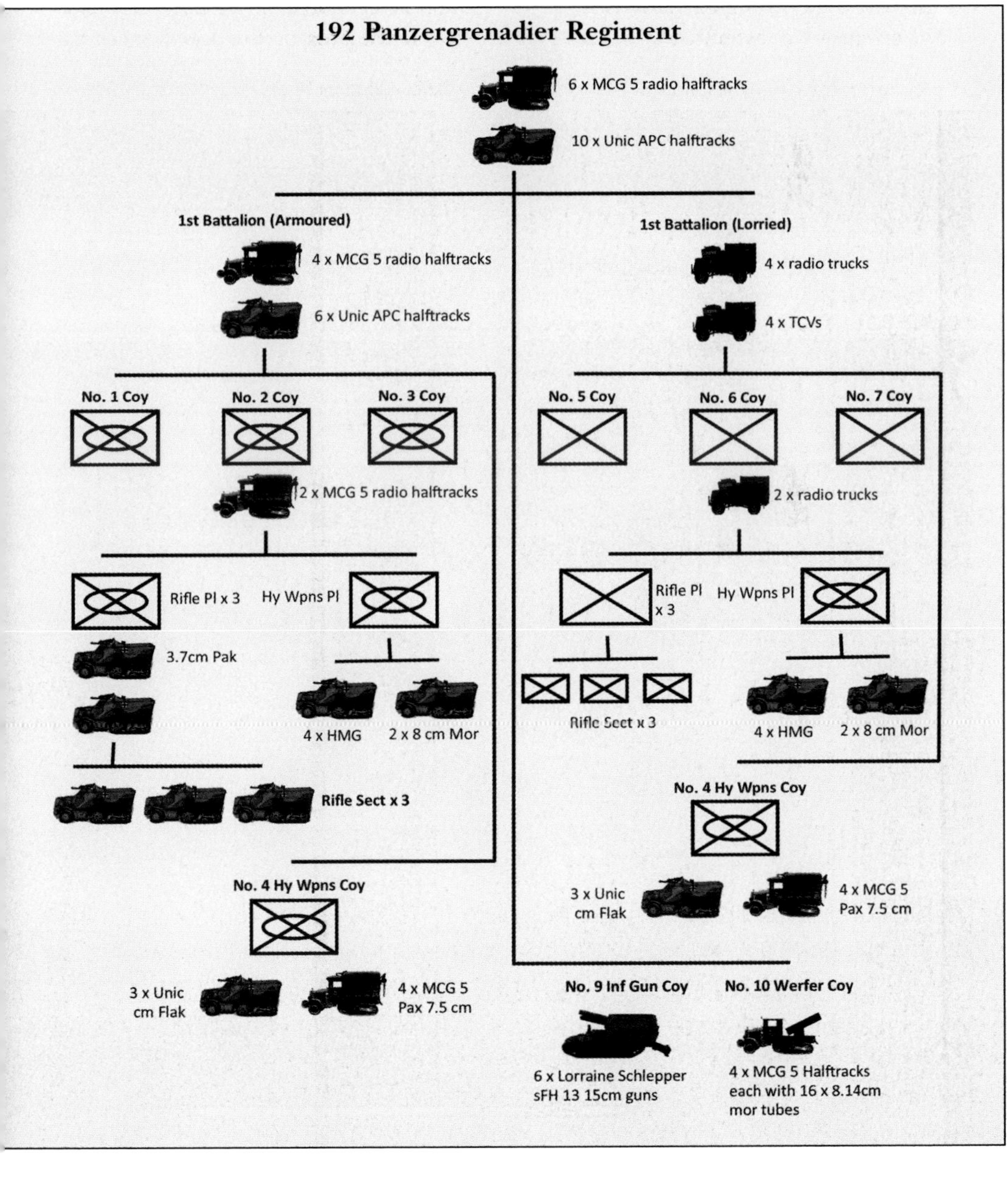

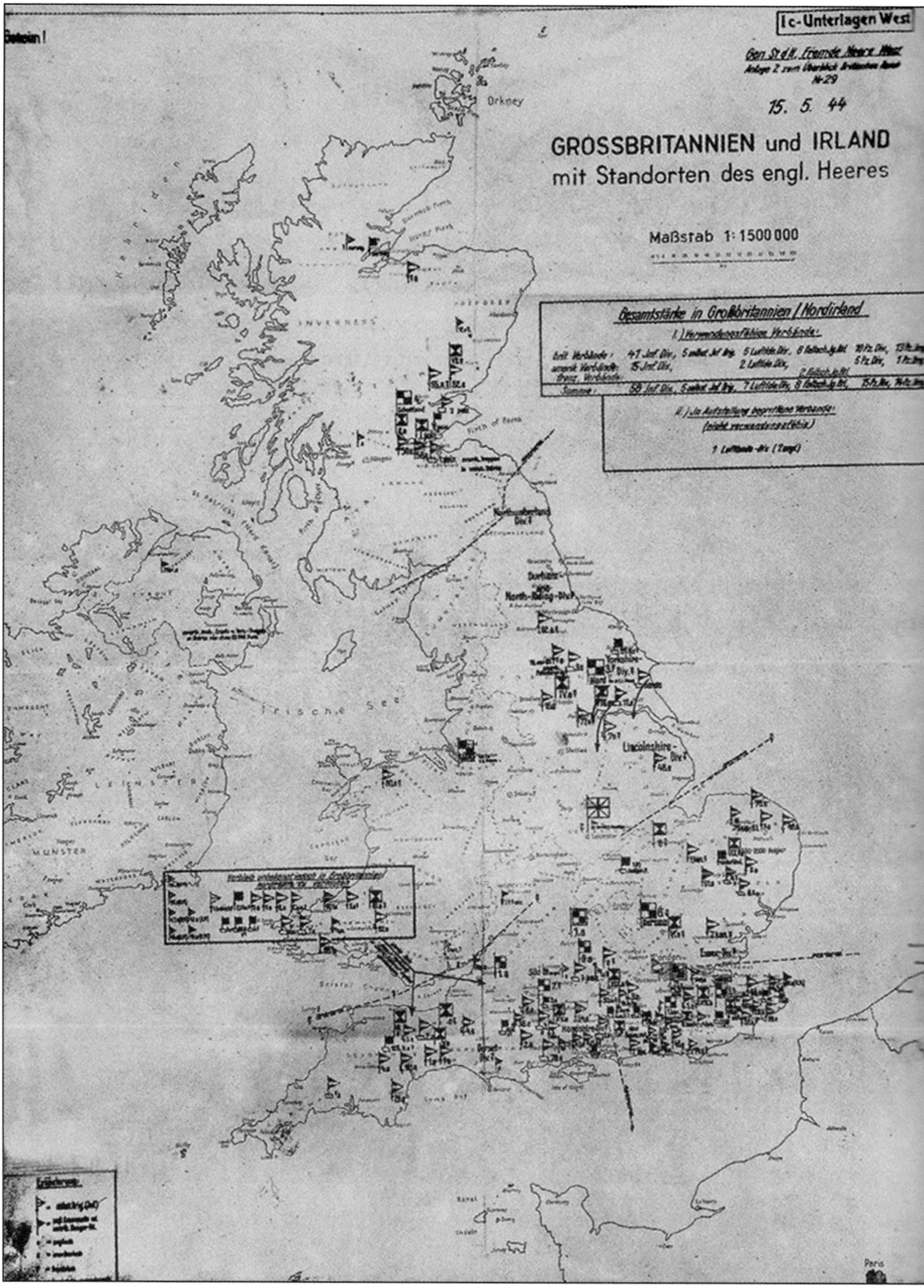

A German intelligence map showing their incorrect understanding of the Allied ORBAT and deployment.

Chapter Three

Preparation for Battle

The 3rd Infantry Division had been preparing to lead a return to the shores of Europe since it was given the invasion role on 1 December 1942. Prior to that, under Major General Bernard Montgomery, the division had fought in the 1940 campaign with distinction, but since Dunkirk, along with much of the rest of the Army, it had been defending Britain from German invasion. The 3rd Division was initially a mobile GHQ reserve formation. With the new role came a move to the Highlands of Scotland, where the Royal Navy and Combined Operations schools were opening to develop amphibious equipment and tactics. In Scotland the division continued its peripatetic existence around camps, training areas and a seemingly endless round of amphibious exercises.

During April 1943, 185 Infantry Brigade joined the division when the experiment of mixed infantry and armoured divisions was abandoned. Having been based in the south of England for most of 1941–43, the brigade spent a period at the Combined Operations Training Centre (CTC) at Inverary on Loch Fyne, before joining the 3rd Division, in the firm expectation of 'proceeding overseas'. The division had trained hard and believed themselves ready to deploy on an amphibious operation, but the 'invasion season of 1943' came and went, with 1st Canadian Division taking their place in Operation HUSKY, the invasion of Sicily.[1]

Life was far from comfortable for the soldiers of the division during the winter of 1943/44, living in huts, or worse, in tents. Gunner Curtis of 33 Field Regiment RA commented, 'We were billeted in bell tents which were camouflaged with a thick layer of snow.' Despite the worsening winter weather, exercises continued, including Exercise GRAB in January 1943. Private Keenan of 2 Lincolns recalled:

> We walked across the sand and up the lowered gangways of the LCIs, onto the boat and then proceeded out into the North Sea. This was pretty traumatic for some of the men as we were caught in quite a severe gale. It was quite amazing to watch these flat-bottomed boats meeting the waves and actually rising in the air before dropping into the next one, seeing the whole of the bottom of the vessel. Many men were sick before we made it into the surf for a very wet landing, wading ashore with water covering our chests.[2]

For the infantrymen aboard the diminutive Landing Craft Assault (LCA) it was if anything worse. Lieutenant Jones of 2nd King's Shropshire Light Infantry (2 KSLI) recalled:

> We sailed in LCAs, flat-bottomed boats, their sides only chest-high and with no overhead cover. Waves crashed over us, soaking us to the skin. We then

Infantry practising an assault landing from an LCA at the Combined Operations Training Centre, Inverary.

> carried out assault landings in the Moray and Cromarty Firths, attacking mock defences and strongpoints. During some of these exercises we were subjected to live ammunition fired just above our heads, accompanied by live shells fired from the supporting RN ships. Then the dismal, wet return across the lochs to our base.

Of these exercises many veterans would subsequently say that the toughening-up process was in many respects worse than the real thing. However, a persistent accusation is that the 3rd Division, thanks to two years of repetitive training, had become 'muscle-bound' or 'over-exercised and under-trained'. In the case of the latter, repeated exercises that focus on process at battalion, brigade or divisional level, and the same for amphibiosity, logistics, etc., leave sub-units as 'pawns, going through the motions', with little training benefit. The imminence of the invasion meant that the normal progression of individual training and building up to the normal larger-scale exercise was badly disrupted in early 1944 by operational rehearsals.

In common with many formations earmarked for Operation OVERLORD during the winter of 1943/44, there were changes of commanders across the 3rd Division. Montgomery's chief of staff, Freddie de Guingand, noted that 'a lot of shuffling around took place in order that at least the commander or his senior staff officer should be one who has proved himself in the war.' As a result, officers who had been tried and tested in the Western Desert and Mediterranean and returned to the UK replaced some of those who had spent years at home training. The most significant of the moves for the 3rd Division was the replacement of Major General Ramsden by Major General Rennie, who arrived at divisional headquarters, which in December 1943 was based in Cameron Barracks, Inverness. At unit level, a significant number of long-serving commanding officers were also moved to meet General Montgomery's edict than no commanding officer was to be older than 36. The 2nd East Yorkshires, for instance, lost Lieutenant Colonel Spicer Hardy and gained Colonel Hutchinson as a part of this process. The disappointment of officers who had trained their battalions for so long can be readily imagined, but Montgomery's view was that battles were won by younger, able commanders, with fitness and resilience.

During the early months of 1944, the division grew in size as specialist units joined for the assault on the coast of Normandy. Brigadier Prior-Palmer's 27 Armoured Brigade travelled to Scotland to come under General Rennie's command. Two of its armoured regiments had been trained in the use of the amphibious DD Shermans in East Anglia, but when it was realized that the width of SWORD Beach was so restricted and the objective so far inland, the assault

Major General Thomas Rennie, commander of the 3rd Infantry Division.

Brigadier Prior-Palmer, commander of 27 Armoured Brigade.

was reduced to a single infantry brigade. Consequently, the East Riding Yeomanry (ERY) lost their DD role and would land behind the DDs of 13th/18th Hussars (13/18 H) and the Western Desert veterans of the Staffordshire Yeomanry. The ERY joined 9 Brigade Group in their role of reserve brigade and took part in a series of amphibious exercises, practising the growing list of anticipated tasks during January and February 1944. Major Ellison described the ERYs' experience:

> The Moray Firth, as most people know, faces north, and it was on these shores that a series of three invasion rehearsals (not exercises) took place. The ground was very similar in all ways to the chosen land on the Continent. The Landing Craft set sail from FORT GEORGE and INVERGORDON in each exercise; pretty uncomfortable exercises they were too, especially for the P.B.I. [Poor Bloody Infantry], wading off tiny L.C.A.s up to their waists,

> small men up to their necks, and even above their steel helmets, in the sea in the North of Scotland in mid-winter. They then slept the night out as they were. CROWN, ANCHOR and LEAPYEAR were the names of the rehearsals.
>
> We actually only took part in the latter in full strength, and the first day it began to snow in the afternoon. It can snow in the North of Scotland, and that day it excelled most days. When it came to sleeping out in six inches of it in a ploughed field during the night, we felt the real thing could not be any worse.[3]

These exercises and a whole series of others at brigade and battalion level were conducted as far as possible with the shipping and landing craft of Rear Admiral Talbot's Force S, which was divided into three assault groups, one per infantry brigade. Captain Kelly of the 1st Royal Norfolks recalled:

> We became used to working with the Navy and to travelling by sea in small craft. In these exercises and in the invasion transport and protection were provided by Force S, inspired by Captain Bush RN [the commander of Assault Group S3], a strong personality who never failed to impress on Brigade conferences. I think the special value of training with the Navy was the confidence it induced during the operation. The Channel crossing seemed to be an exact repeat of the rehearsals, the main difference being the vastly greater number of ships. The exercise feeling was not lost until we came close to the French coast.

For additional security, a small planning staff from the divisional headquarters moved to the remote Aberlour House when the first operational directive was issued. Later, veterans commented that the final series of exercises in Scotland 'bore an uncanny likeness to the real plan'. During April the 3rd Division, by now with numerous attachments that formed the assault group of some 30,000 men, moved south mostly by train to concentrate in Hampshire and Sussex. The division's vehicles and tanks travelled aboard their landing ships and craft.

The final two months' preparation, as more and more formations assembled within striking distance of the south coast ports, were characterized by the issue of additional stores, the endless waterproofing of vehicles, senior officers' conferences and visits to units. Montgomery held a series of briefings for officers down the chain of command to lieutenant colonel, impressing on them how he intended to fight and what was expected of them. However, details of where and when the invasion would take place were only revealed to those who needed them for planning as the date of the invasion approached.

Montgomery joined the King, the Prime Minister and General Eisenhower in paying visits to invasion divisions around the country. De Guingand wrote:

> Having got the Joint Plan off his chest, Montgomery now concentrated upon his soldiers. He was new to many of them, and he lost no time in ensuring that they both saw and heard him. He travelled round and visited

Those who had been let into the D Day secret were referred to as having been 'Bigoted', after the code word that protected 'when and where'.

> all the formations. He would often use a jeep, and tell the soldiers to gather round and, standing up, would give them a few minutes of the 'Monty tonic'. As in the past, he produced in this way great enthusiasm and confidence.

Captain Scarfe recalled a memorable visit to the 3rd Division by General Eisenhower on 13 May:

> His sincerity was impressive. Everyone laughed when he said he knew what some of them thought of the Americans, and that he had the advantage of knowing what some of the Americans thought of them. And everyone knew the truth in his remark about thinking ourselves not Allies, but one indivisible team. 'It is good to see you looking so fit and in such good spirits. I had heard so much about you from General Montgomery: and he certainly did not exaggerate.'

Final Rehearsal

Exercise FABIUS was the final test of 21st Army Group's plans for the invasion. It encompassed the procedure for embarkation, a simulated passage, the assault landing, including elements of the fire plan, the advance to objectives inland and the British build-up. The assault on four of the five replica beaches was rehearsed at the same time, in corps level exercises, FABIUS I–IV.[4] The beaches used by I Corps to land 3rd and 3rd Canadian divisions were near Littlehampton and at Bracklesham, and those by XXX Corps' assault division, the 50th Northumbrian, were on Hayling Island.

A report on the exercise describes the aim:

> No longer was there time for drastic revisions in plan or for retraining units. Minor deficiencies could be corrected, but FABIUS was primarily an

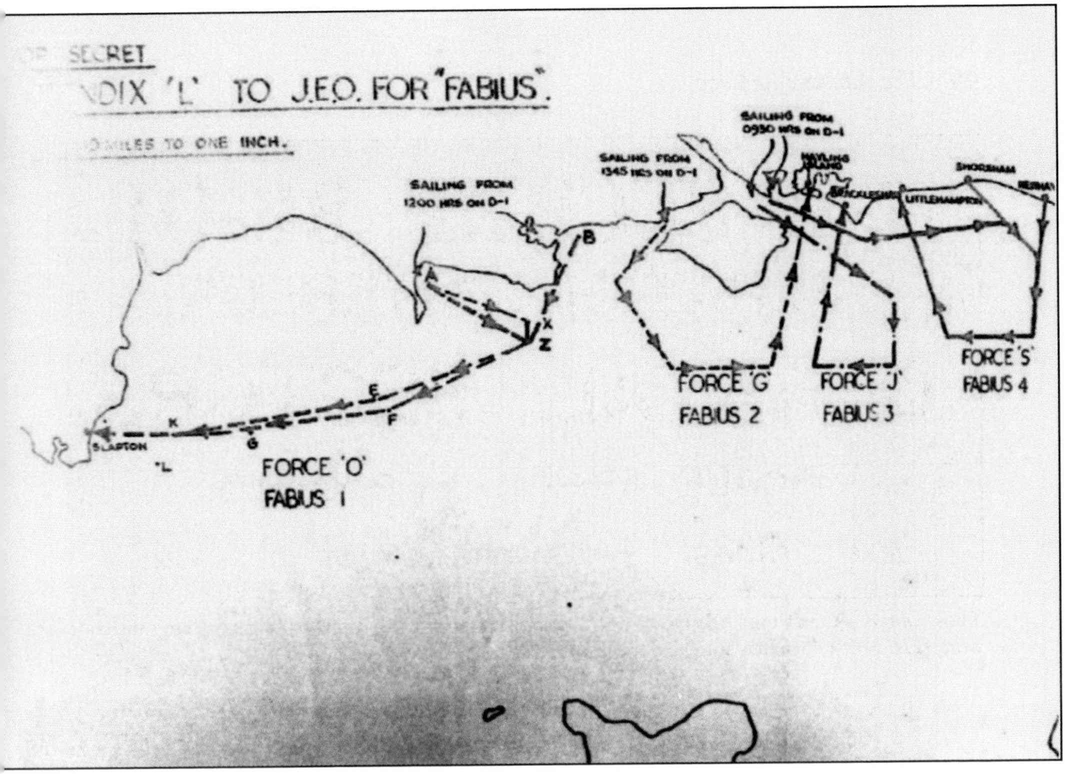

A copy of an original sketch map from the Air Op O showing the four FABIUS exercises.

> exercise to give the troops experience in their tasks and to give the invasion machinery a chance to function as a whole before it would be called upon to perform its primary function. Every effort was made to duplicate the conditions to be met on the Normandy beaches, and planning orders called for the exercise to resemble NEPTUNE 'as closely as limitations of equipment and facilities will permit'.

The Home Guard provided the enemy, and large areas of Hayling Island's farmland inland from the beach had been cleared for use as temporary artillery impact areas.[5]

Most of the 3rd Division's assault troops were already in their as yet unsealed marshalling camps in the Embarkation Areas and began the process of boarding shipping for FABIUS IV on 30 April. Very few members of the divisional group have much to say about FABIUS, which is not surprising after dozens of previous exercises, but Major Ellison of the East Riding Yeomanry wrote:

> On arrival at the 'hards' at GOSPORT we found our craft waiting for us already beached. After taking rations for the journey with us, we backed all our vehicles onto the small craft and put out into the Solent to wait till all was ready. The sea was like a millpond [after a 24-hour weather delay], and after one night on board we sailed and went about 20 miles out to sea and later landed at LITTLEHAMPTON, a round trip of 100 miles. The Navy trailed our coats, and the enemy never responded at all, perhaps fortunately,

> as our American friends lost a few craft to enemy action on one of their practices [Exercise TIGER] about the same time.

It had been hoped that sailing well out into the Channel would provoke the Germans into revealing some of their plans to counter the invasion.

After landing on West and Climping beaches, 8 Brigade advanced inland to 'capture' Yapton (Hermanville), while parts of Littlehampton and Bognor represented the commando objectives of Ouistreham and Luc-sur-Mer, and Arundel, 7 miles inland, was 185 Brigade's objective, Caen. One farmer they encountered on their way from the beaches, 'having watched his beloved hedges get ripped to pieces by the mechanised onslaught of tanks and guns, could stand by and watch no longer. A torrent of profanity-laden abuse rained down upon the dumbstruck soldiers like proverbial machine gun fire.'[6]

Following the exercise, the division returned to its marshalling areas to await D Day. Infantry battalions and artillery regiments from disbanded or re-purposed divisions started to arrive to run 'hotel service' for assault units in the various camps once all unit equipment was packed or sent away with the 'Residue' that would follow during the build-up.[7] These hotel service troops were also

The remains of the four Gosport embarkation hards at Stokes Bay used by 27 Armoured Brigade, the breaching teams of 79th Armoured Division and other vehicles bound for SWORD Beach.

responsible for security, especially once camps were sealed, 'keeping soldiers in, as much as keeping the public out!'

> After *Fabius* it quickly became clear that we were now for it! Wiring round camps was doubled and tents were set aside in each for 'briefing' with strong guards posted outside and C.O.s and I.O.s and staffs working long hours at the preparations within.

The fine weather and smooth seas of FABIUS may have convinced many army units in the assault force that this was a prerequisite for the landing, but following their long experience in the stormy seas off Scotland this cannot have been foremost in the 3rd Division's mind.

Setting the Day and the Hour

As late as 8 May, with the 21st Army Group plan finally approved, General Eisenhower, his three commanders-in-chief and their staffs met to finalize the invasion's D Day and H Hour. The original plan had been to land the assault force three to four hours before high water and about forty minutes after dawn.

> The Navy wanted as many hours as possible of rising tide, and the Army wanted the shortest possible run over the exposed beach. Both wanted adequate daylight for observing shoots and as many hours of daylight as possible for the build-up, in fact a second high water before nightfall. Then [in late February] the under-water obstacles had been reported, and were the most considerable factor. They varied in depth on the different beaches. It was therefore decided that there should be individual H hours, according to the depth of the obstacles. The earliest was fixed at 06.30 hours, the latest [JUNO Beach] at 07.55 [*sic* 0745]. Three days in every fortnight produced suitable conditions. The first timing of H hour depended on which of those days the assault was made. The day was fixed as June 5th. There could be postponement till the 6th, or, if the worst came, till the 7th.

H Hour for the 3rd Division's assault on SWORD Beach was to be 0725 hours.

Embarkation

In the aftermath of FABIUS yet more equipment was issued to individuals and units and needed packing. While commanders pored over operation orders, maps and air photographs, their men laboured at waterproofing vehicles, radios and other equipment. With kit packed and little room in the crowded countryside for training, infantry companies went on route marches until camps were sealed and briefings began. While the broad outline had been steadily revealed on a 'need to know' basis, it was not until after FABIUS that the detailed I Corps Operation Order No. 1 was issued on 5 May. The Corps' order was followed by 3rd Division's on 23 May, brigades on the 25th and units on the 28th. That issued by 2 East Yorks used both bogus names and grid references: '2nd Battn. Group will land on Queen Red Beach at H. plus 5 minutes, destroy the defences, capture

An LCT loading at Gosport. On the right are the carriers of 1 South Lancs, the bulldozer in the centre belongs to No. 5 Beach Group and the carriers on the left are from 2 RUR of 9 Brigade.

CROSSLEY 3816 [St Aubin d'Arquenay], secure RUGGER 399149 [Pont de Bénouville/Pegasus Bridge] and CRICKET 404146 [Pont de Tournant/Ranville Bridge].'[8]

Despite the issue of orders and briefings down the chain of command, the great secret of OVERLORD, the 'where and the when', would only be revealed to most at the last moment.

The Norfolks' regimental historian describes the final preparations:

> Briefing was a serious business. Imagine a series of large store tents each with special lighting and flooring and a 20-foot map. The masterplan was unfolded to every man, but security was such that bogus place-names were used throughout, and even now any reference to any part of the immediate bridgehead is still referred to as Hillman, Rover, etc.
>
> During and after this period of intensive study of air photographs, maps and models, the Battalion was 'sealed'. That meant that no one was allowed in or out of the perimeter within which we lived. We knew that the hour was at hand and that soon we should go through the marshalling camps to our embarkation hards.

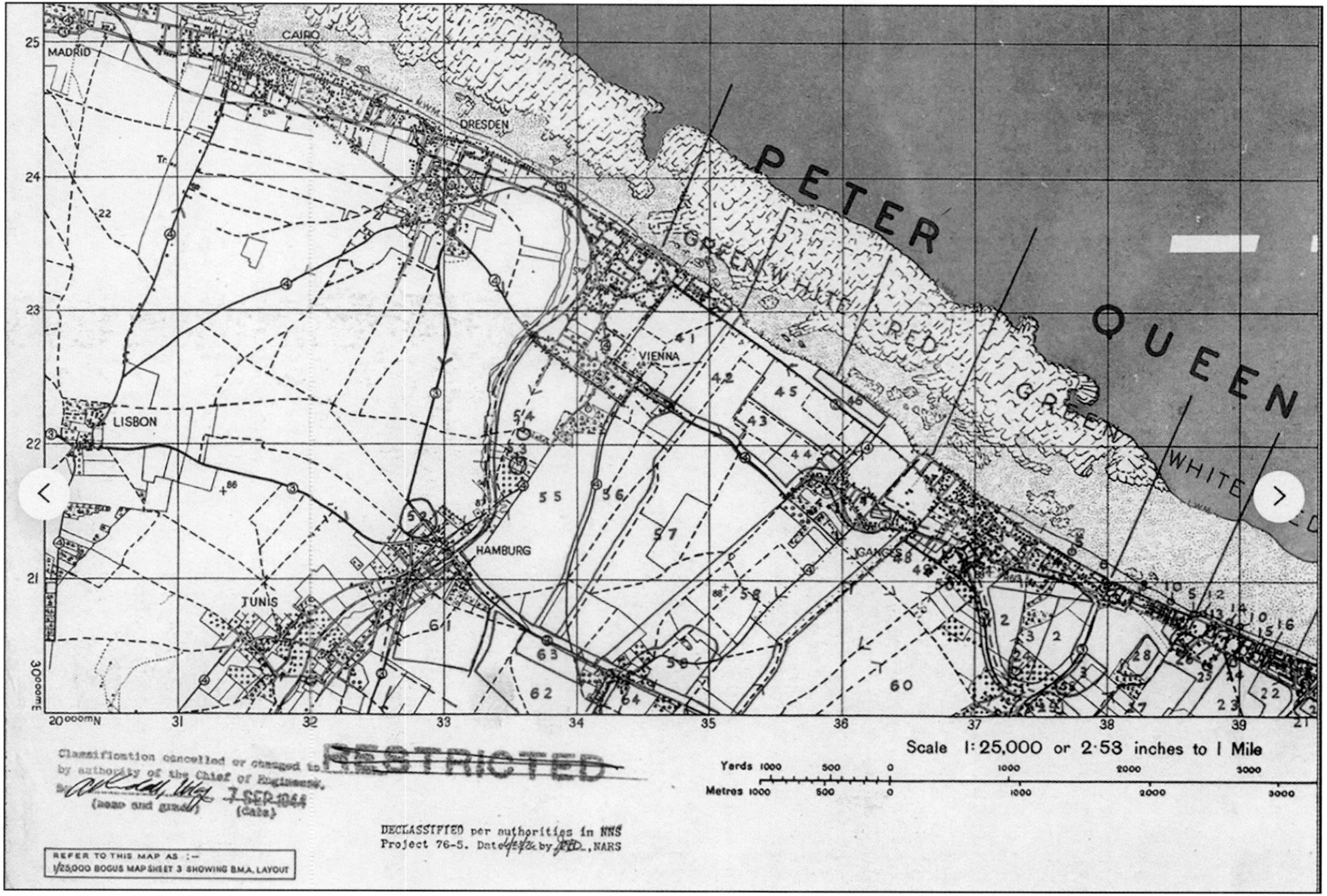

A section of the 'Bogus' map covering the SWORD Beach area, with fake names. These maps were used until after Force S had embarked. Lion-sur-Mer = Ganges. The other markings are the planned logistic layout of Beach Maintenance Area (BMA) MOON.

During the final week of May, units were marshalled into loads for their respective ships and landing craft. Tanks and vehicles that were to land in the first waves were separated from unit transport that would land during subsequent tides and later days according to anticipated requirements. Most unit transport for later in the build-up was sent to Aldershot, from where vehicles would be 'phased into' shipping from Portsmouth, Southampton or the London Docks.[9]

Embarkation began on 31 May. It was an immensely complicated procedure differing from place to place depending on shipping, the composition of the assault force and the availability of piers, hards, etc. Stokes Bay near Gosport had four LCT hards, and Gosport itself, two Landing Ships Tank (LST) hards, while the Portsmouth naval dockyard had a berth earmarked for the larger Landing Ships Infantry (LSI). Loading of LSTs with armour and vehicles that had to be backed on was slow and caused some damage to craft. Major Cotter commanding C Squadron 13/18H recalled:

> After a stay of two days in our marshalling camp where final briefing and instructions were given, and another half of 24 hours where the final waterproofing of tanks was carried out, we eventually reached our port of embarkation, Gosport, on 4 June, and embarked at 10 o'clock in the morning.

Infantry platoons of 3rd Division marching to Southsea Pier for embarkation.

It took a little longer than usual to load the tanks on to the LCTs, as they were all towing waterproofed sledges called 'Porpoises' in which was a reserve of ammunition in case we required more at short notice after landing on the enemy beaches. They were clumsy things and required a certain amount of manoeuvring on the part of the tanks to get them into convenient positions in the limited space on the craft; however, after half an hour my LCT was loaded and we moved out into the bay taking up our positions in line with hundreds of other craft of every type and size. 4 June was a glorious day and I shall never forget the astonishing sight of that invasion fleet of assault craft, lying spread out as far as the eye could see, westwards to the Isle of Wight and eastwards towards Portsmouth and Hayling Island. Surely the Luftwaffe would attempt to do something to such a target and yet there appeared to be no Luftwaffe.

A Sherman backing on to an LCT towing a Porpoise that fitted under the belly of the tank. They normally carried additional ammunition to the beach, where the contents were later collected for replenishment.

As embarkation progressed, the assault elements of the Norfolks were moved to a typical tented camp, Green Camp near Lewes in Area J9. Newhaven could not take the LSIs, consequently the Norfolks were to cross the Channel in the smaller, uncomfortable Landing Craft Infantry (LCI). These lacked anything more than the most basic facilities, so they would only board at the last moment. Major Wilson, the battalion's Second-in-Command, described Green Camp.

> Here we met complete security and were sealed in. However, everything had been thought of even down to entertainment and on Sunday evening we had Vic Oliver to tell us stories and try to sing. The troops enjoyed it and that was important.
>
> Our evenings were quiet and I suppose we were all wondering how we should react under fire intended to kill us. We never talked about this but everyone had his private thoughts on the subject.

With French francs and a *Soldier's Guide to France* issued, the infantry left their camps with 8 and 9 brigades embarking on the LSIs and 185 Brigade boarding the cramped LCIs on the morning of 5 June.

The Weather

No work on the opening of the North-West European Campaign is complete without considering the weather in the final days before the invasion and on D Day itself. In the case of the 3rd Division, it is particularly relevant to their fortunes from the final run-in to the beach onwards.

The weather during the month of May 1944 was typical of a settled early English summer, with eighteen days being 'perfect for OVERLORD and the rest good'. The meteorologists of the two nations and three services, having finally settled down to work with each other, had little to report to concern senior commanders. At the end of May, however, weather stations from as far afield as the North American Arctic and the Caribbean, and ships deployed in the Atlantic, started reporting less stable weather conditions and a decline in the Azores' high pressure; that guarantor of good weather over the Channel.

General Eisenhower and his senior commanders had been receiving weather updates from Group Captain John Stagg on a regular basis for some months, in order that they could gauge their accuracy and the reliance they could place on the meteorologists' forecasts. The first day of June dawned dull and grey, and Stagg noted in his personal diary: 'Fairly optimistic, but obviously a very marginal and difficult situation.' The next day, the meteorologists assembled at Admiral Ramsey's headquarters at Southwick House, near Portsmouth as scheduled at 0930 hours. They reported to Eisenhower and his three service commanders-in-chief that for 5 June 'the situation was not what we hoped for'. Stagg briefed the meeting that 'the whole development was sluggish and slow to show its hand, but on the whole still mainly favourable from the wind point of view though very uncertain about cloud' and that prospects were for 'continuing poor' weather. Admiral Creasy, the naval chief of staff, memorably commented,

Southwick House, Admiral Ramsey's naval headquarters 5 miles from Portsmouth.

'Six feet two of Stagg, and six feet one of gloom'. The prospects for acceptable weather 'became worse and worse'. Eisenhower later wrote:

> The final conference for determining the feasibility of attacking on the tentatively selected day, June 5, was scheduled for 4 a.m. on June 4. However, some of the attacking contingents had already been ordered to sea, because if the entire force was to land on June 5, then some of the important elements stationed in northern parts of the United Kingdom could not wait for final decision on the morning of June 4.
>
> When the commanders assembled on the morning of June 4 the report we received was discouraging. Low clouds, high winds, and formidable wave action were predicted to make landing a most hazardous affair. The meteorologists said that air support would be impossible, naval gunfire would be inefficient, and even the handling of small boats would be rendered difficult. Admiral Ramsay thought that the mechanics of landing could be handled, but agreed with the estimate of the difficulty in adjusting gunfire. His position was mainly neutral. General Montgomery, properly concerned with the great disadvantages of delay, believed that we should go. Tedder disagreed.[10]

With Stagg having overruled the more optimistic American meteorologists, Eisenhower decided to postpone OVERLORD from 5 June for 24 hours. This

Group Captain John Stagg, the Chief Allied meteorologist.

meant that the ships in the Irish Sea returned to port to refuel, and troops endured another day in cramped onboard condition, with the 'consequence of further postponement too bitter to contemplate'. At the 2100 meeting on 4 June Stagg tentatively reported that there was likely to be moderation in the weather on the morning of 6 June. Eisenhower continued:

> When the conference started the first report given us by Group Captain Stagg and the meteorologic staff was that the bad conditions predicted the day before for the coast of France were actually prevailing there and that if we had persisted in the attempt to land on June 5 a major disaster would almost surely have resulted. This they probably told us to inspire more confidence in their next astonishing declaration, which was that by the following morning a period of relatively good weather, heretofore completely

unexpected, would ensue, lasting probably thirty-six hours. The long-term prediction was not good but they did give us assurance that this short period of good weather would intervene between the exhaustion of the storm we were then experiencing and the beginning of the next spell of really bad weather.

They could afford to wait another six hours to see how Stagg's 'rapid and unexpected developments over the Atlantic' played out, and before dawn on 5 June the commanders reassembled in the library of Southwick Park House. Risks that had been discussed the previous evening were covered again – what would the cloud cover, wind speed and sea state be the following morning, 6 June 1944? As far as the likely sea state was concerned, it was assessed by naval advisors as slowing amphibious operations. This was a risk that could, of course, affect 3rd Division's need for speed to reach objectives 10 miles inland on D Day. Conditions were marginal for airborne operations and would reduce the accuracy of air attack, but with the prospect of delay being 'terrible' Eisenhower decided to 'go'.

Across the Channel, with far less complete weather data being submitted by U-boats and a handful of clandestine weather stations, the Luftwaffe meteorologists concluded that the weather over the Channel was likely to preclude an invasion until the middle of the month.[11] Consequently, while orders were being flashed to the great Allied fleet that they were to set to sea, commanders in the German Seventh Army received orders that they were to attend a command post exercise at Saint-Lô on the morning of 6 June. In addition, Rommel was away from his headquarters and on his way to Germany to celebrate his wife's birthday and visit Hitler in order to present his case for command of the panzer divisions.

Sailing

Throughout 5 June, from 0900 hours onwards, shipping and craft bound for SWORD Beach left ports along the south coast on a carefully calculated schedule, based on their speed and the distance they had to travel to be off the Normandy coast at the correct place and time the following morning.

Naval records state that 'The wind was west, Force 5, slackening to Force 3 to 4 and veering west-north-west in the evening, the sea [state] was 3–4, swell 1. These conditions were unexpectedly severe and imposed a high test on landing craft crews.' One of the first to sail, Force S2 sailing from Newhaven with Brigadier Smith's 185 Brigade embarked, 'had a steady beat of 33 miles into a head sea and was hard put to keep to its programme.' According to the battalion's history, the Norfolks aboard the LCIs and LCTs of Force S2 had an uncomfortable passage:

> It was rough outside the shelter of the harbour, and soon the troops were feeling it pretty badly. It was not until we were well at sea that the signal came over the naval wireless that the landing was 'on' and that we could now open up our proper maps and for the first time know where we were going to land. The final briefing took place in the minute cabin of the LCI, with each

> member of the group every now and then rushing out, to come back not quite so green as when he left. And so darkness fell before the most historic day of our generation.

Those ships and craft bearing naval forces S1 and 3 with, respectively, 9 and 8 brigades, passed the Nab Tower at the eastern end of the Solent and were amongst the last to leave sheltered water. Mainly aboard the larger Landing Ships Infantry and Tank, 8 and 9 brigades were heading for POINT ZULU or 'Piccadilly Circus', where the assault forces converged before turning south down the mine-swept lanes, or the 'spout'. Private Gardner recalled what was considered to be 'a marginally better passage':

> Our ship, the [*Empire*] *Battleaxe*, a converted American freighter, was anchored off Portsmouth. Around us, as far as we could see, were ships of all descriptions, all of them with their bows pointing out to sea and France.
>
> On board the boys were playing cards, gambling away their last English money and starting on the French money that had been issued to everybody. At 8.30am the captain spoke over the ship's microphone: 'We sail at 21.00 hours tonight.' This was the message we had been waiting for. At 8.45am the decks were crowded with troops – hundreds of sun-burned, fit young men in khaki, with their safety belts on and everyone with a black triangle on their arms.
>
> On the stroke of nine we weighed anchor. Around us ships were belching black smoke as they got up steam to move off: then we swung into line and began to move out to sea. At 9.30pm, we were all ordered below to get what sleep we could.

One of the many types and sizes of LCI. They had flat bottoms for beach landings so were uncomfortable at sea in anything but fine weather.

Empire Battleaxe, one of six Landing Ships Infantry (LSI) in Force S, including her sister ship *Empire Broadsword*.

Heading south from POINT ZULU aboard a motor launch was Lieutenant Rouse RNVR. As navigating officer of Force S, considerable responsibility lay on his shoulders as he led the flotilla.

> The crossing to Normandy on June 5th was without incident. I had a nasty moment when our navigational equipment became subject to jamming, but I remembered the advice on how to overcome this by changing the RF unit. The whole way over I was subject to what I have later learned is something known to all navigators as 'DMS' (= Dry Mouth Syndrome). This is caused by the fear of making a navigational mistake resulting in the ship – or, in this case, the whole of S Force – ending up somewhere different from where they are supposed to be.

Naval rating and RN beach commando Ken Oakley recalled:

> At 3.30am we queued up with our trays for breakfast of porridge, two hard-boiled eggs, four rounds of white bread and butter and jam and a mug of tea. We gave our rifles the once over, filled the magazines, and made sure our ammunition and grenades were ready for use.
>
> At 4.45am the word came over the loudspeaker to get dressed, and at 4.50 the captain spoke. He could see the French coast, he said: it was a blazing inferno … the RAF are still bombing it. He said that in a few moments we would be starting off on the biggest landing in history.

An Allied poster showing some of the landing craft used on D Day.

Chapter Four

Invasion

SWORD BEACH Met and tidal times.
Weather forecast – Wind WNW force 4–5 (16–20 knots), five eighths cloud cover at 2,000–3,000 feet and 'a short steep sea' of 4 to 6 feet.
Low water AM 0615 hours (Double British Summertime), high water PM 1300 hours, low water PM 1830 hours.[1]

From POINT ZULU the ships and craft of Force S sailed overnight through the marked and swept lanes in the German minefields. While the soldiers aboard slept as best they could, their nerves and thoughts of the following day rendering a good night's sleep almost impossible, above them the air forces were already in action.

Over the Channel a series of coordinated deception measures were underway. To the east Operations GLIMMER and TAXABLE simulated attacks using strips of foil, while surrounding the invasion area in Normandy in Operation TITANIC, dummy parachutists were dropped, along with patrols from 1st SAS. To the west of the Cotentin Peninsula the Royal Navy in Operation BIG DRUM jammed the surviving German radars. The overall intention of these and other measures was to blind and confuse the enemy, and to overload their command systems with contradictory reports.

The German commanders, having received the forecast of poor weather,[2] were mainly away from their headquarters, and the soldiers had manned their defences on all too many occasions as a result of false alarms.[3] There was thus no clear response to the unprecedented levels of Allied activity. Despite Gestapo interrogators having discovered that the invasion would be between 20 May and 10 June and that various messages broadcast by the BBC would alert the Resistance that the invasion would begin within 48 hours, no coordinated alert was issued. Fifteenth Army in the Pas de Calais raised the state of readiness on its own initiative, as had some divisions in Seventh Army. Crucially, with its commander and 1a (chief of staff) in Paris, the 21st Panzer Division had not been placed on heightened alert. Thanks to successful security and deception, the Allies were to achieve tactical surprise. For 3rd Division the resulting time gained would be all important if they were to take Caen.

The drop of three Allied airborne division that began shortly after midnight was of course an indicator that an invasion was underway, although the question for the German commanders was: is this the invasion or only a preliminary attack? They were concerned that a precipitate response would draw their

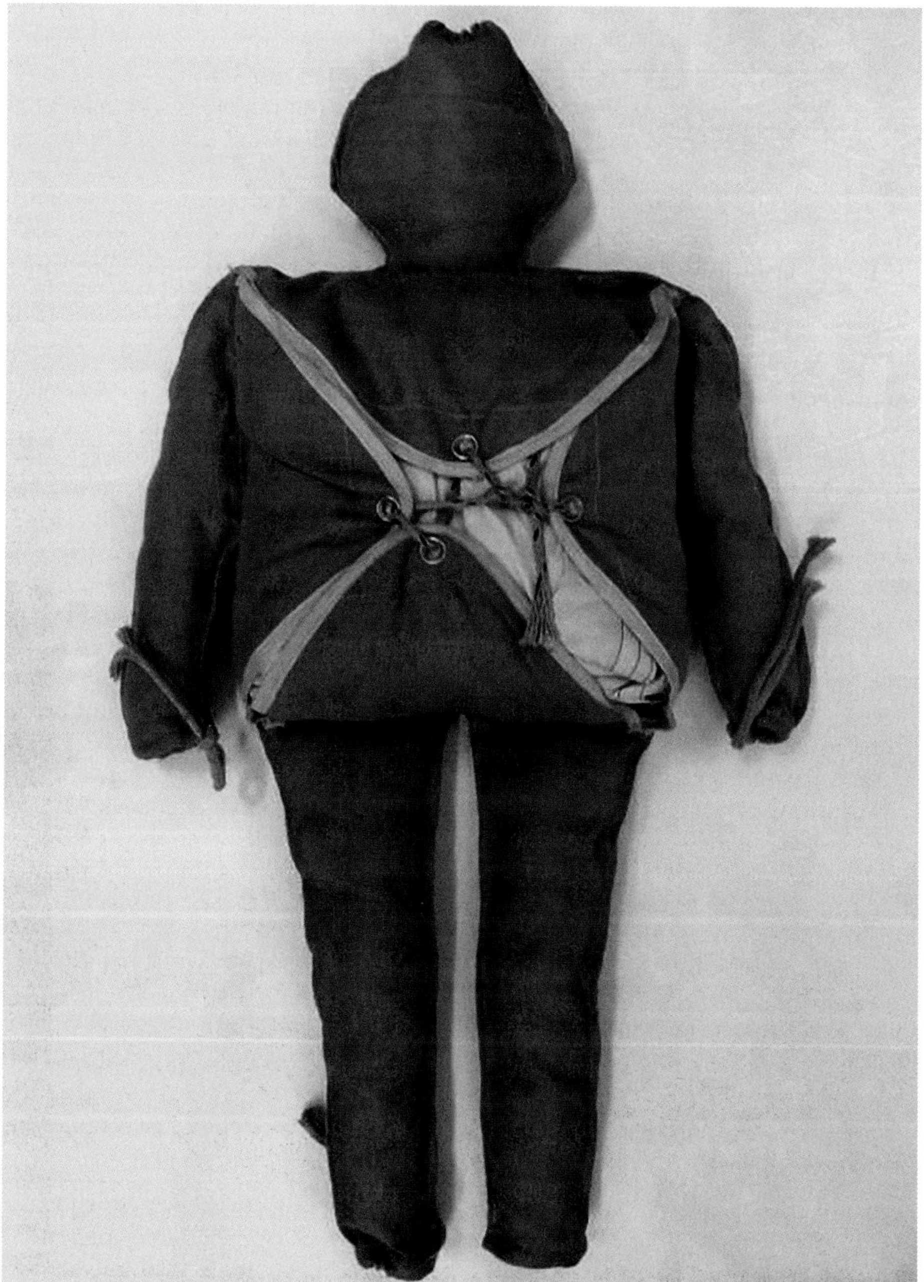

Officially GINGERBREAD MEN or SAINTS, but known as 'Ruperts' (a traditional nickname for young British Army officers). They came with a variety of devices to simulate a firefight and were designed to spread confusion.

reserves away from a second larger landing, which thanks to FORTITUDE they firmly believed would be in the Pas de Calais.

At the headquarters of 716th Division, located in the tunnels of a quarry just to the north of Caen, the phones were ringing shortly after midnight with reports of parachute landings across the eastern half of the divisional area. They immediately went to the highest alert state, but the situation was confused by the dispersal of 6th Airborne Division's drop, with poorly dropped sticks of paratroopers and Ruperts landing as far west as Douvres-la-Délivrande. Significantly, the dispersal included drops across the army boundary in the 711th Division's area to the east of the Dives Estuary.

6th Airborne Division

In the opening act of the land battle, D Company Group of 2nd Ox and Bucks LI seized a pair of vital bridges, Objectives RUGGER and CRICKET, over the Canal de Caen and the River Orne in a glider coup de main. The bridges had been held by a reinforced platoon of 3 Company I/736 Infantry Regiment, but without an alert the bridge guard was at a minimal manning level. These bridges were the only crossings of a double water feature between the lock gates at Ouistreham and bridges on the outskirts of Caen, and their capture would secure not only communication with 6th Airborne Division but also the left flank of 3rd Division for its advance on Caen.

With a thoroughly rehearsed plan, taking the bridges by surprise within fifteen minutes may have been straightforward, but holding them until the arrival of the 3rd Division would be a harder task. Members of the bridges' garrison, who had been off duty in nearby villages, approached from several directions under NCOs and sniped at the Ox & Bucks. A company of self-propelled guns from *Panzerjäger* Battalion 716 was also soon prepared to counter-attack the bridges from its billets in Biéville just 3 miles to the south-west. When the leading Marder I (a Hotchkiss H35/39 tank converted to mount a 75mm PaK 40) approached the junction leading to the bridge, it was knocked out by a PIAT fired by Sergeant Wagger Thornton of D Company, and the rest withdrew. Throughout the day, Colonel Pine-Coffin's 7 Para and D Company of the Ox & Bucks LI fought hard to hold the area of Bénouville and its bridge against determined attacks by 192 *Panzergrenadier* regiment and detachments from 716 Division, until relieved by the 3rd Division on the evening of D Day.

Generalleutnant Richter, who had elements of 21st Panzer Division under his tactical command, recalled:

> At about 0200 hrs the commander of the 716. Div issued the order to the commander of 21. Pz. Div. to attack the enemy east of the Orne with the entire Pz. Div. and to clear the area east of the Orne together with the units of 716. Div. which had been placed in action.[4]

Also immediately in action were parts of 125 *Panzergrenadier* Regiment of 21st Panzer Division that were in the area of 6th Airborne Division's drop. Major

Marder I

The Marders issued to the self-propelled anti-tank company of *Panzerjäger* Battalion 716 was a product of *Baustab* Becker. Designated the *Geschutzpanzer* 39H(f) 7.5cm PaK40(Sf), it was based on Hotchkiss H35/39 French tanks that had been captured in 1940. The conversion work to twenty-four of these tanks entailed the removal of the turret and its replacement with a splinter/small arms-proof, open-topped armoured superstructure, in which a German 75mm PaK L/46 anti-tank gun was mounted. The gun had a traverse of 30° left and right of centre, therefore for any correction beyond this, the vehicle had to physically turn in the direction of the target. The gun crew numbered four including the driver. The fighting compartment provided a generous working space for the gunners, but they were exposed to airburst munitions. SP *Panzerjäger* companies in *Panzergrenadier* regiments or divisions had an establishment of ten Marders.

The Marder I, based on the Hotchkiss H35/39 tank.

von Luck was in his headquarters at Vimout, 6 miles to the south-east of Caen, preparing orders for a training exercise the following day:

> About midnight, I heard the growing roar of aircraft, which passed over us. I wondered whether the attack was destined once again for traffic routes inland or for Germany herself. The machines appeared to be flying very low – because of the weather? I looked out the window and was wide awake; flares were hanging in the sky. At the same moment, my adjutant was on the

telephone: 'Major, paratroops are dropping. Gliders are landing in our section. I'm trying to make contact with No. II Battalion. I'll come along to you at once.'

I gave orders without hesitation: 'All units are to be put on alert immediately and the division informed. No. II Battalion is to go into action wherever necessary. Prisoners are to be taken if possible and brought to me.'

I then went to the command post with my adjutant. The 5 Company of No. II Battalion, which had gone out with blank cartridges, was not back yet from the night exercise – a dangerous situation. First reports indicated that British paratroops had dropped over Troarn. The commander of No. II Battalion had already started a counter-attack with uninvolved elements and had succeeded in penetrating as far as Troarn, to which elements of the 5th Company had already withdrawn under their own steam. We telephoned the company commander, who was in a cellar: 'Brandenburg, hold on. The battalion is already attacking and is bound to reach you in a few moments.'

Having informed divisional headquarters, the majority of 125 *Panzergrenadier* Regiment spent the following day fixed fighting the 6th Airborne Division. Both the divisional commander, *Generalmajor* Feuchtinger, and his 1a (chief of staff) were absent from the headquarters at St Pierre-sur-Dives on 'personal business' in Paris. At 0200 hours a junior staff officer issued the alert for the division to be ready to move in ninety minutes. Having been contacted by phone, Feuchtinger set out to return, but he would not be back at his headquarters until 0520 hours. In the meantime, the 1b (logistic staff officer), Major Scharnhorst, drove to St Pierre-sur-Dives from his rear headquarters, arriving around 0300 hours. Without experienced leadership there was paralysis across the division, as the staff were unsure whether to commit the division without Rommel's express permission to attack the airborne landing. With the panzer regiment of the 21st being under command of Army Group B, no orders were issued by either Seventh Army or LXXXIV Corps.

Further from the coast, the 12th *Hitlerjugend* SS Panzer Division's duty staff officer received a call from the Luftwaffe shortly before 0100 hours alerting him that dummy parachutists had been dropped near their airfield and that real paratroopers had landed near the coast. 'Calls to 711th Infantry Division on the coastal sector confirmed that they had the same dummies … They also added that there were no indications of activity out to sea, concluding that the weather was poor, with wind and occasional rain.' The initial assessment at Corps level and above was that the dropping of the Ruperts was an Allied attempt to bluff them into action to reveal their plans. So effective was the combination of the dispersed airborne drops and the Ruperts that only gradually did the insistence of those on the ground that there were significant numbers of real paratroopers cut through the confusion. Even so, at 0215 hours General Speidel at Army Group B dismissed Seventh Army's reports with the words, 'They're still localized encounters.'[5]

General der Artillerie Erich Marcks, the commander of LXXXIV Corps, correctly predicted the combination of tides, time of dawn and moonlight the Allies would use on 5 or 6 June.

Selected entries in the Seventh Army telephone log concentrating on the Caen area reveal the passage of information and the development of opinion amongst German commanders.[6] At 0220 hours Allied time, two hours after the first airborne landing, LXXXIV Corps reported to Seventh Army (AOK 7):

> Parachute landings from 0030 hours onwards in area east and north east of Caen, St Marcouf, Montebourg, both sides of the Vire and on the east coast of Cotentin.

And at 0300 hours:

> Further landings in the 716th Infantry Division sector ... Two strong points [concentrations of airborne troops] can be recognised in the 716th Infantry Division sector and east coast of Cotentin.

The situation was reasonably clear to Seventh Army, but at Army Group B, *Generalmajor* Speidel, Rommel's chief of staff (1a) was not convinced – 'Chef H.Gr.B considers the operations at the moment to be still only local encounters.' However, Seventh Army disagreed: 'Chef d.G. believes that the activities point to a greater action coming.' Half an hour later, '1a H.Gr.B. reports that shortly after midnight considerable parachute landings were made in area of 711th Infantry Division from troop-carrying gliders.'

The Fifteenth Army, which had been at a high state of alert, was consequently able to send coherent reports of airborne landings that had overlapped their left flank to Speidel far more quickly than the Seventh Army. Consequently, they requested the deployment of the *Hitlerjugend* to the 711st Division in the Grainville area (south-east of Houlgate) in order to confront an airborne landing – essentially the *Hitlerjugend*'s deployment option B. This airborne landing in the 711th area was in fact a few cross-boundary objectives on the Dives, the Ruperts and some poorly dropped British paratroopers, mixed in with TITANIC. The resulting urgent requests contributed significantly to diverting a powerful armoured response away from the assault area and delaying its arrival in the Caen sector until D+1. This was another significant success for FORTITUDE.

At 0600 the situation became clear:

> Chef d.G. [AOK 7] gives following clarification of position to H.Gr B. Large-scale enemy assault indicated by depth of enemy airborne landings up to 20km in Orne sector. Enemy forces west of the Orne estuary mopped up. Position eased. Parachute landings in Falaise-Mezidon area. Gliders flown

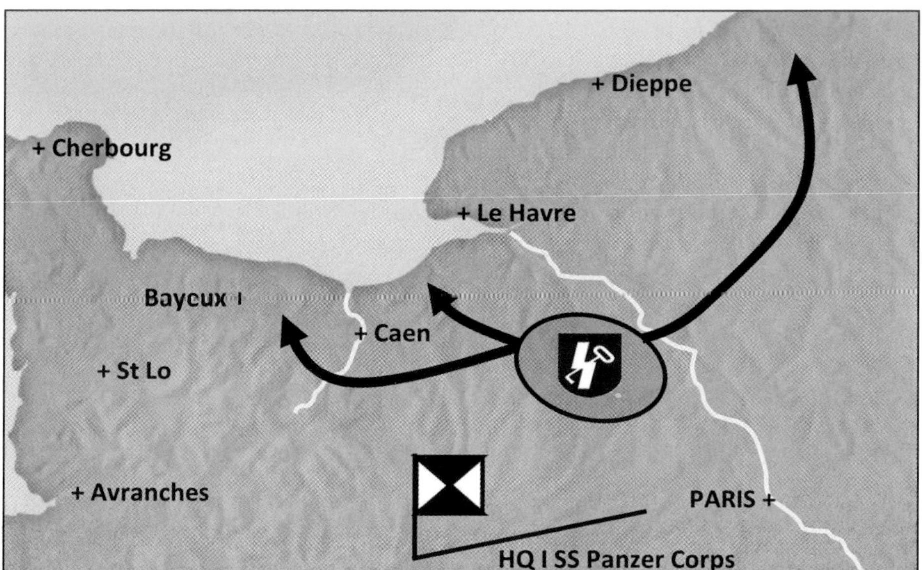

The deployment options prepared for the 12th *Hitlerjugend* Panzer Division.

> over Caen. British 1st Airborne Division on right flank. Airborne landings on south-east of Cotentin Peninsula, and capture of crossings over the Carentan–Pont l'Abbé causeway, taken in conjunction with radar-located targets at sea off the Orne mouth, between Port en Bassin and the mouth of the Vire and to the north of Cherbourg.

Speidel was becoming convinced that this was the invasion, but the higher levels of command, having expected a preliminary landing to draw away reserves, were still convinced that the landing on the coast of Lower Normandy was a distraction.

The Passage

Lieutenant Commander Brown, commanding one of the craft in the LCT Squadron recalled:

> It was a long night's watch on the bridge but one full of tension for us, the reality of it all being brought home by a constant stream of aircraft droning overhead. Finally, with the flotilla still about 10-miles off the coast, we could see the flickering of exploding bombs dead ahead of us, reflected on the clouds, and hear their distant rumble.
>
> The troops were now moving about in the darkness, cigarette ends marking their progress as they unlashed tarpaulins from the vehicles below me. By now all this was a familiar routine but this time leavened with real nerves and expectation.[7]

LCTs with the tanks of 27 Armoured Brigade aboard, photographed from the craft's bridge.

Of the passage aboard a Landing Craft Tank (LCT), Captain Airey Neave, the Adjutant of the 13th/18th Hussars, wrote:

> It was roughish but after a seasick tablet which only served to make me feel ill in a different but almost equally unpleasant way I remember sleeping rather well. We got up at about 4.00 a.m. and it was dark, blustery, cold, rough and uninviting on deck when I went down to my tank at the rear end of the well of the craft to find Goodall, Cook and Suggitt trying to do something about breakfast. There *was* quite a lot to do by way of warming-up the various wireless sets ready to break wireless silence and putting the final touches to the wading apparatus. By this time the seasick tablets had properly turned my inside into what seemed to be plaster of Paris, I certainly could not have been sick but felt awful which had the compensating effect of deflecting my attention from the somewhat alarming prospects of what lay ahead.[8]

The lucky soldiers were lowered in their LCAs from LSI's davits, in this case during the flat calm of Exercise FABIUS.

Starting at 0530 hours, the lowering, or for the unlucky, the clamber down from the landing ships into the LCAs was difficult and very different from the still waters of Exercise FABIUS. In the rough sea, and fully equipped with weapons, ammunition pouches, etc., all seemingly designed to snag on the wet scramble net, the final jump into the LCA required good timing.

The Fire Plan

Ahead of the naval force, the last of ten strikes by 1,136 aircraft of RAF Bomber Command on major gun batteries across the assault area was under way. However, as the airmen had warned the assembled C-in-Cs, due to cloud cover the results were not as successful as had been hoped. Considerable accuracy was required, and the Merville Battery east of the Orne, for example, which was thought to house 155mm guns capable of engaging SWORD, was almost entirely missed, with the bombs falling on the nearby village of Gonneville and just

The Fire Support Programme

The joint fire plan [for the Western Task Force] falls into the following phases:

Phase 1. Preliminary 'softening up' bombardment prior to D Day. This was entirely an air commitment. Some 30 bomber attacks were made on coastal batteries in the assault area before D Day.

Phase 2. Silencing of hostile batteries during the seaborne approach. This was a joint naval and air responsibility. The plan included:

(i) Night D minus 1/D attack on 10 battery positions each by 100 Brit night bombers. 5,300 tons of bombs were dropped.
(ii) Prior to H Hour. Heavy day bombers of US Air Forces on battery positions and defended localities. Over 5,900 tons of bombs were dropped.
(iii) Prior to H Hour. Pre-arranged silencing of hostile batteries by 6 battleships, 2 monitors and 22 cruisers.

Phase 3. Close support of the assault troops during the run-in to the beaches and the assault across them. This was a 'free-for-all' period when destroyers, close support naval craft, the Royal Marine Armed Support Group in LCTs and the self-propelled div artillery all engaged pre-arranged or opportunity targets, while medium and fighter-bombers engaged areas farther inland. 93 destroyers were available for the operation; there was a total of 147 close-support craft of various types equipped with guns, mortars, spigot bombs, etc.

Phase 4. Support of inf as they worked inland, until their own artillery could come into action ashore.

After completion of primary task of silencing batteries, the battleships, monitors and cruisers were available to bombard opportunity targets as necessary. The more intimate support was to be provided by the Royal Marine Armed Support Group. Equipped with 75mm [*sic*] CENTAUR tanks, there were available 5 batteries, each of 4 troops.'[9]

missing 9 Para. The results of the bombing of DAIMLER/Ouistreham and the HILLMAN/MORRIS batteries similarly were unimpressive.

With the departure of the aircraft, the ships of the bombardment forces that had arrived in position 6 miles out to sea were at anchor and at nautical twilight, 0550 hours, opened fire.[10] In a forty-minute engagement Bombardment Force D targeted three batteries in the SWORD area, Merville Battery and three major batteries further east on the coast of the Baie de Seine. The heavy shells of the observed and adjusted fire, while doing little damage to the substantial concrete casemates, significantly downgraded the infrastructure, ground defences and in some cases the guns as well.

As the naval bombardment ceased, the medium bombers of the Allied air forces swept in. For the synchronization of the attack by these aircraft, the wristwatches of the crews had been set using a time signal broadcast by the BBC. The attacks were to be made between 0630 and 0650 hours from 9,200 to 13,200 feet. The targets were the German coastal defences, but with the risk of greater inaccuracy as a result of low cloud, decisions were made to add a few seconds to their bomb runs in order to ensure that the ordnance would not crater the beach. The result was that rather than falling on strongpoints like SOLE, COD and TROUT on SWORD Beach, most of the bombs fell between 1,000 and 3,000 yards inland. Some aircraft could not identify their targets. Objectives HILLMAN and MORRIS were to have been struck by, respectively, six and thirteen B-17 Liberators, but at 15,000 feet, thanks to cloud and smoke, only six dropped their bombs on MORRIS. The remainder returned to their bases in the UK with their bomb loads still aboard. It is impossible to say what difference the tonnage of these bombs on SWORD's coastal strongpoints would have made, but their absence was a result of the risk Eisenhower had little alternative but to take.

The next phase of the fire plan was for the Fleet and Hunt class destroyers escorting the craft of Force S3 to target the German strongpoints and intermediate defences with their 4-inch and 4.7-inch guns.[11] Commander Edwards described of the third phase of the naval fire plan that was designed to 'drench the beach with a crescendo of fire', involving all ships and craft:

> This was the 'drenching' of the beaches and their immediate approaches from landward by the guns of the destroyers and the LC(G)'s [Landing Craft (Gun) with 4.7-inch guns]. Destroyers mounting 4.7- and 4-inch guns and a great collection of other craft ranged up and down the beach, literally 'drenching' every square yard of them from water line to vegetation line with high explosive shells. Behind that curtain of fire the landing craft laden with assault troops made for the beaches.[12]

One of the specially developed fire support craft was the Landing Craft Tank (Rocket) (LCT(R)). Five of these craft that had a range of 3,500 yards were allocated to Force S3. Capable of delivering a very heavy weight of fire in a matter of seconds, they exploded mines and ripped up barbed wire. Fired at about H–10,

HMS *Ramillies*. Her 15-inch guns were a key asset in Bombardment Force D's firing on German batteries to the east of SWORD.

the LCT(R) suffered the drawback of only having one shot before having to withdraw to rearm.

At 0650 hours a run-in-shoot by gunners of the 3rd Division three field regiments began.

The Run-in Shoot

The question of using all available firepower to support a landing was raised following Dieppe in 1942. The Canadians' report on the raid states the case for

> the necessity for fire support in any operation where it has not been possible to rely on the element of surprise. This fire support must be provided by heavy and medium Naval bombardment, by air action, by special vessels or craft working close inshore, and by using the fire power of the assaulting troops while still sea-borne.[13]

The aim was to provide 'drenching fire against beach defences from all weapons'. 50th Division noted:

> For some time extensive trials and exercises had been going on with the object of evolving the best method of providing artillery support during the approach to the beaches and immediately after the first landings. It had been found that artillery 'deployed' in Landing Craft Tank (LCT) could fire accurately on to land targets. For technical reasons, SP artillery was found to

The LCA (Hedgerow) mounted twenty-four spigot mortars that fired bombs on to the beach just before the assault troops landed, in order to set off mines. The picture taken during trials shows four mortars ready to fire.

> be the best for this type of support, and it had obvious advantages for the actual landing and immediate support after landing.[14]

Thus, the seventy-two M7 105mm guns of the 3rd Division's three artillery regiments, plus the sixteen 95mm Centaurs of 5 RM Armoured Support Battery, were to fire a run-in shoot from adapted LCT(A)s. Each craft would carry four Priests, plus an OP tank and other battery vehicles. The fire was controlled by Forward Observation Officers (FOOs) aboard Landing Craft Support (Medium) that were at the front of the invasion flotilla with the motor launches that were navigating the DD tanks. They used a basic ranging radar to initiate the fire plan.

> The fire of each troop [of four M7s] was controlled by the GPO [Gun Position Officer] from the bridge of the LCT. The fire of the Regiment was co-ordinated by the GPO in the control LCT at the centre of the leading line.[15]

Once on target, GPOs used Coventry Clocks developed by a Royal Artillery gunnery instructor matched to the vessel's speed and range to the target to the elevation of the gun. With the Priests firing on a fixed line, the LCTs were underway at a steady 5 knots, straight towards the target, which in the case of SWORD Beach was COD.

> This made necessary a steadily decreasing elevation on the guns. The rate of close on the beach had to be calculated constantly in order to keep the fire where it was wanted, 'just where the grass starts to grow on the beach'. This was done by the regimental Fire Control Officers operating radar apparatus in navigational motor launches. For the SP artillery the schedule of fire support was as follows. [Coventry] Range clocks were started at 15,000 yards; ranging with smoke began at 10,000 yards and fire for effect at 9,000 yards. This latter had to be timed so as to commence at H minus 35 minutes. From then until H minus 5 minutes (i.e., at a range of 2,000 yards, having covered 1,000 yards per 5 minutes) each gun fired 3 rounds in every 200 yards. The total HE expenditure at H Hour was thus [theoretically] 105 rounds per gun [a total of 7,560 rounds].[16]

Lieutenant Turnbull of 76 (Highland) Field Regiment RA recalled that on his LCT:

> Two of the guns were at the front of the craft on a well deck and two were at the rear of the well deck with two Sherman [OP] tanks between each pair. All available remaining space on the LCT(A)s was taken up with ammunition to fire once we were ashore. The LCTs were manned by the Royal Navy, who would be responsible for taking us to wherever we were to go.
>
> After a couple of ranging rounds, the seventy-two guns of the Divisional Artillery started firing and continued for the next thirty-five minutes.[17] Concentration was paramount; the sailors had to keep the LCTs pointing in the right direction, and we had to keep shortening the range every minute as the

> craft approached the shore. In all, the Divisional Artillery fired over 110 tons of high explosive in that time.
>
> [As planned at H–5 minutes] the firing was stopped as the assaulting battalions of infantry with their supporting services approached the beach. Whilst they went ashore, the LCTs with our guns wheeled out to sea again, returning to land an hour later.

The artillery report continued:

> At this point, the LCTs, now 2,000 yards offshore, did not continue on their course in order to touch down and offload the guns, for the beach was not yet ready to receive them. Instead they turned off to a flank to a waiting position.

While waiting for their turn to land, the gunners bombed up their Priests with sixty-nine rounds from the first line ammunition stacked around the gun. Further ammunition was in the watertight Porpoise sledges under the vehicle, which were pulled onto the beach when the vehicle landed.

The M7 Priest

Most of the 105mm M7 self-propelled guns, known in British service as 'Priests', used on D Day were procured through the Lend-Lease programme in 1943, with additional vehicles being borrowed from the Americans for the invasion.

The need for tracked artillery to cross the beaches during D Day is self-evident; in addition, the towed 25-pounder gun, tractor and limber, unlike the Priest, could not be waterproofed sufficiently for it to wade ashore. The alternative was the Canadian-built Sexton that mounted a 25-pounder on an RAM chassis, but there were only sufficient available to equip the regiments supporting 50th Division on GOLD Beach. Consequently, 3rd and 3rd Canadian divisions of I Corps were both converted to US 105mm Priests on loan from the Americans.

The M7 was given the British name 'Priest' due to its pulpit-like mount for the .5 calibre Browning machine gun.

The M7 Priests were returned to the Americans from late July onwards and replaced with either towed 25-pounders or Sextons in armoured formations and some AGRA regiments. There were several reasons for this, despite the significantly larger shell (105mm *v* 88mm):

- They were on loan or D Day and the Americans needed them back for replacements.
- The Priests were well used, and the Headquarters RA of Second Army was concerned about barrel wear and the resulting loss of accuracy. This was compounded by a lack of replacement barrels and spares for the vehicle.
- Second Army wished to simplify its artillery ammunition supply chain.
- In the aftermath of GOODWOOD there were concerns over the level of stocks of 105mm ammunition.[1]

There were also doctrinal reasons for reverting to the towed 25-pounder in the field regiments RA and RCA:

- The Royal Artillery preferred towed guns to support of infantry formations.
- The advantages of the lighter 25lb British shells – reduced gunner fatigue, extended range and reduced logistic tonnage – meant it was preferred to the larger shell.
- The 105mm was outranged by the 25-pounder (12,000 *v* 13,400 yards) and it was quicker for 25-pounder crews to make a significant changes of target. Speed and flexibility were key tenets of British artillery doctrine and excellence.

The gunners bemoaned the loss of the Priest, presumably for its mobility, protection, and because it did not need digging in! The Royal Artillery consistently pointed out that with a towed gun, the weapon is not lost as it would be if an SP broke down.

Chapter Five

The Landing of the Assault Brigade

The assault on QUEEN Sector of SWORD Beach was allocated to Brigadier Cass's 8 Brigade group. Their mission was:

> With under command 13/18 H, 5 Assault Regt RE (less two squadrons) and 4 and 41 Commando will carry out the assault on QUEEN RED and WHITE beaches and secure the beachhead to include high ground about PERIERS-SUR-LE-DAN – ST AUBIN-D'ARQUENAY 0976.

Their first task was defined as:

> Assault and clear the beach of aimed fire to enable 5 Assault Regt RE and Divisional RE to construct vehicle exits and clear beach obstacles.

While the navies and air forces worked their way through the fire plan, the various landing and support craft of Forces S1 and 2 assembled in assault formation and shortly after 0600 hours started to pass through Bombardment Force D's line of battleships and cruisers. Ahead of them were Force S3's LCTs bearing the DD tanks, self-propelled guns and the 79th Armoured Division's breaching teams. Private Wilkinson aboard an LCA bearing B Company of the South Lancashires recalled:

> We passed between a couple of cruisers that were shelling targets somewhere inland. The noise as they fired off their guns all at once was tremendous and hit you like a blow. Off to our left we could see the big ships and the sound of their broadsides rolled across the water several seconds after we saw great gouts of orange flame and smoke. After that we could hear the sound of shells passing overhead. I wasn't too bad, but some were too sick to care![1]

With the landing craft of Force S3 having passed through the bombardment line, Combined Operations Pilotage Party 6 (COPP 6) took up their positions at 0630 hours in front of the LCTs aboard a variety of small craft. With the assistance of a navigational fix from the pre-positioned X23 mini submarine, they were to pilot the two squadrons of 13/18 H's Sherman DD tanks and the flotilla bearing the eight breaching teams to their sectors of QUEEN Beach. As the smoke from the naval bombardment cleared, the navigators were able to pick up their marks on the coast ahead of them.

> Houses in Lion-sur-Mer and cliffs westward of the town were clearly visible at this time, and the conspicuous house marking the right-hand edge of

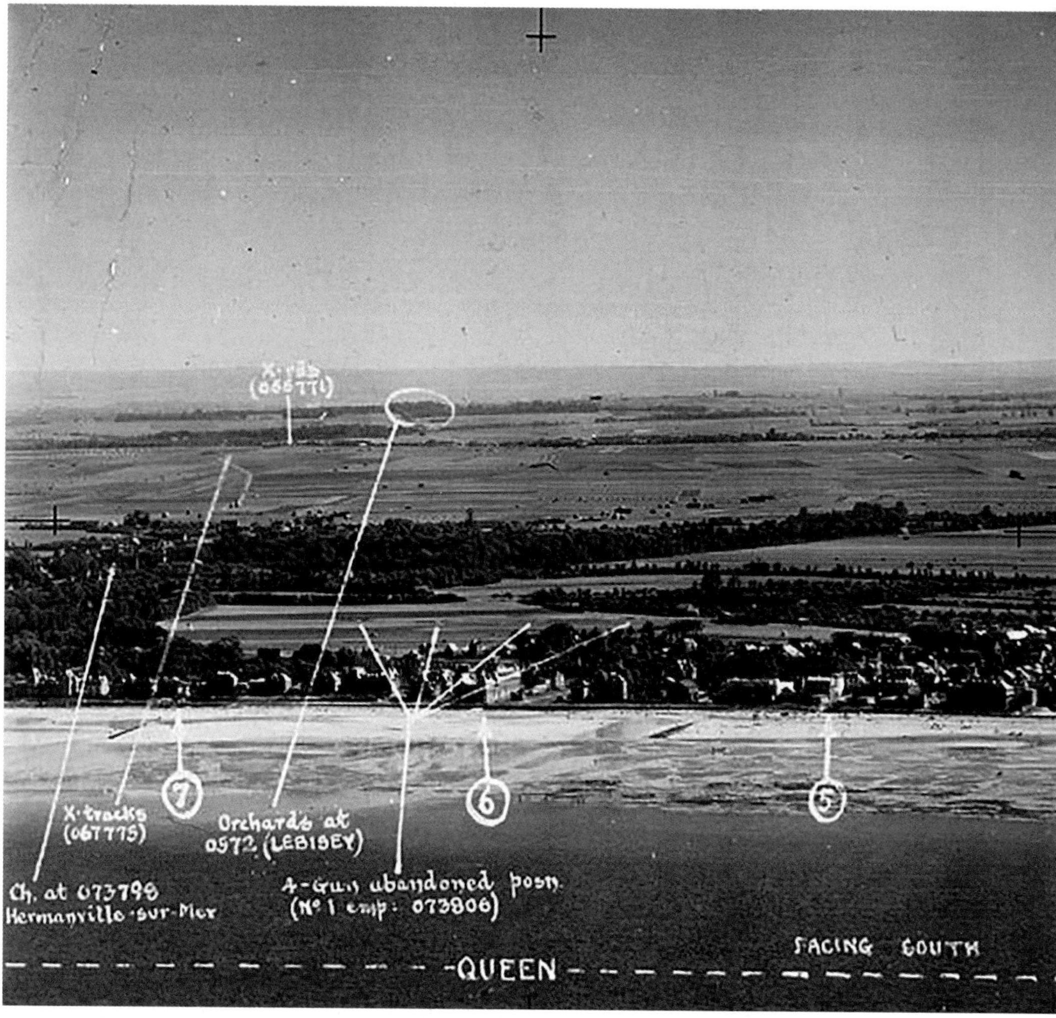

(**Above & opposite**) Oblique air photos of the QUEEN Sector and an example of the low-level coastal profiles issued to navigators and landing craft coxswains. The later sorties by PRU aircraft were often under fire and were known to the aircrew as 'dicing' (dicing with death)!

> White Beach [was] positively identified at 0650. Bearings taken on this house indicated that the tidal set was less than that allowed for, and course was altered.[2]

COPP officer Major Mackenzie aboard an LCP(N) (Landing Craft Personnel (Navigational)) reported that 45th LCT Flotilla's E Squadron was five minutes behind schedule and needed to speed up. 'At 5,000 yards landmarks stood out well, and the exact position for touching down was pointed out to the Flotilla Officer, allowing him to take the necessary bearings before smoke from shells temporarily blotted out the beaches.' The Royal Navy's account states that 'weather conditions were recognised as being unsuitable for swimming DD tanks.' The decision was, however, made by Captain Bush and Brigadier Prior-Palmer not to launch the DDs at 7,000 yards out to sea but to send the codeword

ORNE
OUISTREHAM

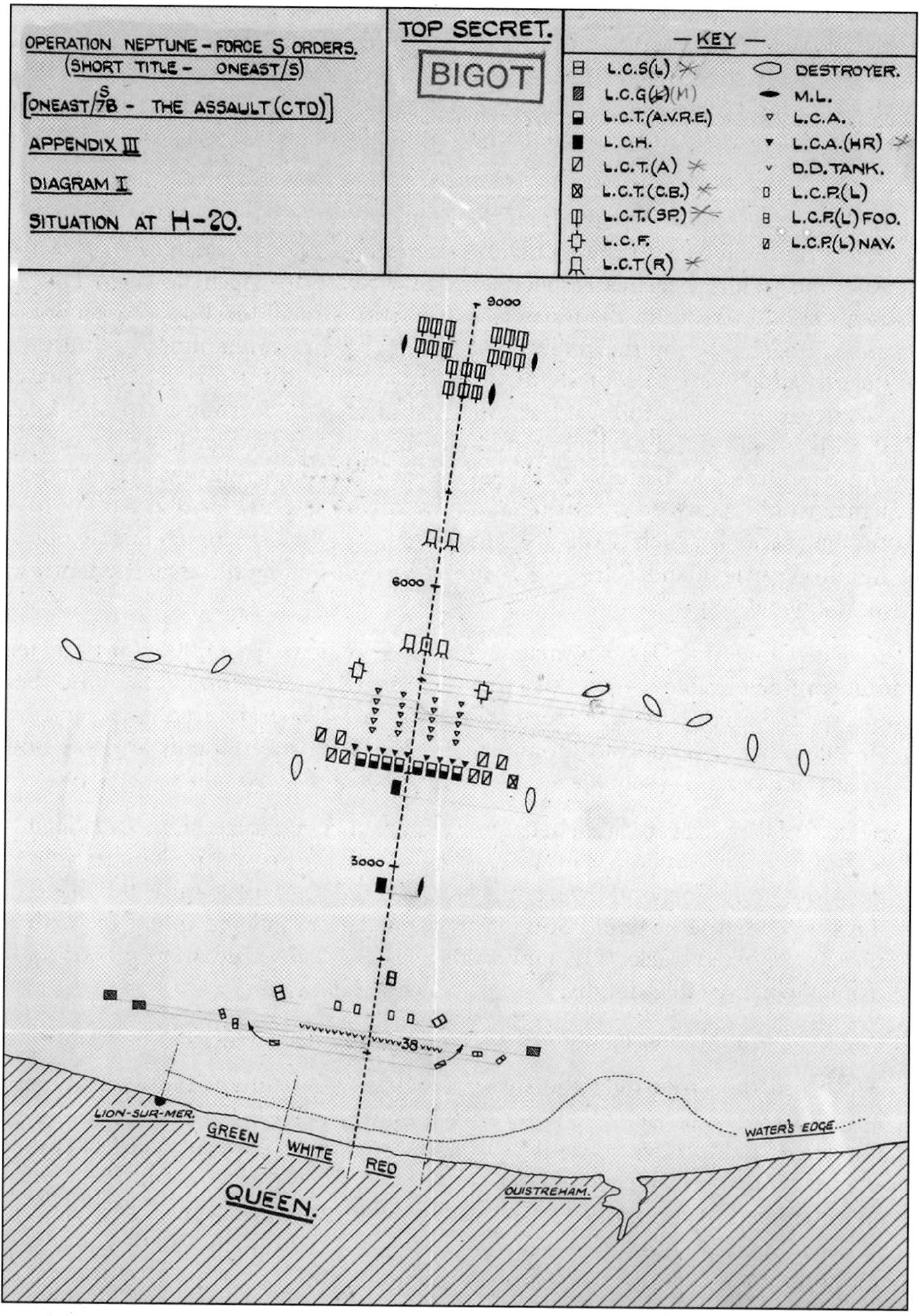

The intended assault plan for the DDs of 13th/18th Hussars on SWORD Beach. 'Just before their tracks engaged the sand it was planned that the DDs would deploy into a single line evenly spread across the assault frontage. Needless to say, with the sea state this did not happen.'

'FLOAT 5,000', which took the LCTs a further 2,000 yards inshore to launch. Even so, Rear Admiral Talbot described this as 'a courageous decision'. Of the 13/18 H's thirty-eight DD Shermans, thirty-three were successfully launched, with a leading B Squadron DD being damaged on LCT 467's ramp, stopping the remainder on that craft from launching. The Regimental historian describes the task of the DDs:

> A Squadron (Major Wormald) on the right, and B Squadron (Major Rugge-Price) on the left, with their D.D. tanks, were to lead the assault on Queen Red and White beaches respectively. They were to touch down at H–7 minutes and remain in the water and subdue by fire all local opposition not already destroyed by the preliminary naval and air bombardments. Subsequently, they were to support the infantry ... inland in a normal tank role.
>
> They were to be followed at H–5, minutes [i.e., 2½ minutes later] by the Flails and AVREs which would clear the mines on four lanes on each squadron front, by flailing over the beach as far as the sandbanks. The sandbanks would be scaled by a bridge, thence there would be further flailing to the first lateral, which was a road running parallel to the beach, about one hundred yards inland. The AVRE would be followed by the assault infantry at H hour [0725].

The speed that the DD Sherman could make equated to 1,000 yards in ten minutes in favourable water, but in the marginal sea conditions of 6 June they could make barely half that speed. The risk that General Eisenhower and his senior commanders took in 'going' in far less than ideal conditions was now affecting the carefully sequenced assault plan. Major Wormald wrote:

> At 06.16 all tanks were launched, after closing to 5,000 yards. The sea looked alarming from the craft but FLOATER (launch) proved to be the right decision. Only Corporal Sweetapple's tank failed to swim towards the shore. This was because he could not get his propellers to fall and to engage with the drive off the tracks. His tank sank but he and his crew were picked up from their inflatable dinghy.[3]

Lance Corporal Hennesey commanded an A Squadron DD tank:

> We heard the order over the ship's Tannoy, 'Down door, No. 1', and we knew this was our cue. The ramp on the bow of our LCT was lowered into the sea, the ship hove to, tank engines started, and Sergeant Rattle's tank moved forward down the ramp and nosed into the waves. We followed, and as we righted in the water I could just see the shore line some 5,000 yards away; it seemed a very long distance and in a DD Tank, in that sea, it certainly was!
>
> Slowly, we began to make headway. The crew were all on deck apart from Harry Bone who was crouched in the driving compartment, intent on keeping the engine running because, as we all knew, if that stopped we stood no

chance of survival. The . . . sea appeared even rougher from this low point of view, with only a flimsy canvas screen between us and the waves. We shipped a certain amount of water over the top of the screen from time to time, so Trooper Joe Gallagher, whose task it was to man the bilge pump, was kept hard at work.

We battled on towards the shore through the rough sea. We were buffeted about unmercifully, plunging into the troughs of the waves and somehow wallowing up again to the crests. The wind, fortunately, was behind us, and this helped a little . . . Seasickness was now forgotten. It took over an hour of hard work to reach the beach and it was a miracle that most of us did.

Major Wormald noted:

Naval and air bombardment was tremendous and occasional glimpses of the shore were possible, due to the offshore wind which carried the smoke of the bombardment towards us. The tanks were performing well beyond what we thought to be practicable for the apparatus. Four columns each of five tanks (less Cpl Sweetapples) followed the lead of a Landing Craft Personnel (Navigational), the task of which was to lead us to the correct point of 'TOUCH DOWN' on the beach.

COPP officer Major Mackenzie continued his account:

The smoke cleared at 1,000 yards, enabling all craft to locate their marks. Rockets from the LCT(R) were falling short about the craft at 600 yards,

DD tanks training off Swanage in a moderate sea.

> and the flotillas were in danger of running down the DD.[4] The Flotilla went astern for a minute, and then on to touch down 5 to 10 minutes late about 300 yards from the back of the beach, within 15 yards of the exact position.[5]

Captain Denny, the second captain of A Squadron, described his approach to the beach:

> Wireless comms for the launching drill worked well and my craft load launched at about 4,500 yds had some mech trouble, but otherwise everything went according to plan. The sea was rough and the tk stood up to it far beyond my expectations.
>
> At about 1,500yds from the beach the AVREs LCTs passed between the port and starboard colns. Shortly afterwards, stopped engines and then went astern, and we passed them again. The rockets then began their cones, and were falling short amongst us. The Sqn kept good station in spite of these intrusions. Enemy fire began at about 800yds from the beach, and the crews got inside their turrets. Up to 1,000yds I could pick out the required landmarks and check that we were steering in the right direction.
>
> At about 800yds, I was rammed by an LCT, and we sank immediately, the tk going over on its beam and sinking for about 25ft, ending upside down. Although the crew were wearing ATEA and Mae Wests they never appeared again, as I did not see them during the 30 mins I was in the water. The rest of my coln beached satisfactorily, but three of them got swamped by the incoming tide and only one got through the gap onto the shore.

The ship's log of LCT 947, which was leading the landing craft of E Squadron, with the assault engineer's armoured breaching teams aboard, confirms that at '0720 the LCTs started overtaking the DD tanks that were "swimming" towards the shore.' In doing so, however, one or possibly two DD tanks were run over and sunk. Major Wormald noted that 'Our tanks touched down at 07.23. Sixteen tanks [of A Squadron] got their tracks on the seabed, moved into water sufficiently shallow to allow them to drop their screens and to engage the beach defences.'[6] A Squadron's account records that 'the leading AVREs were wading ashore before our DDs had moved in to deflate.' These were vital minutes, during which time, from positions hull-down initially some 250 yards out to sea, the tanks were to have engaged the embrasures of enemy weapons casemates with direct fire. With the forty assorted 'funnies' of the breaching teams that had caught up with the DDs landing around them and heading across the beach in front of them, the Shermans' arcs of fire, and hence targets, would have been increasingly restricted. To further reduce the DDs' effect, A Squadron landing further west than intended also limited their contribution. It is, however, noted in the 3rd Division's Narrative Report that 'the flail tks of 22 Drgns filled the gap with accurate gunfire on enemy guns and saved the situation.' However, this was still a greatly reduced level of support compared to that which was planned.

The rear view of a Sherman DD tank with the screen erected and the two duplex propellers for propulsion when swimming.

Corporal Hennesey's DD having successfully swum in, and with its propellers disengaged, motored on to a point where he could drop his screen:

> As we approached, we felt the tracks meet the shelving sand of the shore, and slowly we began to rise out of the water. We took post to deflate the screen, one man standing to each strut. When the base of the screen was clear of the water, the struts were broken, the air released and the screen collapsed. We leapt into the tank and were ready for action. '75, HE, action-traverse right, steady, on. 300 white fronted house first floor window, centre.' 'On'. 'Fire!' Within a minute of dropping our screen we had fired our first shot in anger. There was a puff of smoke and brick dust from the house we had aimed at, and we continued to engage our targets. Other DD Tanks were coming in on both sides of us and by now we were under enemy fire from several positions, which we identified and to which we replied with 75mm and Browning machine gun fire. The beach, which had been practically deserted when we had arrived, was beginning to fill up fast.

Corporal Hennesey's action was brought to a halt by the rising tide and by waves that swamped his engine and shortly afterwards the tank as well. Two other A Squadron DDs were swamped, while other armoured vehicles were knocked out by enemy fire from COD and the other *Wiederstandsneste* to the flanks. Major Wormald recalled:

> I still remember very clearly the 'brewing-up' of the leading AVRE Churchill tank as it drove down the ramp of an LCT which was beached a few yards to my left front. The turret and the contents thereof spun into the air after a violent explosion, presumably caused by a penetrating direct hit by an anti-tank shell which detonated the explosive charges which the AVRE was carrying for the purpose of destroying concrete emplacements.

It is estimated that eighteen of the 13/18 H's Shermans got off the beach, which in broad terms equates to half of A and B squadrons' original strength.

The Defenders

The Orne Sector of the Atlantic Wall was held by *Oberst* Krug's 736 Infantry Regiment, with his headquarters south of Colleville in Objective HILLMAN (WN-17). One battalion, the I/736, was concentrated astride the Orne at Ouistreham, and further west, Major Pipor's III/736 held the coastal defences between Ouistreham and Luc-sur-Mer, the latter with 9 Company. SWORD Beach itself was held by *Hauptman* Kuhtz's 10 Company, while 11 and 12 companies manned positions in depth/reserve at Douvres-la-Délivrande and near Cressons, where their battalion headquarters was also located. Additionally, *Osttruppen* of 3 Company 642 *Ost* Battalion were in depth behind WN-20 (COD). The rest of this battalion, along with II/736 Infantry, were deployed east of the Orne.

The main physical defences covering what would become SWORD Beach were the three *Wiederstandsneste*: in the centre, COD (WN-20) on Colleville Plage, to the east on RED Beach at La Brèche, SKATE (WN-18), and to the west of Lion-sur-Mer, TROUT (WN-21).[7] In common with other positions along the Atlantic Wall, the exact grouping of troops and weapons depended on the particular tactical problem that the Germans were presented with. The *Wiederstandsneste* were well prepared with concrete casemates and shelters linked up by revetted trenches, and surrounded by mines and barbed wire, with machine guns to cover the approaches. The basic garrison of a *Wiederstandsnest* was plus or minus a platoon. In addition to the above, WN-21 (TROUT) at the west end of Lion-sur-Mer consisted of an artillery OP for the direction of the 105mm guns at WN-16 (MORRIS). This battery also included a French 75mm gun, two obsolescent but still effective tank guns, the 50mm KwK L/42, a 20mm flak gun and an 81mm mortar.

SKATE (WN-18), the other flanking position just east of La Brèche, was altogether smaller, with a Great War-vintage French 75mm gun and a 50mm gun captured in 1940. WN-20 COD, however, was a substantial position incorporating captured weapons including a French 75mm and a pair of 50mm guns, plus a 37mm Skoda gun. The up-to-date German weapons included a PaK 40 75mm anti-tank gun, 20mm anti-aircraft guns, mortars and machine guns.

Grenadier Hubbne, III/736 Infantry, recalled an alerted before dawn:

> We slept in a bunker not far from the shore and went to bed as usual that night. We were roused by our *Stabsfeldwebel* who yelled that we must get to our alarm positions at once. We rushed about in great confusion and fear, trying to eat something and drink coffee while pulling on our equipment. It took us almost fifteen minutes to reach our position in a fortified bunker which included a machine-gun post overlooking the beach.

The fortified casemates of WN-21 (TROUT) at the western end of Lion-sur-Mer accommodated coastal and army Forward Observation Officers.

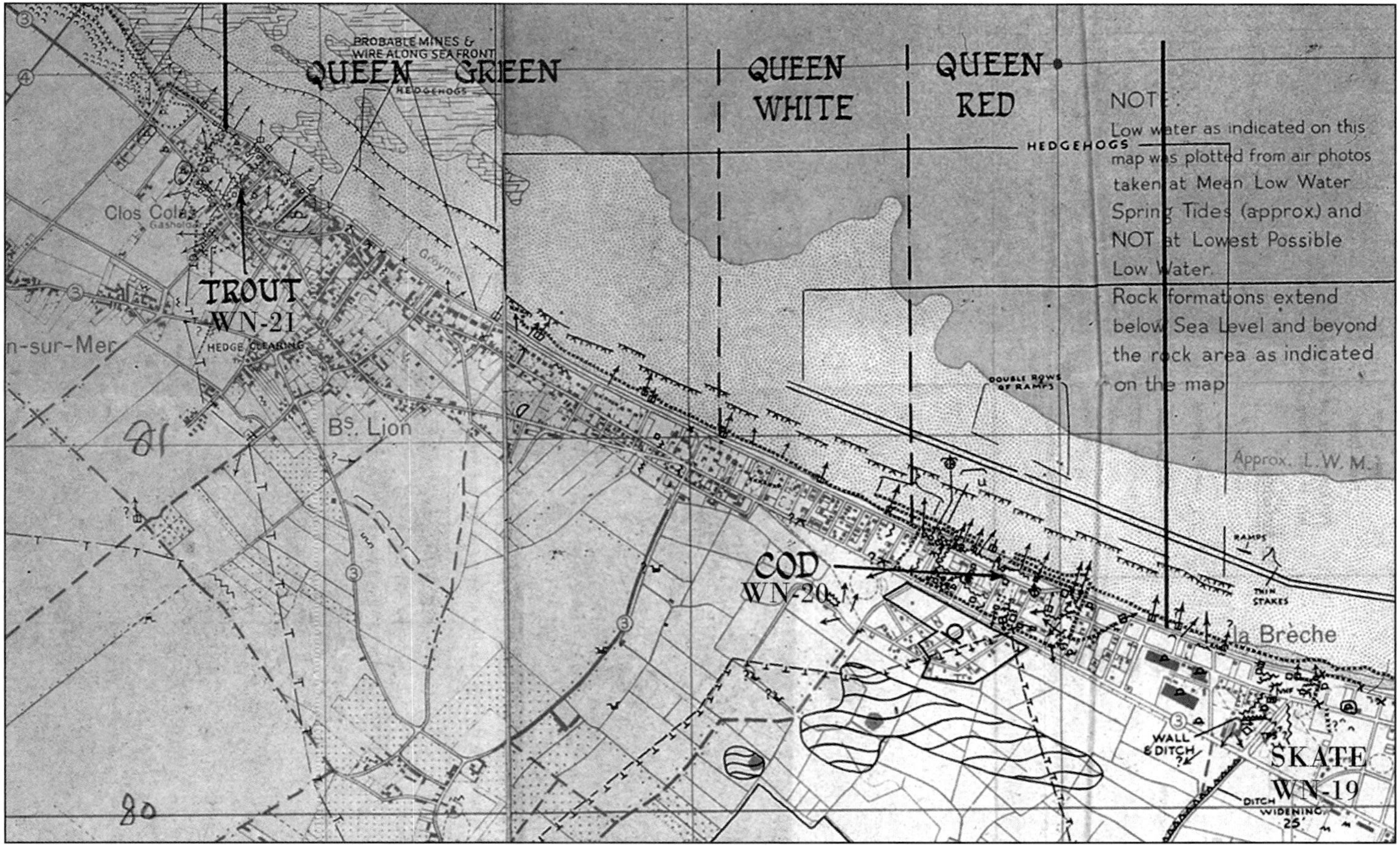

SWORD Beach obstacles and defences. Note the machine-gun (↑) positions between the *Wiederstandsneste*. 1:25,000 Defences overprint.

The Breaching Teams

Due to have landed no more than five minutes after the DD tanks, 77 and 79 squadrons of 5 Assault Regiment RE, with the flail Crabs of A and C squadron of the 22 Dragoons under command, were each to provide four breaching teams. Their task was to blast and beat exit lanes from the beach across the dunes to the roads beyond. Landing twenty minutes behind them, two Field Companies of dismounted engineers were to clear 225 yards of obstacles on QUEEN RED and WHITE.

There were no fewer that twenty-six identified tracks and roads, from a track immediately behind SWORD Beach which led through the seaside villas and gardens to the main coast road, the D 514, in most cases referred to as the 'lateral road'. Of these tracks, eight in QUEEN had been selected to be exit lanes from the beach. Once a pair of Sherman flails had cleared the beach of mines and reached the sand dunes or sea walls, the minefields and barbed wire of the coastal defences would need breaching. The teams of funnies consisted of six vehicles needed to get through sand dunes or over the low sea walls. Originally, the former required the use of the Boase Bangalore which, when the explosive-packed steel pipes were driven at speed by an AVRE into sand dunes and exploded, created a ramp sufficiently low for the vehicle to pass. Each team had one Bangalore-equipped AVRE and another carrying a Small Box Girder Bridge (SBG), which was used to climb over sea walls but in practice also to get up onto sand dunes. By D Day some of the Bangalores had been replaced by carpet-laying AVRE Bobbins and log carpets to deal with the clay outcrops on the beach. Of the final two vehicles of the breaching teams, one had dozer blades mounted on an AVRE and the other was a D7 armoured bulldozer. These were to fill craters blocking routes, remove barricades and other obstacles, and later assist in removing beach obstacles that could not be demolished with explosives. Each team with its own challenges and enemy to face has its own story. What is provided here is a snapshot of how the opening of routes off the beach affected the capture of Caen.

As the British armour waded ashore onto RED and WHITE beaches, the Germans, who had been hitherto neutralized by the 'drenching fire', started to recover and man their weapons. To the east, on QUEEN WHITE Beach, 77 Assault Squadron enjoyed initial success. No. 1 Team, furthest away from COD to the right, despite taking fire as it approached the beach and landed, saw two flails promptly beating their way across the beach and over the sea wall, dunes, mines and wire to reach the main lateral road. However, with plenty of enemy small arms fire, during the first attempt to put up the windsock to indicate the presence of an open gap, a sapper was wounded. Clearly, as indicated by Major Wormald of A Squadron 13/18 H, a second attempt was not made again for some time:

> As no 'exit open' signs (windsocks on poles) had been erected I decided to dismount from my tank and to walk along the beach to our right to inspect a

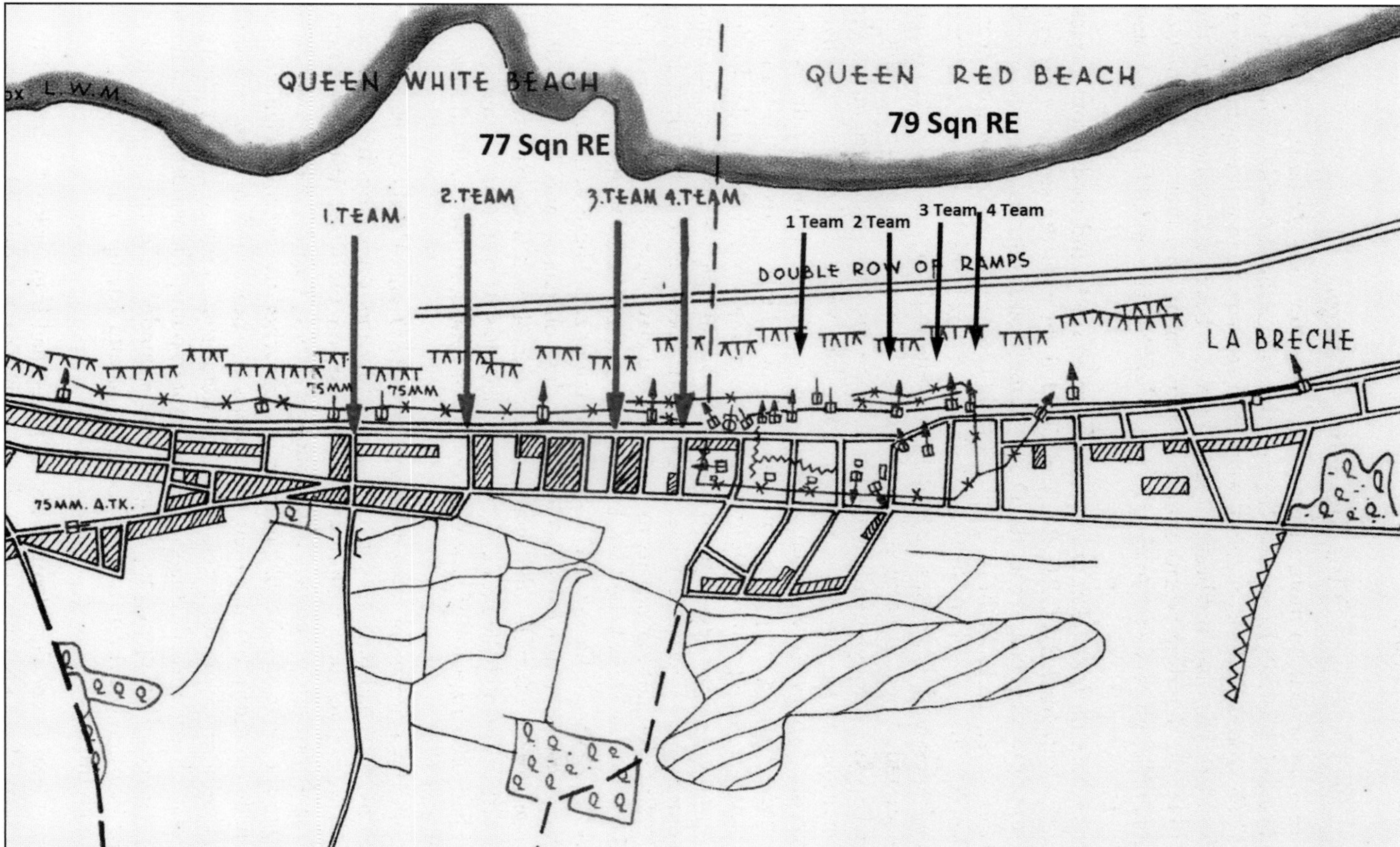

The 5th Assault Regiment RE's breaching plan.

> road which I could see led straight onto the beach. When I got there, I was surprised to see that the German anti-tank mines, which should have been placed in prepared holes in the road surface, were stacked up on the side of the road. I hurried back to my tank and remounted. By then the beach area was becoming a distinctly unhealthy place, due to mortar and shell fire. The time must have been about H+15. The four 'windsocks' had still not been erected so I ordered my Squadron to follow me from the beach via the exit that I had found.

Even though six tanks were soon off the beach, No. 1 Team's exit was, however, not properly marked as open until 0820 hours.

With only machine-gun positions immediately in front of them, 77 Squadron had modest opposition to cope with but was enfiladed by a 75mm Pak 40 in an R677 casemate sited in COD which covered the western part of RED sector and onto WHITE. This gun fired sixteen rounds during the first few minutes of the landing before being knocked out, and it is probable that it was responsible for most of the early vehicle casualties out towards Lion-sur-Mer. In the view of a Combined Ops survey party, the Pak 40 was hit by either a 4.7-inch shell or a petard bomb from an AVRE, but the 79th Armoured Division's history attributes its destruction to a 75mm shell fired by a Crab. It was, of course, not unusual for a target of any type to be engaged and 'claimed' by multiple parties.[8] In total, seven funnies on WHITE Beach were knocked out while crossing it or tackling the defences on the sea wall.

On WHITE Beach, 77 Squadron lost No. 4 Team, which was hit by a shell while still aboard its LCT and could not land. The resulting explosion of ammunition stacked in the craft killed the commanding officer of 5 Assault Regiment, Lieutenant Colonel Cocks. The remaining two exits from WHITE Beach took some time to complete, at the cost of casualties to Crabs, AVREs and men.

On RED Beach, 79 Squadron had an altogether more difficult task. They were to land in front of WN-20 COD and force their way through the defences all the way to the main lateral road. An entry in the squadron's war diary timed 0725 describes their landing:

> All serials touch down. CRE orders SEARCH FRONT over the air ... The sea is rough and a cloud of smoke overhangs the hedgehog COD. For a minute or so there is no fire from the enemy. From the water's edge up to the back of the beach is about 250yd not 400yd. The first 100yd is thick with obstacles. First two rows of ramp-type obstacle every alternate one mined with a 1935 Tellermine on top is in 4 feet of water. Then three rows of heavy pitprops sunk into the ground again each alternate one fixed with a Tellermine. And inland of these, rows of reinforced concrete Tetrahedra and steel girder hedgehogs with alternate obstacles wired up with shells with German Push Igniters DZ.35. Flails and AVRE were unable to drive in between obstacles.[9]

Assorted assault armour on QUEEN WHITE with the tide rising around the obstacles. Note the distinctive 'Twin Villas'.

Four flails and five AVREs were lost to a combination of anti-tank fire and the thickly sown mines around COD. Sapper Beeton driving an AVRE of 79 Assault Engineer Squadron recalled:

> As I came down the ramp I could see German mines everywhere, fixed to cross-pieces on the obstacles about 2 feet above ground level. Further up the beach I could see the German pill-boxes.
>
> I was instructed by my officer to pick my way up the beach as best I could. My luck held and I was almost off the beach when we hit a mine which blew the bogey off. Fortunately, the tank track held, but the officer and sergeant in our crew were killed. Over half the squadron was wiped out before we cleared the beaches.

Leaving aside the six Shermans of A Squadron, tracked vehicles were only able to leave the beach in most cases between 0845 and 1000 hours, with lanes suitable for wheeled vehicles eventually opening during the late morning. Behind the breaching teams, other engineers were to clear mines and obstacles from the beach, but this was far more difficult than expected due to the earlier and higher than calculated rise of the tide. As recorded in 79 Squadron's war diary, at H Hour the beach was estimated as being 250 yards rather than 400 yards wide. This miscalculation added another element of difficulty and delay.[10]

Amongst the significant factors in slowing the breaching were the mining of vehicles while clearing the lanes or failure to follow the track exactly. Accurate bombing of the beach defences would have reduced the number of mines through sympathetic detonation. The overall delay in clearing the lanes through to the main lateral road, which were planned to be open by H+20, caused significant traffic jams on a narrow stretch of beach at high water. From the outset, delays in creating the exits off the beach contributed significantly to an inability to develop the necessary tempo for a successful advance by the 3rd Division on Caen.

The Infantry Assault

The DDs and the funnies had landed with the tide lapping around the obstacles furthest down the beach, but given the beach's shallow profile, the tide advanced rapidly across the sands. The combined effects of inaccurate tidal calculation and the recent strong westerly winds meant the tide was flooding thirty-minutes ahead of the expected time. Consequently, the infantry's LCAs were having to avoid the numerous beach obstacles rather than landing below them. The 21st Army Group Royal Engineers' report detailed the number of obstacles on the beach in QUEEN Sector:

52 × Hedgehogs – recycled from the Czech pre-war border fortifications.
67 × Stakes.
76 × Timber ramps.
46 × Element 'C' – Belgian Gates recycled from that country's roads and bridges on the frontier.
Making a total of an obstacle for every 3 yards of beach. [11]

The plan was for the two assault battalions of 8 Infantry Brigade to lead the assault, each with a pair of rifle companies and supported by the squadrons of DD tanks, their principal objective being WN-20 COD. They were to be followed

An example of an Element C obstacle, referred to as 'Belgian Gates'. They were recycled 1940-vintage gates originally designed to keep the panzers out of Belgium!

twenty minutes later by the two reserve companies per battalions, with their support weapons schedule between H+60 and H+120. Having secured COD and SKATE, 2 East Yorks were to take SOLE and DAIMLER and then advance to Objective RUGGER (Pegasus Bridge). The brigade's third battalion, 1 Suffolks and the non-DD C Squadron 13/18 H, were planned to start landing at H+60. Their objectives were MORRIS, HILLMAN and the Périers Ridge. Once the Suffolks had passed through their positions, 1 South Lancs would become brigade reserve with a number of 'Be prepared to' tasks, as anticipated by Brigade Headquarters. Subsequently, 185 Brigade, landing at H+150, was to conduct a passage of lines through 8 Brigade's centre in a dash to take Caen.

Lieutenant Colonel Burbury's plan for 1 South Lancs was to land on WHITE Beach at H Hour, with A Company on the right, which was to fight through the coastal defences as far inland as the main lateral road and wheel right to cover that flank until such time as 41 RM Commando arrived. Landing on the boundary between WHITE and RED, C Company's task was to attack and clear WN-20 COD, along with 2 East Yorks to their left. They were supported by breaching detachments of 246 Field Company RE, who were to clear mines and blow the barbed wire with Bangalore Torpedoes carried ashore by sappers. At H+20 B and D companies were to touch down as the second wave, with a light section of 8 Field Ambulance. With the four 1 South Lancs rifle companies ashore, B, C and D companies, with the support of B Squadron 13/18 H, were to advance and clear Hermanville, while A Company would join with the commandos (landing at H+75) in an advance to Lion-sur-Mer, where Objective TROUT WN-21 was to be taken by 41 Commando.

The 8 Infantry Brigade plan for the assault on WN-20 COD.

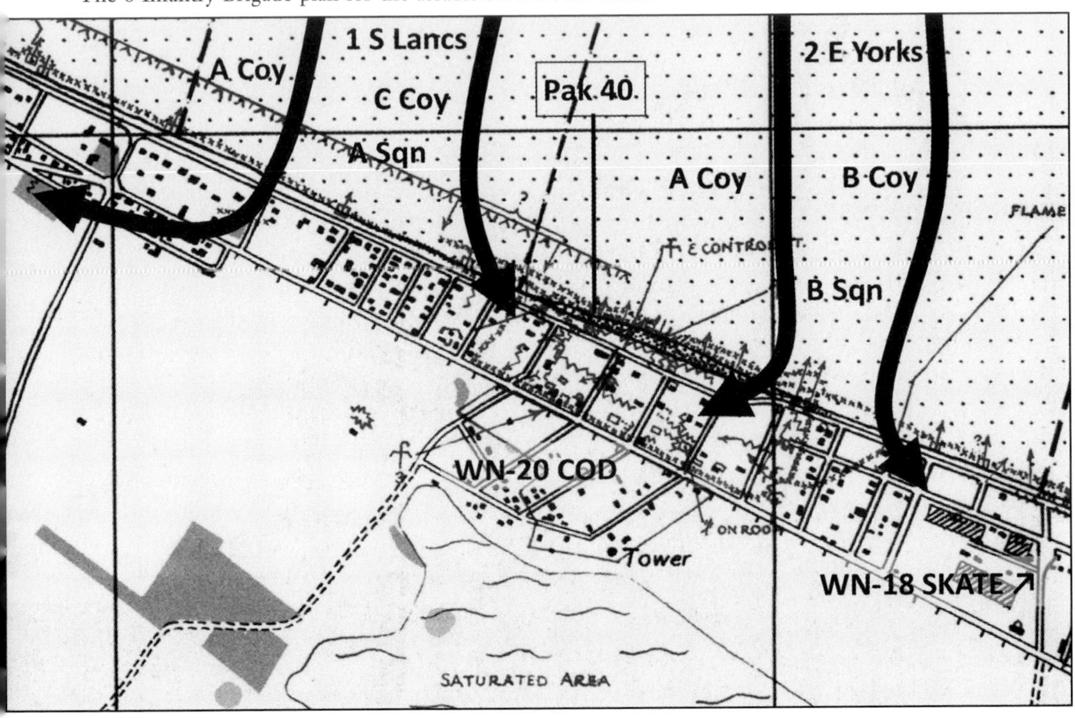

The detailed tasks for 2 East Yorks on landing on QUEEN RED were set out in their operation order:

> A Company
> (a) Will land about the middle of RED BEACH at H+5 minutes, swing South West and in conjunction with C Company 1st Battalion THE SOUTH LANCASHIRE REGIMENT, destroy the enemy in COD 3820
>
> B Company
> (a) Will land on left of RED BEACH at H+5 minutes, swing East and destroy enemy in beach defences all exclusive of COD and up to and inclusive SKATE 398202

On the assumption that A and B companies' objectives had been taken, C and D Companies landing at H+20 would head straight for the battalion's assembly area inland beyond the lateral road.

As the LCAs approached the beach, the coxswains could see that they had to steer through the obstacles, many of which were tipped with shells or mines. Many were the tales of near-misses, soakings and 'miraculous dry landings'.

Captain Rouse of battalion headquarters 1 South Lancs recalled:

> The boat crews had been ordered to go in at 4 knots and hit the beach hard. During the last 100 yards of the run-in everything seemed to happen at once. Out of the haze of smoke the underwater obstacles loomed up. We had studied them on air photographs and knew exactly what to expect but somehow we had never realized the vertical height of them, and as we weaved in between iron rails and ramps and pickets with teller mines on top like gigantic mushrooms we seemed to be groping through a grotesque petrified forest.
>
> The noise was so continuous that it seemed almost like a siren. The seamanship was magnificent. The LCAs weaved in and out of the obstacles and we almost had a dry landing. I have very little recollection of wading ashore, there was too much going on above and around to notice it. It was however, apparent from the beginning that it was by no means an unopposed landing. Mortar fire was coming down on the sands, an 88mm gun was firing along the line of the beach and there was continuous machine-gun and rifle fire. Immediately ahead of us a DD tank, its rear end enveloped in flames, unable to get off the beach, continued to fire its guns.

Grenadier Hubbne was in a bunker ashore in COD or SKATE awaiting the onslaught:

> Then our Lieutenant came to remind us of all the drills we had done and not to fire until the enemy was in the water when they were most vulnerable. We knew all that, but wondered if we would still be alive to act at all … The great shells from the battleships made a fantastic noise and the concrete

An air photograph of WN-20 COD of the type used for briefing the assault troops.

> shook when they exploded. We guessed that all the seafront houses and our defences were being smashed. The bombardment seemed to go on for a very long time and all the while the air was also filled with the sound of bombers.

There are some claims that the infantry's assault companies landed before the DD tanks. They had expected to pass through a line of DD tanks as they had in FABIUS, but in the exercise the unwaterproofed tanks had made an assumed landing on the beach, while in the real thing the infantry were sheltering low in their LCAs and had probably not seen the DDs hull-down in the surf. The leading infantry were, however, touching down amongst the last of the breaching teams. Grenadier Hubbne was waiting as a part of a machine-gun team:

> Then, the noise seemed to lessen and our *Feldwebel* told us to stand up as the enemy were about to land, so we jumped to our weapons, trembling with fear and from the effects of the bombardment noise. One of the units on our left was composed of Eastern 'volunteers' from the *Ost*, I believe, who looked very Asiatic in appearance; I wondered if they had survived and would surrender at once. Then we could see the enemy landing craft coming into the shore and the warships still firing. We forced ourselves to get ready.

Machine-gun fire greeted the infantry of 8 Brigade as their platoon and company commanders led the way out into the waves to wade ashore. Major Harwood of A Company 1 South Lancs was mortally wounded. Private Cartwright of the same unit was luckier. He stepped off his LCA into a foot of water:

> We tried to get off that damned beach which was covered by Jerry fire and I thought, if only I could run faster, but it was impossible with all that stuff on me. There were lots of bits of debris in the sea swell and smoke and noise and it seemed an age before we reached the shelter of a knocked-out DD tank with no sign of the crew. Our Lieutenant and NCOs ran up to urge us on behind them, but we were very reluctant to do this because of all the fire going on.

Private Hansen of the 2 East Yorks recalled:

> We went in with none of the yelling you see in films. It was every man for himself as we tried to get up the beach in one piece. No one wanted to stop for a wounded mate, though I did see it happen. One bloke who stopped and tried to pick up his pal was himself killed. That shook me as I'd never seen anything like it. I was really too soft to be in battle; the noise upset me a good deal and I preferred to keep my head down. But with so much going on I was too curious and ... when I looked back and saw our own lads struggling up that beach I was amazed that so many made it. And I felt relieved and began to feel better.

The dismounted engineer breaching teams that accompanied the two infantry battalions suffered casualties and lost some of their equipment during the landing, facing machine guns in concrete *Tobruckstände* unsubdued by the bombardment. Private Wellings was with A Company 1 South Lancs:

> Our first holdup after landing was the wire. It must have been 8′ high and 12′ deep so our Bangalore team went into action. The first 6′ length was slid under, then the second length was locked in and pushed under, and the third length was connected. The third man ran back and I think he forgot to light the fuse for it didn't go off. Our OC Major Spook Harwood told us to keep our heads down while he went off to investigate. On his way he caught a burst of Spandau fire. He crawled forward and managed to light the fuse. He must have been in acute agony. As I ran through the gap in the wire he looked at me with a half-smile on his face and I heard him say, 'Carry on, Wellings, I'll catch up later.' He died of his wounds about 0315 hrs on 7th June. We managed to get to the safety of the seaside villas. To my left CSM Murphy stood beckoning the next wave to come forward, the Coy runner Dickie Dallow by his side. Suddenly there was a fierce explosion and they both were killed instantly.

The companies on the outer flanks of the two battalions were able to break through the mines and wire in the direction of Lion-sur-Mer and WN-18 SKATE, while those in the centre were making slow progress against WN-20 COD, where the defenders were putting up stiff resistance.

A CANLOAN[12] officer of C Company 2 East Yorks, Lieutenant Roberts, described the landing of the second wave:

> Bullets, shrapnel and what have you was flying around like a swarm of angry bees ... Blood was flowing and bodies of other pl[atoon]s from A and B Companies were floating face down in the water here and there. Things were moving so fast that one had hardly time to think or be scared. Our main thought was to get the hell off the beach ... We were on the beach and soon organized and on the move. 15 Platoon was the first in the Coy to get moving as a unit and with the least casualties ... two killed and two wounded, the lightest in the battalion, I believe. We felt very lucky indeed. My men were just grand all the way, even finding time to joke.

Lieutenant Roebuck, also of the East Yorks, wrote:

> All around was a scene of utter destruction, wrecked boats lay broadside on, dead comrades floated face down in the tide, others lay in grotesque positions on the beach. Exploding shells fell as we raced on towards a gap in the defences. It was being made wider by brave stalwart REs who swept the sands with their mine detectors, then laid out white tapes to mark a safe track. The sand dragged on our feet and slowed down on our progress. The gap was to the left of the beach strongpoint COD in process of being put out of action by A Coy E. Yorks and C Coy S. Lancs. On the sloping grassy bank which covered the huge bunker were three dead Germans. They were immaculate in their grey overcoats and smart uniforms, caught as they

An obsolescent 50mm tank gun on a locally manufactured mount sited in a Nr. 1694 gun pit to cover the inland approaches to COD, adjacent to the D514. A similar gun can be seen at Pegasus Bridge.

> had run away, they lay, two of them face down in a neat line. The track led away from the beach going towards the lateral road.

The South Lancs war diary entries read:

> 0745 hrs. The second wave Battalion HQ, B & D Companies HQs touched down, met by small arms fire, mortars, and firing from an 88mm gun firing down the beach. The Battalion landed almost on strongpoint COD which was still active.
>
> Battalion HQ moved towards the sand dunes near the enemy 88mm [*sic*] position and the C.O. Lt Col Burbury was killed whilst directing operations.
>
> B Company proceeded to deal with the strongpoint COD and their company commander was killed on landing. The officer taking command was killed during the attack on the pillbox.

The CO's tac HQ had been carrying a small camp colour to mark his position. A handy device while on exercise, but against a real enemy with live ammunition, not such a good idea, when commanders tend anyway to be all too obvious.

It took until 0900 hours to subdue the defences of COD, but even then, the South Lancs and East Yorks were being sniped at from the ruins of adjacent buildings and scrub, and the beach was still under mortar and artillery fire. The companies that had been able to get through needed reorganising and were, except on the right, without the tanks necessary for the planned all-arms advance inland. Nonetheless, B and C companies of the South Lancs had pressed on with their advance to Hermanville, which they had secured by 0900 hours. No mention is made in the accounts of resistance by the *Osttruppen*, only 'isolated snipers'. Meanwhile, on the opposite flank, C Company of the East Yorks was preparing to advance on SOLE, the battalion headquarters of I/376 Infantry Regiment.

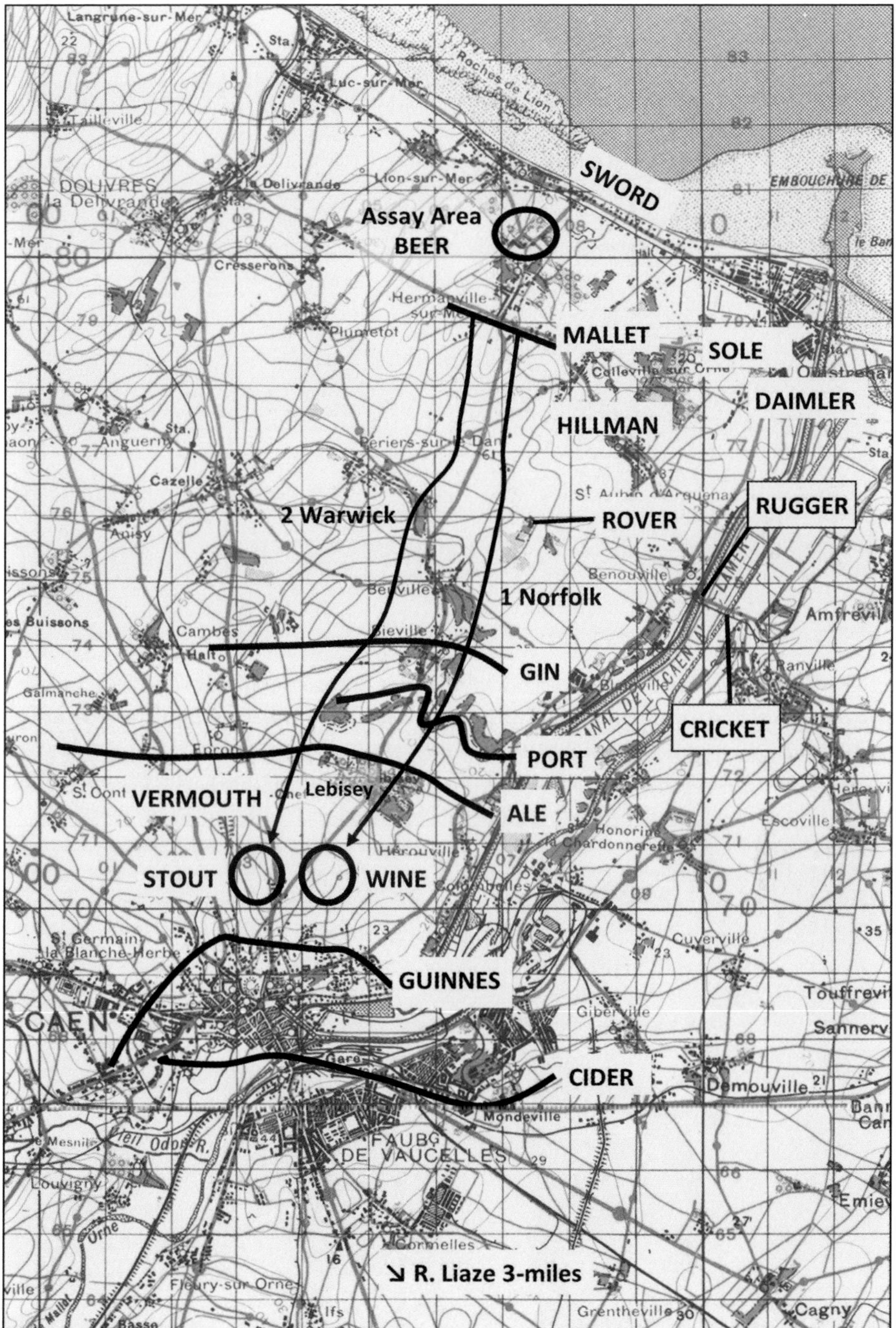

Trace A of 3rd Division's Op O No 1 showing the objectives and report lines during the advance on Caen.

An extract of the 1:12,500 tactical overprint map showing the complex ground of marshes, woods (partly felled for the construction of beach obstacles) and open areas covered with 'Rommel's Asparagus' anti-glider poles that the Suffolks would have to cross to reach Colleville.

Chapter Six

MORRIS and HILLMAN

Within an hour or so of H Hour, the coastal strip may have been 'cleared' by 8 Brigade, and the leading battalions had begun to make their way inland to their objectives. SWORD, however, was far from secure, with small arms, mortar and shell fire falling on the beach and its immediate vicinity. Nor, as recorded by their regimental historian, was it much better for 2 East Yorks away from the beach, as their leading company advanced south-east. Their historian wrote:

> Under enemy observation, mortared and shelled, the move across country to 'Sole', the first objective, was slow. The naval artillery Observation Officer could not be found when naval artillery fire against 'Sole' was wanted, but 76 Field Regiment shelled the place, and 'C' Company finally took it. 'A' Company had meanwhile been clearing the beach area but arrived at 'Sole' in time to help in consolidating.

Meanwhile, with less far to go to their objective and facing the dubious quality of 3 Company, 642 *Ost* Battalion, 1 South Lancs, according to their war diary, were getting on well:

> 0900 hrs. Hermanville was captured and Battalion HQ was then established in the area of the church. Communications with B & C Companies which were previously out of commission were now working well. They fulfilled their roles to plan and consolidated. A Company was out of contact.There was street fighting in the village and odd snipers were still active around the village.[1]

1 Suffolks – The Reserve Battalion

One of the key arguments over the failure of 3rd Division to capture Caen on D Day has traditionally revolved around the operations of 1 Suffolks to capture Objectives MORRIS (WN-16) and HILLMAN (WN-17). Starting to land at H+60, Lieutenant Colonel Goodwin's battalion was to advance just under 2 miles inland, through the coastal defences secured by the East Yorks and South Lancs, and clear the village of Colleville. Then they were to take Objective MORRIS and, a further 1,000 yards south, capture HILLMAN. Finally, they were to establish a defensive position around Beauvais Farm on the Périers ridge. The Suffolks were to be supported by C Squadron 13/18 H, a pair of 105mm batteries from 76 and 33 Field Regiments, a detachment of 246 Field Company RE, a machine-gun

A section of 1 South Lancs' 6-pounder anti-tank guns positioned at the south-west corner of Hermanville … and the same spot on the D35 today. The Périers Ridge rises to the right.

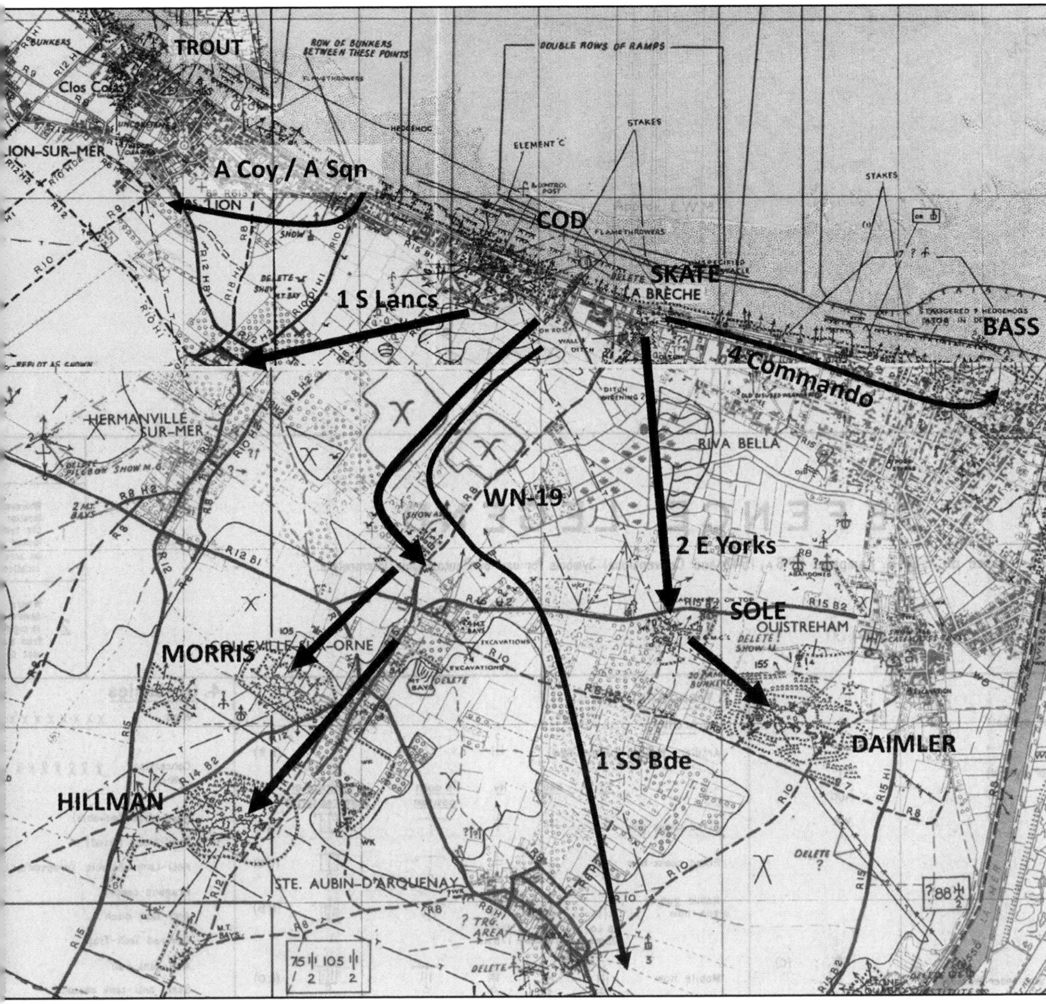

8 Brigade's advance inland.

platoon of 2 Middlesex and a section of 8 Field Ambulance. The sequencing of the battalion's plan was:

Phase 1. Landing on SWORD Beach, they were to move to an Assembly Area 1,000 yards inland.
Phase 2. C Company was to clear Colleville from north to south, allowing B Company to have a clear run in an assault on MORRIS with one breaching platoon of D Company (the battalion's reserve) and a pair of 13/18 H's Shermans.
Phase 3. Having taken MORRIS, B Company were to provide fire support for C Company's attack on HILLMAN. Also fire support from C Squadron.
Phase 4. A Company with the RE detachment and a breaching platoon of D Company were to assault HILLMAN.
Phase 5. The Battalion was to consolidate on the Périers-sur-le-Dan feature south of HILLMAN.

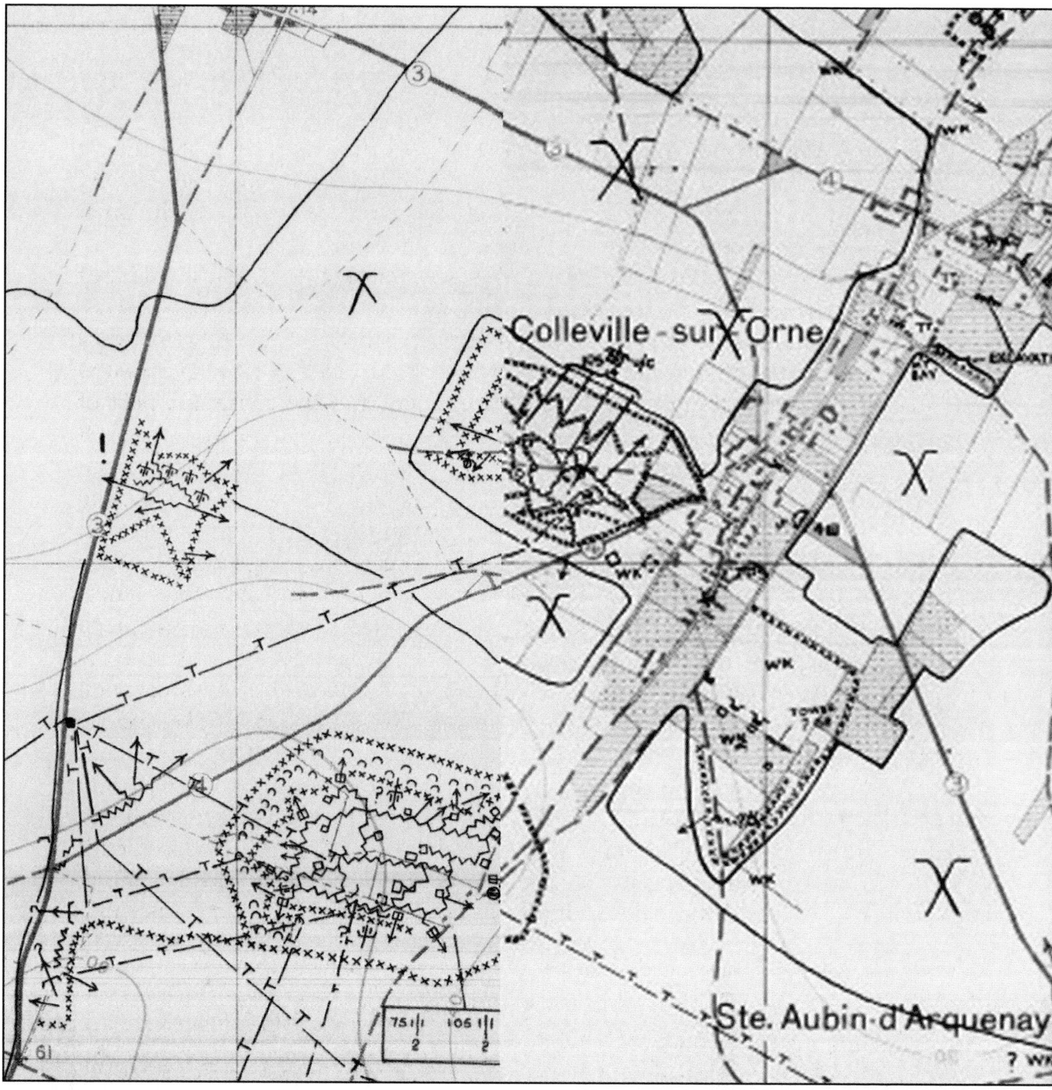

An extract of the 1:25,000 overprint map showing Objectives MORRIS (WN-16) and HILLMAN (WN-17) along with the dummy position to the west.

Both MORRIS and HILLMAN were to have been subject to air attack prior to H Hour and naval gunfire support was to be provided by a Forward Officer Bombardment who had the guns of a 6-inch cruiser and a destroyer on call. This plan only partially worked due to causalities.

To the north of Colleville, the first opposition the Suffolks expected to encounter was a small enemy defensive position (WN-19) consisting of a couple of *Tobruckstände* covering the road and the open ground leading from the beach to the village. Beyond WN-19, Colleville was a 1,000-yard-long straggling village, orientated north-east to south-west, built of the usual honey-coloured Norman limestone. It was dominated by the church, the *mairie* and several substantial farm complexes, all naturally strong.

Objective MORRIS (WN-16) lay immediately to the south of Colleville. It consisted of four 100mm Skoda guns. The battery was surrounded by barbed wire, and the guns were in the process of being casemated, with three of the open gun pits having been replaced by R669 concrete bunkers.

Clearly marked with a '!' on the Defences Overprint map to the south-west of MORRIS is a dummy four-gun position.

HILLMAN (WN-17) stood on a dominating position on the forward edge of the Périers Ridge that was known to the Germans as *Hohe* 61. It was the headquarters of *Oberst* Krug's 736 Infantry Regiment and the command post of Major Hof's 1/1716 artillery battalion. Both were in largely subterranean H608 bunkers which were well sited for observation over the beaches and country from the Orne at Ouistreham to Douvres and Lagrune-sur-Mar in the west.[2] The fields of fire from the three *Tobruckstände* machine-gun positions, plus a French 75mm and two French 47mm anti-tank guns, were equally impressive. The whole HILLMAN position was surrounded by thick concertina-wire fence, a mixed minefield of anti-tank and anti-personnel mines some 40–60 yards deep and another barbed-wire obstacle. Sited inside the perimeter defences, on the forward slope, were the two massive H 608 bunkers with steel cupola observation positions. In addition to other shelters there was an R605 concrete bunker for the anti-tank guns.

MORRIS, like many other batteries, had been bombed prior to D Day. On the evening of 1 June, Ninth US Air Force's Marauders struck with 2,000lb ordnance, and the following evening thirty-six aircraft of the RAF returned with 1,000lb bombs. Air photography showed that the 'results were poor to good', with bombs impacting 500 yards north on the edge of Colleville, killing a number

A French anti-tank gun designated in German service as the 4.7cm Pak 181 (f).

of Germans in the battery headquarters in the village. Amongst other 'hits', a bomb fell alongside Casemate No. 3, and a number caused sympathetic detonation of mines laid around HILLMAN. Some of the craters reported within the latter position's boundary could have resulted from this bombing.

The Landing

C Squadron 13/18 H landed on time at H+45. The regimental historian described the scene:

> Everything was very confused, due to the influx of men and vehicles, which increased rapidly while the pace of dispersal was still very slow. There was little opposition in the form of direct fire, except from a few concealed snipers, but shelling and mortar fire from concealed positions was heavy and the sea front displayed an amazing scene of burning craft and 'brewed up' tanks and vehicles.[3]

Meanwhile, the Suffolks, having transferred from the LSIs *Empire Broadsword* and *Battleaxe* into LCAs, touched down on QUEEN WHITE Beach at H+60 (0825 hours) under fire with 'bullets and shells flying about in all directions'. Having run the gauntlet of fire across the beach, A Company's radio operator Private Varley and other members of company headquarters took cover under the seawall. 'No one was keen to get moving as there was plenty of fire. Moments later, CSM Leatherland strolled past with his rifle crooked over his arm. "Are you lot staying there all day?" We sheepishly follow him.'

The Suffolks, having gathered at the back of the beach, were able to leave by some of the first exits that had just been opened.

> On arrival at the wood previously selected as the Battalion assembly area we found what we had suspected – so much had been cut that no decent cover was left. There was a sniper among the bundles of brushwood; but he was killed or made off at once.
>
> Decided to move forward to the next cover about two or three hundred yards ahead as planned. On arrival here, an orchard, we were greeted by an officer and about five other ranks of a Canadian parachute unit who had been dropped over the wrong area during the night. They were very pleased to see us as they had had an uncomfortable time during the early hours, being bombed by our own people. However, they were determined to go on with the battle and later joined 'D' Company for the morning.[4]

One crucial loss to a mortar bomb during landing was the battalion's FOB party, without whom contact with the supporting ships, the Polish cruiser ORP *Dragon* and the destroyer HMS *Kelvin*, was not possible. Thus, the Suffolks were unable to call for timely, heavy and accurate fire. These ships had, however, already engaged MORRIS and HILLMAN during the preliminary bombardment with predicted fire.

The Commandos

No. 4 Commando had landed on RED Beach at H+30 with the mission to advance east to clear the coastal defences, ultimately securing the lock gates at the entrance to the Canal de Caen. Behind them, landing on QUEEN at H+75 (0840–0910 hours), were the main body of 1 Special Service Brigade, who rushed through the wreckage on the beach. Following behind his commandos, Brigadier Lord Lovat, landing on RED Beach, waded through the surf and ran across the sands through the 'men of the 2nd East Yorks [who] lay dead and dying at the water's edge … These crumpled khaki forms seemed to confirm the worst fears of the follow-up troops.'[5] Despite the scenes of chaos, the commandos, following their credo of 'Get off the beach', had quickly made their way through the coastal belt to their assembly areas beyond the main lateral road, only pausing to clear several pillboxes that barred their way. Their mission was not to fight on the beach or in the immediate hinterland but to cut across nearly 5 miles of enemy-held country to Objective RUGGER (Pegasus Bridge) and join 6th Airborne Division in pushing west towards the Dives inundations.[6]

Commandos of 1st Special Service Brigade making their way off QUEEN WHITE Beach.

Having got across the beach to the assembly area, shortly before 1000 hours Colonel Mills-Roberts, No. 6 Commando, led the brigade's four units south to the first contact with the enemy at WN-19, which covered the approaches to Colleville. This was just forty-five minutes since the last of their landing craft had touched down. Colonel Mills-Roberts wrote:

> Suddenly the column came to a halt. I pushed my way up a little lane with high hedgerows on either side and came to a gap where the hedge had been broken. On the far side of this gap was a clump of bushes and there I saw Bill Coade, my Second-in-Command. His face was a mass of blood he was temporarily blinded. He had been hit by a grenade.
>
> Someone shouted, 'Look out! There's a sniper covering that gap.' I got across it all right, but Corporal Smith, who followed me, was shot through the forearm.
>
> Bill Coade was in a shocking mess; knowing that speed was essential, he had gallantly tried to rush a pill-box and received a stick grenade right in the face.
>
> Somehow this had to be sorted out really quickly. There was no possibility of an alternative approach without running into more trouble. A wireless message came from Shimi [Lord] Lovat: 'Why are you halted?' The rest of the brigade, it must be remembered, was following in our tracks. It was our job to blaze the trail.
>
> About 70 yards away on the right I saw a British DD tank, which had come straight up a track from the beach . . . I cut back to the tank and asked for fire. It lumbered forward and fired two rounds: the first one did no damage, but the second one split the pill-box like a rotten apple.[7]

The tanks of C Squadron 13/18 H had taken a route across the open country and come up behind the commandos, while the Suffolks worked their way through the woods to the west.

No. 6 Commando did not, as has sometimes been claimed, clear through Colleville but turned east as always intended through the woods before reaching the village. The rest of the brigade followed on a variety of routes, leaving the Suffolks to clear Colleville. Advancing from the assembly area some time after the commandos, Colonel Goodwin caught up with Lord Lovat's brigade headquarters around 1030 hours near WN-19.

At this point a salvo of *Wurfkörper* rocket mortars screamed down near the commandos and Suffolks, causing large explosions. Presumably because of the telltale smoke trail identifying the launch site, Lord Lovat detached a troop of 3 Commando, assisted by two of C Squadron's tanks, to clear it, but by the time they deployed there was no sign of a launcher or the enemy.

At about the same time, the leading batteries of 76 (h), 33 and 7 regiments RA were off the beach and opening fire from gun positions around the assembly areas. Other batteries were receiving calls for fire from FOOs and engaging targets from the beach as the tide rose around their Priests. In contrast to the

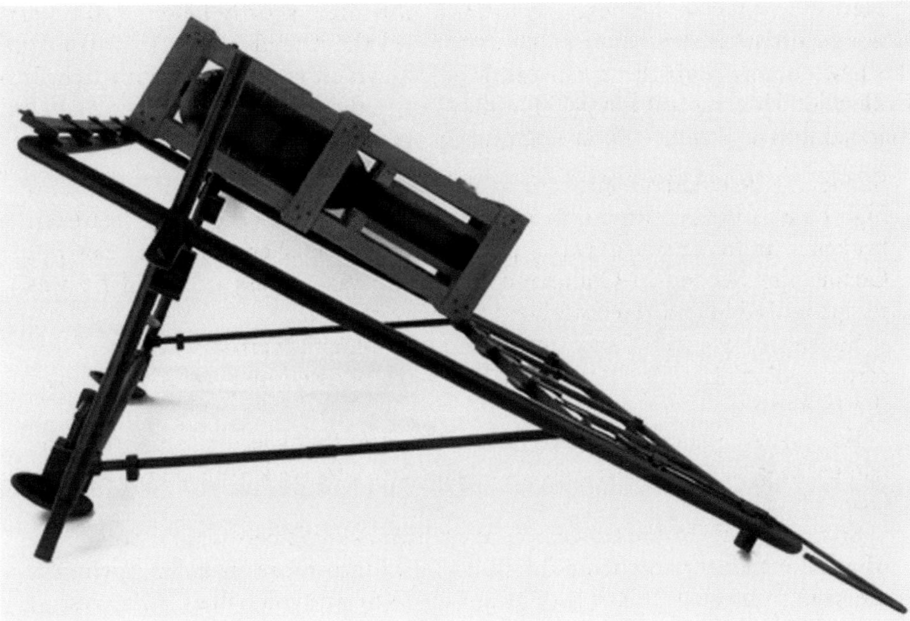

There were no *Nebelwerfers* on the establishment of 716th Division. From the description of what happened, the weapon most likely to have engaged the Suffolks and commandos was the *Wurfkörper*. They were fired direct from crates mounted on stands, or simply dug in at the appropriate angle to engage a target.

normal practice of an artillery regiment being in support of a particular brigade, and batteries supporting specific battalions, on D Day FOOs of all three regiments were deployed across the division's nine infantry battalions. Given the uncertainty of amphibious operations, it was thought that this was the best and most flexible way to guarantee fire. By D+1 normal grouping had been resumed.

Colleville and Objective MORRIS WN-16

Colleville proved not to have been held in any strength, and Major Boycott's C Company worked their way through the village with a troop of C Squadron in support against negligible opposition. Each platoon and section knew their well-briefed and rehearsed tasks. Lieutenant Smith and two tanks of his troop made their way down the main street behind the infantry. He recalled:

> The task was much easier than we had anticipated. Two tanks worked through the village, street by street, with the infantry in the approved manner, while two more tanks nosed through the surrounding orchards. We, of course, expected to see something or be fired upon, but, in fact, we had no occasion to fire a shot. Much to our surprise, the Boche and a number of the inhabitants had cleared out. Perhaps they had been alarmed by the landing of the 6th Airborne Division nearby earlier in the morning, and

> probably did not like their defensive position after tasting the furious onslaught of the initial landing. I can recall two memories of Colleville. Firstly, the reluctance of my driver and myself to run over a dead German body lying prostrate across the road, and, secondly, the bewildered and haunted expressions of the inhabitants, who must have thought that their houses would be completely destroyed, and probably doubted our ability to remain in Normandy for any length of time.[8]

Meanwhile, the remaining Shermans out on the open right flank were already 'exchanging some shots with Hillman' and its anti-tank guns. With negligible opposition in the village, Colonel Goodwin sent B Company forward into Colleville, no doubt heartened by reports from Major Papillon out on the right with a platoon of D Company that there appeared to be no movement in MORRIS. However, he added that they should be careful, as it could be a trap. Corporal Byatt of B Company recalled the attack on MORRIS. As planned, Major McCaffrey's B Company and two troops of tanks had approached the battery with the intent of blowing the barbed-wire entanglement with Bangalore Torpedoes.

> We went at the double from the beach, leaving snipers and other pockets of resistance to be mopped up by others following. 'Morris' was still firing on the beach and with shells going overhead the noise was terrific. We managed to find some cover on the approach and got in position to attack ...
>
> The air photos we had studied had shown the trenches round the gun emplacements, so each section knew where to make for. I remember laying flat by the Bangalore torpedo team, ready to blow the wire, wondering what it was going to be like. The shelling stopped and we were just going to blow and attack when white flags were waved. We hoped it wasn't a trick, but they surrendered, sixty or seventy officers and men, which was just as well for us. Their positions were well covered and formidable, but the shelling and bombing had softened them up, although the emplacement looked intact. I think the speed with which we got there also helped a lot. So, the 'Success' signal [flare] went up.

Sixty-seven mainly Polish *Beutedeutsch* soldiers serving in 2 Battery of 1716 Artillery Regiment came out with their hands up, clearly 'pleased to be out of it'. Captain Lummis later wrote:

> So, at midday the Battalion was able to report that 'Morris' had been cleared. Ten minutes after B Company had satisfied themselves that there were no enemy left, the position was shelled by guns firing from the south-east (perhaps from the battery just north of Périers-sur-le-Dan or from the self-propelled 155mm battery of 1716 Regiment at Plumetot) but there were no casualties as they were secure in the concrete defences they had just taken or were well outside the position. B Company then moved on to take up positions to support A Company in its attack on 'Hillman'.[9]

One of the three R669 artillery bunkers of MORRIS that survive, now in a housing estate.

Objective HILLMAN WN-17

Thus far, the Suffolks had been lucky, with B and C companies clearing their objectives easily, but HILLMAN, the well defended headquarter location of *Oberst* Krug's 736 Infantry Regiment, was to prove an altogether sterner test. Apart from the fact that there was to be no naval gunfire support, the barbed-wire was thicker and mines had been more densely sown than thought.

With MORRIS in the hands of the Suffolks, their attached battery of 79 Field Regiment and the 3-inch mortars of their own mortar platoon began the process of registering targets on HILLMAN. This was not quick or easy as radio communication via the No. 18 set to the guns and mortars was 'difficult'.[10] Colonel Goodwin, however, had a stroke of luck as he moved south of the village when another mis-dropped Canadian paratrooper met him. The officer, who had been in the area since the early hours, showed the CO a covered position in standing crops 150 yards from HILLMAN from where he could see the formidable outer barbed-wire obstacle. The view was restricted, but one of the steel observation cupolas could be seen.

The guns reported 'ready', and as Captain Ryley's A Company approached HILLMAN via a sunken track.[11] the Colonel gave the codeword GRAB at 1310 hours to initiate the fire plan, with the Shermans of C Squadron joining in with 75mm HE and 17-pounder AP.[12] Lieutenant Russell's breaching platoon was able to approach the obstacle by crawling from the sunken track, under cover of the exploding mortar bombs and shells, with the long grass and scrub that had grown up in the minefield helping to conceal the final few yards to the barbed-wire. An officer of C Squadron wrote:

> It was these mines and quantities of wire that caused trouble and delayed us. After reaching the edge of the objective the infantry made two attempts to clear a gap by hand, while being covered by the tanks, but the mine lifters were pinned down by intense machine gun fire and suffered some fatal casualties. The machine guns were difficult to locate as the concealed Germans were not firing tracer and continually changed their positions.
>
> At first my troop was well out on the left flank again with a view to shooting the infantry and tanks in on to the position.[13]

Sapper Ellis was one of the detachment of 246 Field Company tasked to clear a path through the mines for the infantry:

> We were told to tape a path through the minefield, where we came under machine-gun fire. I led the way into the minefield at the crouch and dived

The assault by A Company 1 Suffolk on HILLMAN.

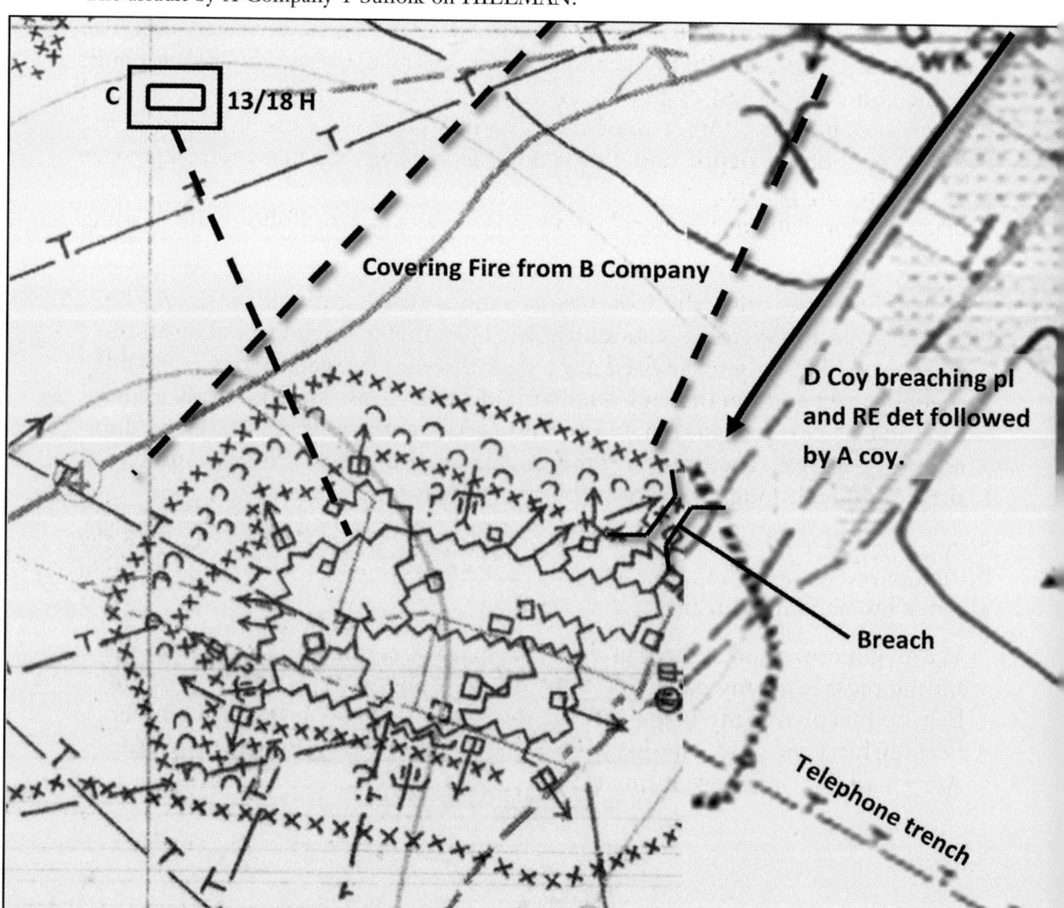

> behind a small mound; the machine-gun rounds were bouncing off it and the third man of our team was hit in the chest. After lying there for a while I began to ease myself forward. Pinning marker tape around the mines, I picked up on the detector and crawled on until I reached a triple barbed-wire fence. I then crawled back down the tape, very aware of an extremely dry mouth and perspiration running down my face.

Corporal Rayson of Lieutenant Powell's 9 Platoon, which were to carry out the assault of the breach, wrote that 'We crawled through a field of barley and waited till the Engineers lifted some mines and taped a track through. Another party [the breaching platoon] got rid of the wire with Bangalore torpedoes. Then we went in.' Another member of 9 Platoon, Private Rowland, wrote:

> Eventually, word was passed back that we were to dash, one at a time, through the gap and into a small crater just inside the wire, and from there get into a trench. I relayed this message to the chap lying behind me and told him to pass it on – the rest of A Company being in among the corn. I then carried out the order and managed to get into the trench unharmed and joined the small party gathered there.

The soldiers' accounts all focus on machine-gun fire from the two heavy steel cupolas, but in this case, these were both the observation post version. The machine guns in the H 608 bunker were mounted in adjacent *Tobruckstände* built into the concrete structure; an easy mistake to make for 'soldiers under fire and on their belt buckles'. Other fixed machine-gun positions were firing from the flanks, at least one in depth, and light-role *Spandaus* and riflemen would also have been able to engage the area of the breach.

Section commander Corporal Rayson was waiting to follow the leading section:

> Suddenly, along came the Company Commander. 'Come on, Rayson,' he said. I got up only to be knocked down by someone running behind him. I followed him, only to be fired at as I got through the gap. I got down and then up again and ran through a hole in the bank where the others had gone. I found myself in a deep trench. I couldn't see over the top, but following the trench to the left, then to the right, and so on, I eventually caught up with the others – although there weren't many of us left.

Several men of 9 Platoon and Company HQ were killed in the dash through the breach to the shallow shell hole and trench. Private Rowland was pinned down in a crater by machine-gun fire:

> We all got down and he kept us down. Bullets whizzed above our heads. One hit the pickaxe on my back, one went through my gas cape rolled up on my belt ... this proves my behind was higher than my head. The Bren gunner, lying behind me, had one hit his shovel, the bits going into his backside. After a while, things went quiet.

(**Above**) The commanding view down to the beach from the surviving OP cupola, a part of *Oberst* Krug's headquarters bunker in HILLMAN. (**Below**) The *Tobruckstand* machine-gun position just yards from the heavy steel observation cupola.

Captain Lummis wrote:

> Lieut Powell then came forward with a PIAT team (the infantry rifle platoon's anti-tank weapon). Three shots were fired at a cupola which was causing most of the trouble. They had no effect. The platoon had advanced into the trenches in the position, but this did little good as the enemy merely withdrew into their concrete shelters and opened up with machine guns at any attempt to move against them. A message was sent back to say the platoon was held up, but the runner was killed on the way back and a second runner had to be sent.

Corporal Rayson in the German trenches recalled that 'As we were wondering what to do next, a runner came round the corner and told us to get out as quickly as we could. We didn't need encouraging.' They passed the body of Captain Ryley, who had followed the assault platoon and had been killed while going back to fetch reinforcements. Other wounded from the area of the breach were dragged back through the corn to the cover of the sunken track, from where stretcher-bearers took them back to the RAP in Colleville. Lieutenant Powell received the MC for leadership and courage, but A Company's assault on HILLMAN had failed. As an objective it was far stronger than expected and would remain dominating thousands of yards of country in the centre of the advance on Caen with machine guns as well as observed artillery fire. HILLMAN was not taken, and across the 3rd Division delays and difficulties were multiplying and time was slipping away. The momentum necessary to capture Caen was not being generated.

It was probably during this first attack by the Suffolks that *Leutnant* Schaaf was ordered to intervene with his battery of three SP 155mm guns acting as assault guns. They had just returned to their position near Plumetot from a failed counter-attack in the Lion-sur-Mer/Hermanville area, when Major Hof, Schaaf's battalion commander, rang the battery command post and ordered him to again leave his gun position and head east, as the battalion command post at HILLMAN was under attack. Captain Lummis recalled:

> The Divisional Commander (Major General Rennie) came up at this time to the CO's OP and asked how the battalion was getting on. When he was told the situation, he said, 'Well, you must get it ('Hillman') before dark and in time to allow you to dig in before dark as the enemy armour is about and they will probably counter attack about first light.' The CO assured him that 1 Suffolk would succeed. He left with a cheery 'Good luck'. General Rennie was wounded a few days later and then killed at the Rhine crossing in the following year.

It has been suggested that the statement by General Rennie allowed Colonel Goodwin to take no less than four hours to plan and widen the breach in the minefield for the second attack. However, as will be explained, at 1500 hours 185 Brigade's battalions were advancing past HILLMAN; to the west the KSLI

Lieutenant Colonel Dick Goodwin, the commanding officer of the Suffolks.

were already on the Périers Ridge; and to the east, the Norfolks were heading for the 2,000-yard gap of open fields between the two, between HILLMAN and St Aubin.

1 Norfolks

While Colleville was being cleared, the Intermediate Brigade had landed on QUEEN Beach at 0950 hours and 1 R Norfolk had assembled by 1100 hours; but ahead of them, with HILLMAN yet to be taken, their part in 185 Brigade's dash to Caen was stalled. The battalion's objective was the Bellevue farm complex on a ridge 3½ miles inland nicknamed ROVER. Their designated route would take them through Colleville, where it was planned they would conduct a passage of lines through the Suffolks at HILLMAN. To facilitate this, the Norfolks had moved forward into Colleville, where after a long wait, at 1500 hours, Brigadier Smith ordered them to bypass HILLMAN to the east. They were instructed that 'on no account were they to become involved in either HILLMAN or St Aubin.'

Being in a different brigade from the Suffolks, and with the inadequate radio communication of the day, particularly when on the move, the Norfolks could not easily be informed that the Suffolks had yet to take HILLMAN and that they should thus avoid the area. Consequently, A and B companies went out into the open cornfields east of the German position, where they were in full view of the enemy and came under fire from a pair of machine guns. Private Evans recalled:

> Once off the beach we advanced slowly along narrow dusty roads with Jerry snipers banging away at us. So far we had covered 2 or 3 miles and were

> doing well until we came up to a cornfield. Then Jerry machine guns in a small pill box [*Tobruckstand* in HILLMAN] opened up. The lads were soon being cut to pieces as the machine guns, with their tremendous rate of fire, scythed through the 3-foot high golden corn. I remember one of the company cooks behind me getting a bullet in the neck. That was the day I first saw the red poppies of France as I dived to the ground.

Lance Corporal Seaman MM commanded a section of stretcher-bearers:

> I was detailed to go with 8 Platoon across cornfields where the Brigadier put us in front of our own tanks and we really got slaughtered. We had so many killed and wounded that I was the only stretcher bearer left . . . I had one rifleman to help me bandage and carry them down to an old track across the field where RAMC ambulances picked them up.

The Military Medal.

Private Duncan of B Company added that under mortar fire it was a long crawl back out of trouble:

> Going through the corn on one's belly with all the gear we were carrying was a punishing experience, the sweat poured down my face and I thought to myself, what the hell am I doing here, why hadn't I joined the Royal Artillery like my brother.

At some point, the FOO from 76 Field Regiment that was supporting the Norfolks, or the Staffordshire Yeomanry's liaison officer (sources differ), went forward in a Sherman thinking he could deal with the German machine gun holding up the battalion. This expedition did not last long as there was a loud explosion and the tank commander came back on foot to report that his Sherman had gone up on a mine. The tank was 'a complete write-off, one track being blown off and the vehicle burnt out. The LO came back to say he had a slight headache.'

The majority of the Norfolks' 150 D Day casualties were suffered during this action.[14] Their war diary also adds that they had 'several casualties in [the] 2 Coys from our own tks which thought they were enemy getting out of HILLMAN and fired on them'. The leading companies were pinned down for some time before being extricated. The Norfolks' advance had been halted and a further delay incurred while a longer route south to ROVER was taken.

The Second Attack on HILLMAN

It was clear to Lieutenant Colonel Goodwin that he needed close support of tanks on the objective if his infantrymen were to subdue the enemy defences. The Shermans' firepower would help greatly, and their armoured bulk would act as mobile cover to enable the Suffolks to get within assaulting distance of individual German positions within HILLMAN. This, of course, would require the minefield breach to be widened significantly, ideally to 15ft, to enable the tanks to lead the infantry into the enemy position.

While Colonel Goodwin was requesting mine-clearing assets to be sent forward to his aid, the tanks of C Squadron 13/18 H remained active. No. 4 Troop was sent left to cover the flank out towards St Aubin d'Arquenay, which had earlier been transited by 1 SS Brigade on their way to Objective RUGGER. With 2 East Yorks still involved with SOLE and DAIMLER, the Germans had taken the opportunity to temporarily reoccupy the village.[15] Two of the Shermans were hit before being called back. The troop commander wrote:

> Soon after this bad spell, I returned to the north-eastern point of 'HILLMAN' and here we immediately got our own back shooting up a machine gun post which had exposed itself, and an anti-tank gun near which we apparently set fire to some petrol cans and oil drums. The anti-tank gun had been caught while one of its crew was at the front of the muzzle turning the gun round; somehow or other after being shot up his body found itself suspended over the gun barrel – a grotesque sight!

An air photograph of WN-17 HILLMAN.

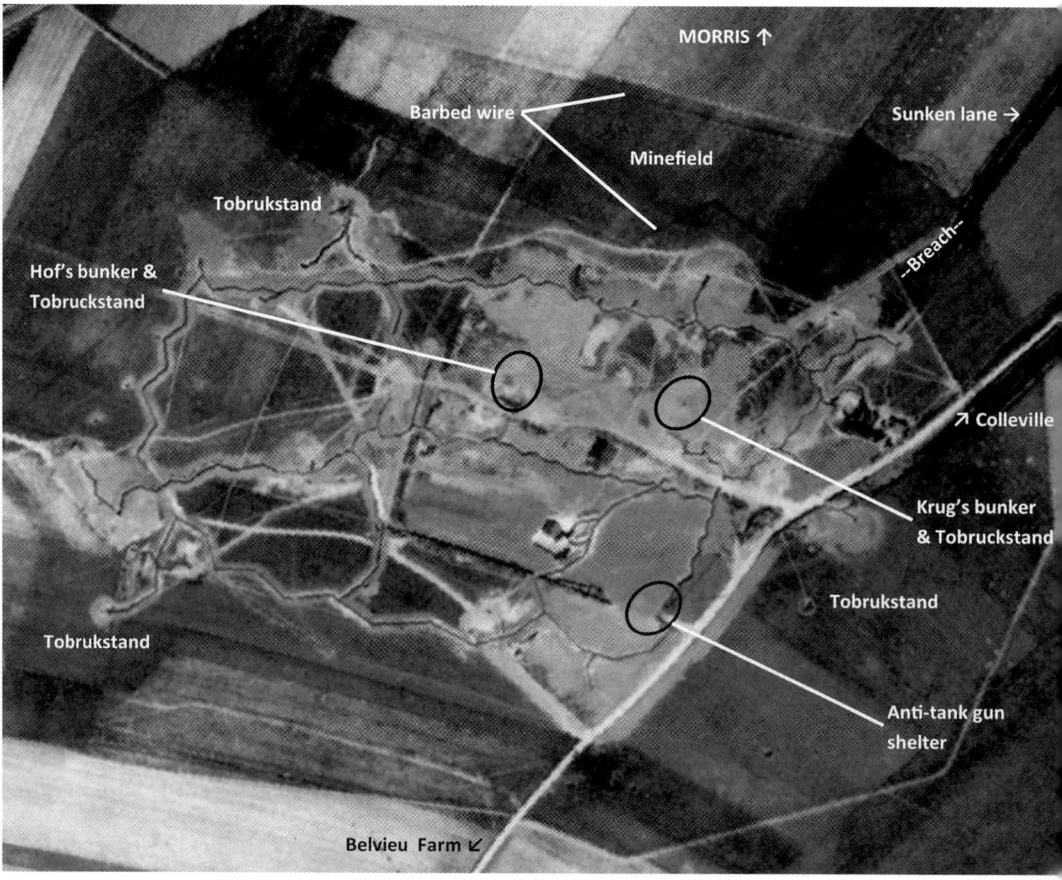

Captain Lummis wrote that the commanding officer turned to his attached 246 Field Company RE and

> sent for the RE officer Lieut Arthur Heal and told him the gap had to be widened to 9 feet [*sic*]. Heal told the CO that the quickest way was to use flails ... He went off to reconnoitre. He and LCpl Boulton and a sapper from his detachment crawled flat on their bellies to find out more about the minefield. It was thought possible it might have been a dummy one. However, Arthur Heal found a mine and started carefully examining it. He had made himself familiar with all types of German mines likely to be found but here was one that he could not identify. With some trepidation he pulled it out and examined it more closely: he was relieved to find it was an obsolete British Mk III mine captured at Dunkirk. He found the mines were in 4 rows at about 5 yards intervals. He returned to the CO to report his findings.

Having been told that flail tanks were not available, Colonel Goodwin had to resort to tasking Lieutenant Heal to widen the breach by hand.

> He was asked how long it would take to make a proper gap. Heal said about an hour but suggested he could do a quicker job using gelignite charges to blow a row of mines providing a gap of 5 yards. The tank commander was agreeable to this so he set off once again with his Lance Corporal working flat on the ground under fire to clear sufficient mines for a tank gap. Covering fire was provided by Mike Russell's platoon and one of the tanks.

Lieutenant Heal earned the Croix de Guerre with silver star. His citation reads:

> During the attack on COLLEVELLE-SUR-ORNE on 6 June 44, it was necessary to clear a forty-yard lane in the perimeter minefield to enable tanks to enter the locality. The gap was under enemy small arms and mortar fire. This officer commanded the assault engineer platoon supporting the attacking Battalion: he organised and personally carried out the clearing of the gap under very heavy mortar and MG fire, from short range.
>
> During the whole of this period the work had to be carried out lying flat on the ground. It was entirely due to his work that the tanks were able to enter the locality and destroy the enemy. Throughout the operation he set a splendid example to all ranks, his exceptional courage and determination in this action being a major factor in its ultimate success.

During the late afternoon, A Squadron of the Staffordshire Yeomanry were re-deployed to add their weight to the second attack, but they had not even been briefed when orders came at 1615 for them to return to the right flank, where the first signs of 21st Panzer Division's counter-attacks were developing.

At 1900 hours, with the minefield breach widened, the plan was for a repeat bombardment of five minutes at Rate 4 by two batteries of artillery, followed by C Squadron's Shermans leading the way through the gap, but 'The leading tank ... baulked at driving over the dead body still obstructing the path ahead.' The tank commander was told in no uncertain manner to drive on, and the infantry following the tanks spread out into the enemy position, dashing from shell hole to shell hole The tanks engaged the cupolas from which it was assumed that the machine gun fire came from, but the infantry had spotted the real culprit – the *Tobruckstand* adjacent to one of the cupolas which covered the area of the breach. Captain Lummis recalled:

> Corporal Lawson and Private 'Tich' Hunter of 8 Platoon found themselves within 20 yards of the cupola. Suddenly one lone German came running towards them, hands raised in surrender. A shot rang out and he was killed. The tension had been too much for one soldier. Soon afterwards Hunter suddenly stood up from his shelter in a bomb hole and slowly and determinedly walked towards the cupola, firing his Bren gun from the hip. This had the desired effect as no further resistance came from this direction and the mopping up began. Hunter was deservedly awarded the DCM for his bravery …
>
> The network of trenches was found to be deserted except for one dead German. Hunter jumped down and was looking at the body when Cpl Lawson glancing to the right saw a lone German rifle raised. Lawson shouted a warning and the bullet just grazed Hunter's forehead. The German disappeared round the corner of the trench which led into one of the heavily concreted emplacements.

A *Tobruckstand* with its dual-purpose ground and anti-aircraft mount. Note the low profile the machine-gunner would have had.

Private 'Tich' Hunter received the Distinguished Conduct Medal for his action at HILLMAN.

The regimental historian of the 13/18 H recorded:

> It was, consequently, late in the afternoon [*sic*] before tanks and infantry succeeded in breaking through the enemy resistance, when tank commanders had a great time winkling Germans out of their trenches by throwing grenades from their turrets, whilst other tanks moved round to the far side at full speed to cut off the retreating enemy.

What the regimental historian does not mention is that the squadron leader's tank ended up in HILLMAN's latrine cesspit with a broken track and needed heavy recovery to extricate it.

Captain Lummis commented that in their enthusiasm the tanks went too far ahead and had to be called back to provide protection for the infantry. The combined effort of tanks and infantry had finally subdued HILLMAN, but most of the garrison had withdrawn to the concrete bunkers. Sappers were called on to use their shaped beehive charges to blow in some of the bunkers, but the smaller versions they had were ineffectual as the concrete was so thick. Corporal Rayson described how other Germans were persuaded to come out and surrender:

> We couldn't get down into the position owing to some steel doors which we couldn't open, but to wake them up we put several grenades down the ventilation shafts, plus a few smoke ones. After this we dug in around the place. Things got quieter, so we opened the 48-hr [compo] ration packs and brewed up some tea in our tin mugs. The tea [tableted], sugar and milk, looked like an Oxo cube, but at least it tasted like tea, although even Naafi tea was better.

In an hour firing had stopped, and at 2010 hours HILLMAN was eventually reported as being secure, but there were still a significant number of enemy troops underground, not least in the large headquarter bunker where *Oberst* Krug, his staff and a number of infantry had taken shelter.

During the short hours of summer darkness 1 Suffolks had consolidated on the Périers Ridge.

> The enemy posn now being under control 'B' and 'D' Coys (the latter having collected its breaching platoon) moved fwd S.W. and S.E. of the village [of Colleville] respectively to take up def. posn for the night. 'B' Coy moved up without further interference and were established by 2215 hrs. 'D' Coy on moving up were confronted by a farmhouse locality about 300 yds ahead of their consolidation area.

Of the final incident of the day Captain Lumis recorded:

> Just after troops had left 'Hillman' the enemy opened up with artillery and mortars but the shells fell beyond Battalion HQ except for one mortar bomb which hit the office truck, setting it on fire and causing three casualties.
>
> In the D Company consolidation area was the farm called Beauvais. As they approached it two snipers were met in the corn and were dealt with. The CSM (CSM Franklin) said he could see movement through a window of the farm about 250 yards away. He fired a round and saw someone fall down. 17 Platoon under Lieut Johnny Vaughan ... was given the task of clearing the buildings.
>
> They approached by a line of trees but then had about a hundred yards of open space to dash across. No sign of life was to be seen; the Bren guns were positioned to cover the farm from the right flank and the platoon prepared to dash across. With a burst from the Brens, the platoon was off, but they immediately saw, on the left, troops climbing out of slit trenches with their hands in the air, shouting '*Kamerad*!' All surrendered, two officers and forty-eight men in total. They left behind four machine guns and their rifles together with a great many stick grenades. Their packs and parcels were all laid out in threes – ready for surrender – when the farm was reached. The Company Commander (Major Papillon) decided to stand back about 250 yards from the position to dig in. This was a wise decision as the enemy position was mortared off and on for about an hour with no casualties to D Company.

Surrender

During the night, *Oberst* Krug rang headquarters 716th Division from this bunker on HILLMAN, as recalled by *Standartenführer* Kurt 'Panzer' Meyer:

> At 2400 hours I was standing before the commander of 716.*Infanterie-Division*, *Generallettnant* Richter ... [who] briefed the situation to me. The silence was broken by a ringing telephone. One of the regimental

Oberst Krug conducting an inspection prior to the invasion.

> commanders, *Oberst* Krug, reported from his bunker asking for orders. He stated: 'The enemy is standing on the top of the bunker. I have no means of engaging him, nor any contact with my units. What should I do?' An icy silence settled in the bunker. Everybody looked at the divisional commander. The tone of the man's speech was shocking: 'I cannot give you any further orders; do what you have to do. Goodbye!'[16]

It was not until the following morning that HILLMAN's garrison finally surrendered. At 0645 hours the Germans started to emerge from the bunker, followed by the smartly dressed *Oberst* Krug in polished boots carrying a briefcase with his batman carrying two suitcases. He was quickly relieved of the briefcase containing maps and documents, and with, as recorded by 185 Brigade, 'much saluting and heel clicking', Krug took leave of his staff and was taken to 8 Brigade's headquarters for questioning.

* * *

After the war, members of the Suffolk Regiment were at pains to explain the strength of HILLMAN and the challenge that they faced in taking it. The fact remains, however, that WN-17 in its dominating location on the Périers Ridge, in the very centre of the 3rd Division's drive on Caen, did disrupt and delay the advance of 185 Brigade. A brief glance at the expanse of open ground to the east and west of HILLMAN confirms this point. In planning it would seem that the staff of neither 3rd Division nor 8 or 185 brigades appreciated the strength or dominating position of HILLMAN or doubted that its capture was within the capacity of an infantry battalion. Without being allocated flail tanks, which were to support 185 Brigade, and under time pressure, Colonel Goodwin resorted to a hand breach by his engineer detachment for an infantry assault. For a timely capture of the objective, it can be argued that the Suffolks required flails to permit the deployment of AVREs and C Squadron's Shermans in close support of A Company's assault. Shermans on the enemy position, of course, proved to be the key to the final capture of HILLMAN.

Other factors that made the capture of HILLMAN far more difficult for the Suffolks included the poor results of the pre-H Hour bombing by the air forces; this being the result of the risk to 'go' in marginal weather condition. The loss of the naval FOB party that would have enabled the position to be heavily pounded, undermining enemy morale prior to the assault, was a substantial addition to the difficulty.

An allocation of assault armour from 79th Armoured Division to HILLMAN would have made all the difference to the Suffolks' attack.

Chapter Seven

The Intermediate Brigade and the Drive on Caen

With the assault battalions of 8 Brigade clear of the beach, the LCIs bearing the Intermediate Brigade, Brigadier Smith's 185 Brigade, could start to land. They threaded their way to the beach through the now nearly submerged obstacles, drowned vehicles and wrecked landing craft. The first battalion of the Brigade to touch down on QUEEN Beach at 0950 hours was 1 R Norfolk. Like others, Private Plant contrasted the organization of the FABIUS beaches with the chaos of the real landing just weeks later:

> We knew all about bad weather from our Scottish winter but the recent schemes had been in good conditions and we thought that our landings behind the first lot would be on an ordered beach. Not a bit of it for the real thing. Nowhere were the signs and marked exits to be seen. Instead, there were bodies, burning vehicles and exploding mortars. Absolute b***** chaos. Weighed down with all kinds of clobber, all I could do was get across the beach as quickly as possible. I passed wounded and men taking shelter in whatever cover they could find. I didn't fancy stopping one little bit. I flopped down gasping and when I looked up from the sand there were these boots belonging to a severe looking naval officer with a tin hat of many colours.[1]

The Gunners

Having completed the run-in shoot and turned back out to sea to recharge the ammunition racks from the piles of shells around the guns, the first five Priests of Major Pirie's battery of 76 Field Regiment were ashore at 0840 hours. Under fire themselves, they were almost immediately in action on the beach, while their recce parties went forward to proposed gun positions. The battery war diaries noted at 0920 hours that 'By this time the beach was crammed full of all types of vehicles and armour. During its action on the beach, the guns of the Battery fired an average of 50 rounds each.' The gunner plan was for 76 Field Regiment to remain firing from the beach while 33 Field, landing at 0945 hours, leapfrogged through to inland gun positions, followed by 7 Field at 1045 hours. Landing of each wave prioritized the infantry, tanks and guns, but once ashore getting off the beach was another matter.

SWORD Beach under fire. The men on the right wearing Mk II helmets with bands painted on them are from the Beach Group.

With the tracked vehicle exits finally having been opened, 33 Field, after twenty minutes stuck in congestion on the beach, was able to make its way off the fast-reducing stretch of sand to join the battle inland as the tide rose.

> DF [Defensive Fire] on the beach had now increased both with shells and with an occasional incendiary mortar bomb, and owing to the landing being not quite in the expected place some difficulty was found in getting off the beach.
>
> 109 Field Battery were the first to reach the main axis and come into action in a cornfield about 500 yards from the beach at about 1000 hours. 101 Field Battery followed and went further forward on the left of the axis and came into action near RHQ. It had been planned for 113/114 Field Battery to be prepared to come into action on the beach, but as the area occupied by 109 Battery was large enough for two batteries and shelling of the beach had increased, they were brought in alongside 109 at about 1050 hours.[2]

When 7 Field Regiment got off the beach just before midday and motored out to the right flank, the only battery positions they could find were in front of the South Lancs and overlooked by the Périers Ridge. One officer commented that 'We seemed to be leading the whole Second Army for a while.'

A 105mm Priest of 33 Field Regiment 300 yards inland from SWORD, in the relatively close country north-east of Hermanville.

The Beach Group Lands

By late morning the beach group on QUEEN was beginning to take its first faltering steps to establish order out of the confused situation. However, gaining control was further disrupted by the death of key commanders, including the senior naval beachmaster. Into this situation landed Major General Rennie and his tactical headquarters, who were ashore at 1030 hours, with the corps commander being seen shortly afterwards.

With the arrival of the No. 5 Beach Group or 'beach brick' starting at 0810 hours (H+45),[3] the task of establishing order on the beach and dumping 'beach packs' began. These packs contained supplies which the logistic planners estimated would be required to sustain the force ashore until the Beach Maintenance Area (BMA) opened on D+2 or +3. In addition, vehicles landed with at least 50 miles of fuel each, and every man had two or three days' rations, which meant that the main content of the packs was ammunition. With the Luftwaffe launching far fewer sorties than expected, and with little to shoot at by day, there was a surplus of anti-aircraft ammunition, which in turn encouraged the gunners' night-time firework displays of tracer that became so characteristic of the beachhead.

One of the tasks of the beach battalion, 5 King's, was to clear the area of casualties and other stranded personnel. Corporal Warren recalled an encounter with one of the King's warrant officers. He and his two Royal Marine crew struck a beach obstacle that ripped a hole in the wooden hull of their LCA and his load of thirty Suffolks had scrambled overboard into chest-deep water. After attempting unsuccessfully to salvage their craft, Warren recounted that 'The crew and I waded ashore, dashed across the beach, and dug ourselves shell scrapes in the dunes.' He recalled being 'stuck there' for hours 'with shells and bullets whizzing past, when out of the smoke marched an upright Sergeant Major, pace-stick under his arm, who exclaimed: "What the hell are you boys doing on my beach?" Gesturing to a beached LCA, he ordered: "Get your arses on that LCA over there and get off my f***ing beach – now!"'

QUEEN RED. The dead would be collected later. The first priority was to treat the wounded in the cover of disabled AFVs.

The German Reaction

Ten hours after the drop of the three airborne divisions, and two and a half hours since the first amphibious landing, OKW and Hitler in Berchtesgaden were still far from being convinced that the landings in Normandy were the Allied main effort. In anticipation of a landing further east on the Channel coast, encouraged by reports of bombardment of the Baie de Seine as far east as Le Havre, it took time for reality to sink in. It was only when the Fifteenth Army reported there was no amphibious assault in their area did it start to become obvious that the *Hitler-jugend* Panzer Division was concentrating for the wrong deployment option. As late as 1432 hours the division was finally released by OKW to Seventh Army, but by then it was obvious that the panzers would not arrive in time to take part in Rommel's planned D Day counter-strike.

At the divisional level, with the British armour from GOLD Beach KING Sector moving rapidly inland and the problems of congestion on SWORD slowing the deployment of tanks towards Caen, at 0905 hours General Richter ordered the redeployment of the guns of *Panzerjäger* Battalion 200 to the west. This move, though logical at the time, took all but three of the twenty-four 88mm guns away from positions north and north-west of Caen which had been very well positioned to block an advance on the city. It left only a handful of the 716th Division's thinly spread anti-tank guns in depth to confront the 3rd Division and accounts for 155mm SP guns being used as assault guns. If the *Panzerjägers*' 88s had been in left position it is likely that the division's advance would have stalled before the Périers Ridge (see General Fuchtinger's account, Appendix VII, p. 233).

Generalmajor Richter, commander of the 716th Coastal Infantry Division and the division's sign.

Delivering counter-attacks, both immediate and deliberate, lay at the heart of German tactical doctrine, but few were recorded as taking place on D Day, or simply not noticed as such by the assault troops. One of the latter category appears to have been launched against A Company 1 South Lancs and 41 Commando in the Lion-sur-Mer area. Evidence is provided by *Leutnant* Schaaf, who commanded a battery of I/1716th Artillery Regiment. This was the 716th Division's three 155mm self-propelled guns, which had been firing on SWORD Beach since H Hour from a gun position 4,000 yards inland near Plumetot. Communications with the battery's FOO in a *Wiederstandnest*, probably SOLE (WN-21), had been lost early in the battle when the coastal positions were engaged by naval gunfire, leaving the guns firing on pre-registered DFs on the beach.

With the British advancing from the beach, where they were, in Rommel's plan, to have been destroyed, a counter-attack was ordered, probably by *Oberst* Krug, who from his headquarters at HILLMAN could see most of the country

15cm *Geschützwagen* Lorraine Schlepper (f)

The presence of *Leutnant* Schaaf's SP battery of 150mm guns in the 716th Divisions ORBAT is a bit of a mystery, but evidence points to it being one of many unofficial sub-units, which in this case made up an eleventh battery in Artillery Regiment 1716. Early in 1944, strength returns show the 3rd Battery holding three 15cm *Geschützwagen* Lorraine Schlepper (f), but they were replaced by towed 155mm guns of French origin in March 1944. It would seem that the 150mm SP guns were not transferred to 21st Panzer's Artillery Regiment 155 but were retained as the Graff Waldense Battery, which is referred to in several accounts as being in action as an eleventh battery on D Day from the area of Plumetot.

The Lorraine Schlepper was introduced into the French Army as a light personnel and ammunition carrier in 1938. Some were taken into German service as ammunition carriers in 1941, and the first conversions to SP gun carriages were made in 1942 after a demonstration of captured equipment for Hitler. Alkett in Hanover made the first 160 conversions, of which forty mounted 150mm howitzers, sixty the 105mm gun and another sixty the 75mm Pak 40.

This initial batch was followed in 1943 by wholesale conversion of the Lorraine Schlepper and other captured or obsolescent vehicles by Alfred Becker's engineering firm in Krefeld. *Baustab* Becker later also worked in various engineering plants in France. The vehicles produced here included a further forty-two 150mm howitzer conversions, bringing the total of that calibre to 102. By the time of the invasion some 180 Lorraine Schleppers had also been converted to mount the 75mm Pak 40.

The open-top steel structure that accommodated the 150mm howitzer was high; as an artillery piece it should not have been deployed in the direct fire zone of the battlefield, but it did provide protection for the crew from small arms fire and shell splinters. Due to the relatively light weight of the carriage and the size of the gun, a spade ground anchor was used to prevent the vehicle sliding back as a part of the recoil when firing.

The full title of Schaaf's guns was: 15cm sFH 13/1 (Sf) auf Geschützwagen Lorraine Schlepper (f) Sd.Kfz.135/1.

The guns could only carry nine rounds. Consequently, it was normal German practice for SP guns to be accompanied by converted Lorraine Schleppers used as ammunition carriers. The advantage was that the guns could be swapped and mounted in them in the case of mechanical failure.

down to the beaches. Schaaf was instructed to deploy his guns in support of the *Osttruppen* under command of III/736th Regiment who were to launch a counter-attack north towards Lion-sur-Mer.

The German infantry were seen moving forward and were attacked by Allied aircraft and engaged by naval gunfire. Nonetheless, they pressed on towards Lion, the SP guns being used as assault guns, sending shells into farms and the outskirts of the village with direct fire. Schaaf states that he took British infantry prisoner, as without their support weapons, which were still on the beach, they were unable to take on his guns and surrendered. As the volume of Allied fire increased, the German infantry were beaten back, with Schaaf's verdict on the enterprise being, 'Pathetic'. Once back at their gun position in Plumetot,

> they examined their prisoners, and were awed by their superb maps, food and equipment. Schaaf ordered them to be herded into a shell hole. In great agitation, a German-speaking British officer produced a copy of the Geneva Convention which he waved at the artilleryman, declaring forcibly that it was illegal to shoot them. 'Nobody is going to be shot,' said Schaaf brusquely.[4]

As far as other counter-attacks are concerned, 11 and 12 companies of III/736th Regiment are recorded as having been deployed to round up mis-dropped Canadian paratroopers further west, but were seen on the open hillside and hit by naval gunfire. Later, the same companies are said to have launched counter-attacks in the direction of JUNO Beach.

The Intermediate Brigade – 185 Infantry Brigade

At 1000 the first LCIs bearing 185 Brigade touched down. However, several of the LCIs carrying the 2nd Warwickshire Regiment and the 2nd King's Shropshire Light Infantry (2 KSLI) suffered hits from mortars and shells on the way in, and all three of the brigade's battalions suffered casualties amidst the confusion on the beach. The infantry companies were, however, able to get off the beach and through the dunes and villas quite quickly, but not so the vehicles. The rifle companies reached their assembly areas between 1040 and 1100 hours.

The concept of operations of the Intermediate Brigade was given in the divisional operation order:

(a) 185 Infantry Brigade Group with Staffs Yeo in support will land at approximately H+2½ hour and will capture CAEN and a bridgehead SOUTH of the R ORNE at CAEN.
(b) This advance will be carried out with speed and boldness so that the enemy's local reserves can be overcome quickly and the brigade established on its objective ready to meet counter attacks by reserve formations which may develop towards the evening of D Day.
(c) Armour will be used boldly in this advance but when defences are encountered which cannot be overcome by the advance guard a coordinated attack supported by all available artillery will achieve the best results. It is important in an advance of this nature that the commander should retain a reserve battalion in hand and keep control of his armour so that any weakening of the enemy can be immediately exploited.

The Brigade had known since early March that this would be their D Day mission, but after intelligence on the German reinforcement of Lower Normandy had trickled down to them, most commanders subsequently claimed to have thought the capture of Caen to be unlikely on D Day, but entirely possibly soon afterwards. The brigade's tasks in detail were:

<u>Phase I.</u> Assembly at BEER (wood between QUEEN beaches and Hermanville-sur-Mer).
<u>Phase II.</u> Advance to ALE (report line it. Contest, 0072 – Beauregard, 0772).
<u>Phase III.</u> Capture of ALE, WINE and STOUT (high ground immediately 0370, 0470).
<u>Phase IV.</u> Capture of Caen.
<u>Phase V.</u> Consolidation of Caen, both sides of R. Orne CIDER.
<u>Phase VI.</u> Establishment of covering position south and south-east of Caen between the R. Laise and the R. Muance.

The brigade was organized with a Mobile Column and a Main Body. The former consisted principally of 2 KSLI and the Staffs Yeo, and the latter, the brigade's

Trace A from 3rd Division's Op O No. 1 showing objectives and report lines for the advance on Caen.

A Landing Craft Infantry, one of many that beached during the landing. The infantry would have disembarked by the twin gangways forrard.

other two infantry battalions, 2 Warwicks right and 1 Norfolks left. The advance would 'probably' begin at 1125 hours on the orders of the Brigade Commander. Both of these battalions were to send a bicycle company forward, in the case of the Warwicks to take over ground behind 2 KSLI in the area of Le Landel, while 1 Norfolks were aiming for Objective ROVER and the high ground above Bieville, on report line Gin.

When the time came for 185 Brigade to assemble during the mid-morning of D Day and begin its advance on Caen, the sundry delays that had begun with the arrival of the H+45 wave of landing craft were beginning to bite. Cumulatively, they would have a significant impact on the 3rd Division's planned advance on Caen. On the beach, the combination of a soft strip of sand/clay, the sea state and a higher and more quickly rising tide than expected had prevented removal of most of the beach obstacles. This was also an obvious problem for the landing craft, both on the way to the beach and when going astern having dropped off their assault troops. While the German defences on the beach had certainly not stopped the landing, they had slowed it and caused congestion by disrupting the carefully sequenced breaching operation. With the tide rising, there would shortly be only 10 yards of sand at high water rather than the anticipated 30 yards, as well as stronger than expected enemy resistance. This resulted in continuing delays as increasing numbers of tanks and other vehicles queued to get off the beach.

Inland, the slight delay in 1 Suffolks assembling had been followed by finding the defences of objective HILLMAN to be far stronger than had been deduced from intelligence. With machine guns protected by concrete that, as far as dismounted infantry was concerned, dominated the centre of the 3rd Division's advance on Caen, a substantial disruption to the expected rate of progress was inevitable.

More generally, the artillery batteries of 21st Panzer Division deployed by Rommel, along with fire from coastal guns to the east, which the Royal Navy could only partly neutralize, inflicted additional delays on the beach and to progress inland. These cumulative factors resulted in the delays reported in the summary of operations in the Brigade's war diary:

> Headquarters 185 Brigade was established at 1105 hours near the church in Hermanville. At that time, the situation as it appeared to Comd 185 Infantry Brigade was that the infantry of the brigade less their support weapons was in their assembly areas; STAFFS YEO being held up by congestion of the beach exits; 1 S LAN R (8 Bde) at the x rds SOUTH of HERMANVILLE; COLLEVILE-SUR-ORNE not yet clear of enemy; the German strong points HILLMAN and MORRIS reportedly very strongly held but were to be attacked by SUFFOLK.[5]

The classic SWORD Beach photograph showing the Intermediate Brigade landing from their LCIs. Clearly, the beach is under fire, with casualties and men taking cover. The soldiers in the foreground are from the Beach Group.

With the battalions of 185 Brigade waiting in the assembly area for nearly an hour for their missing sub-units, which were still struggling in queues to get off the beach, Brigadier Smith himself abandoned his jeep in favour of an airborne bicycle to catch up. Arriving north of Hermanville:

> The Brigade Commander called 'O' Group at 1200 hrs – 2 KSLI were ordered to commence moving forward on axis HERMANVILLE–BEUVILLE–CAEN: STAFFS YEO to get clear of beaches as soon as possible and catch up and marry up with 2 KSLI vide original plan. 2 WARWICKS were to disengage from enemy in their original assembly area and reassemble in woods EAST of HERMANVILLE church, 1 NORFOLKS were ordered to proceed towards COLLEVILLE-SUR-ORNE ready to pass through 8 Bde directly HILLMAN and or MORRIS were taken.

From the foregoing it is clear that the delays around HILLMAN exacerbated an already deteriorating situation, with the Norfolks only being ordered to advance, bypassing HILLMAN, two and a half hours later. When Brigadier Smith had given his quick confirmatory orders, the situation changed again, as explained in the brigade's war diary:

> At 1215 hrs Commander 185 Inf Bde received information of enemy tanks NORTH of CAEN, of fire from position at PERIERS-SUR-LE-DAN and of heavy fighting on 8 Canadian Bde front, which decided him to put into operation an alternative plan of moving 2 WARWICK to the EAST of the axis behind 1 NORFOLK, taking advantage of [avoiding] the anti-tank obstacle.[6]

Brigadier Smith was clearly concerned that the Warwicks were already tangling with German infantry in their assembly area out towards Cressons even before they began their advance.[7] If committed to their planned route on his western flank, without tanks they would effectively be stalled before they started. Also, with enemy armour reported moving north-west of Caen, Brigadier Smith had little choice but to switch the Warwicks to the left flank. The 3rd Division's report confirms that this information 'caused him [Brigadier Smith] to decide to put into operation his alterative plan of moving 2 Warwick on to the EAST of the axis behind 1 Norfolk, thus taking advantage of avoiding the anti-tank obstacle.'[8] As Major General Rennie was ashore and mobile in the divisional area visiting headquarters, Brigadier Smith 'decided after reference to Div Comd, that 2 Warwick should move up the axis of the canal road.'[9] There is also evidence that Rennie s concern over the German counter attacks on Objective RUGGER contributed to the decision.[10] According to the I Corps report, the 'alternative plan' was one of four options detailed in his orders from division:

> If the enemy should position very strong armoured forces on the high ground west of the brigade axis, it might be necessary to adopt the alternative of directing 2 Warwick, behind 1 Norfolk, east of the axis; the latter

The traffic on the lateral road (D514) behind QUEEN WHITE. The distinctive buildings of La Brèche d'Hermanville can be seen in the background.

> being required to consolidate behind the Mobile Column with FDLs [Forward Defended Localities] on the line Biéville–Beauregard.[11,12]

The Staffs Yeo were to remain supporting the KSLI and covering the right flank.

The Staffordshire Yeomanry

On foot the brigade's infantry were able to leave the beaches with only modest delays, but not so their vehicles and support weapons, especially their tanks, which were essential for the dash to Caen. The armour allocated to 185 Brigade, the Staffordshire Yeomanry (Staffs Yeo), landed almost on time, but according to their war diary that was when trouble began:

> Touched down at 1030 hrs on White Beach and had practically speaking a dry landing. A terrible jam on the beach where no organization appeared to

> be operating and no marked exits were to be seen. The majority of our tanks remained stationary for approx 1 hour. Spasmodic shelling and a considerable amount of sniping. Traffic control seemed non-existent and even after leaving the beach vehicles remained head to tail for long periods on the only available routes.[13]

Two of the problems with SWORD Beach that had been identified during COSSAC planning were the marshes beyond the lateral road (Line PIKE) and the paucity of routes away from the beach. Immediately behind the beach the country was naturally boggy, and with additional German inundations the soft ground extended some hundreds of yards inland. The divisional plan has been consistently criticised for trying to squeeze too many vehicles along too few roads. Consequently, 2 KSLI, who expected the Staffs Yeo at 1115 hours, waited until 1230 hours for the tanks to arrive, and set off on foot as there seemed to be no alternative. The view that 2 KSLI could have reached the bridges in the city 10 miles inland from their assembly area, having conducted an advance to contact

Congestion on the beach, with a rising tide and traffic jams in the exits and on the lateral road.

Shermans of the Staffs Yeo at Hermanville preparing to move forward.

on foot, is delusional. Even with the assistance of the leading squadron of the Staffs Yeo, without substantive support from either the Norfolks (delayed) or the Warwicks (diverted) the capture of Caen proved to be impossible.

The Advance on Caen

Finally, Lieutenant Colonel Maurice was ordered to begin the KSLI's advance without waiting for the Shermans of the still traffic-bound Staffordshire Yeomanry, and all went well to start with. The battalion set out on foot from Hermanville towards Le Homme/Beuville in order of march X, W, Y and Z companies, astride the road leading south to Caen. With them were FOOs from all three of the division's artillery regiments, but little else in terms of support.[14]

At 1300 hours the battalion's war diary noted: 'X Coy came under fairly heavy mortar and artillery fire on the forward slopes of the ridge south of HERMANVILLE (to be known as the PERIERS RIDGE).' Fifteen minutes later: 'X Coy report enemy posts in the fields on top and just beyond PERIERS RIDGE, in particular MG posts holding them up from the right.' The enemy they had encountered was 7 Company of 192 *Panzergrenadiers* dug in on the reverse slope of the Périers Ridge and supported by several anti-tank guns. Corporal Littlar of X Company recalled:

> My company was to be the first one going up the left-hand side of the road, and W Company was to go up the right-hand side [onto the Périers Ridge]. We left a space of at least 5 yards between each man as we moved up the hill, as we had been trained to do. This is to avoid a cluster of men being hit at once. The first bit was all right, but then we got closer and closer to a

A contour layered map showing the ground from Hermanville south, over the Periers Ridge to Bieville.

massive concentration of fire. I was so scared I got down on my hands and knees, and then onto my stomach. It was a baptism of fire; I had never seen anything like it. I think some of the fire was German, but some of it was our ships firing onto the ridge. The concentration of fire on this ridge was incredible, and to this day I have no idea whether it was our boys or the enemy firing. Whoever it was, it wasn't nice.[15]

At 1430 hours, according to 185 Brigade's summary of operations, as the fighting developed on the KSLI's axis, 'No battalions at this time had yet got any [of their] support weapons with them, owing to congestion on the beach.' Without their 3-inch mortars and 6-pounder anti-tank guns the battalion was entirely reliant on external fire support and, as the war diary notes, '33 and 76 FD REGTS were still involved with 8 INF BDE battle.' Consequently, only 7 Field's guns were available. In addition, the carriers with the Vickers medium machine guns and 4.2-inch mortars of 2 Middlesex were similarly held up and only started to arrive at Hermanville at 1300 hours. Initially they appear not to have been sent forward but used defensively, as recorded in the regimental journal: 'During the late afternoon and evening of 6th June, "A" Company established an MG belt along the line HERMANVILLE-SUR-MER to COLLEVILLE-SUR-ORNE [Line MALET]. One platoon of mortars went into action at Battalion Headquarters [in Hermanville] and one platoon about one mile on the left flank [HILLMAN].'[16]

As the KSLI's advance got underway, Leutnant Schaaf, who had just returned with his three SP guns to his battery position at Plumetot, received a call from his battalion commander, Major Hof. He was ordered to again leave his gun position and head east to where his battalion's command post and HILLMAN were under attack. When he deployed onto the Périers Ridge and was moving towards Point 61 he saw the KSLI infantry advancing through the corn and taking cover. But heading his way from Hermanville he also saw the leading tanks of the Staffs Yeo and, deciding that three self-propelled guns engaging a squadron of tanks was beyond the call of duty, beat a hasty retreat. When he found a telephone line to tap into he attempted to contact Major Hof, but an English voice, presumably one of the KSLI, answered the call. It is presumed that this was a telephone exchange in a position below Point 61 that was now in the KSLI's hands.[17]

Meanwhile, on the KSLI's other flank, their war diary records the reaction to enemy encountered in Périers village and the woods to the east at 1315 hours:

C.O. orders W Coy to come up on the right and take on M.G. post. Adjutant reports to C.O. in A.C.V. [armoured command vehicle] having just got forward from the beaches. Advance continues on two coy front, leading coys still meeting enemy parties in the fields on the reverse slopes.

By now B Squadron of the Staffs Yeo, accompanied by flail tanks, had arrived on the ridge along with the naval FOB, and with artillery and naval gunfire support for the KSLI, the Périers Ridge and its reverse slope were cleared. The battalion's adjutant noted: 'W Coy overcomes some opposition in Church Area West of

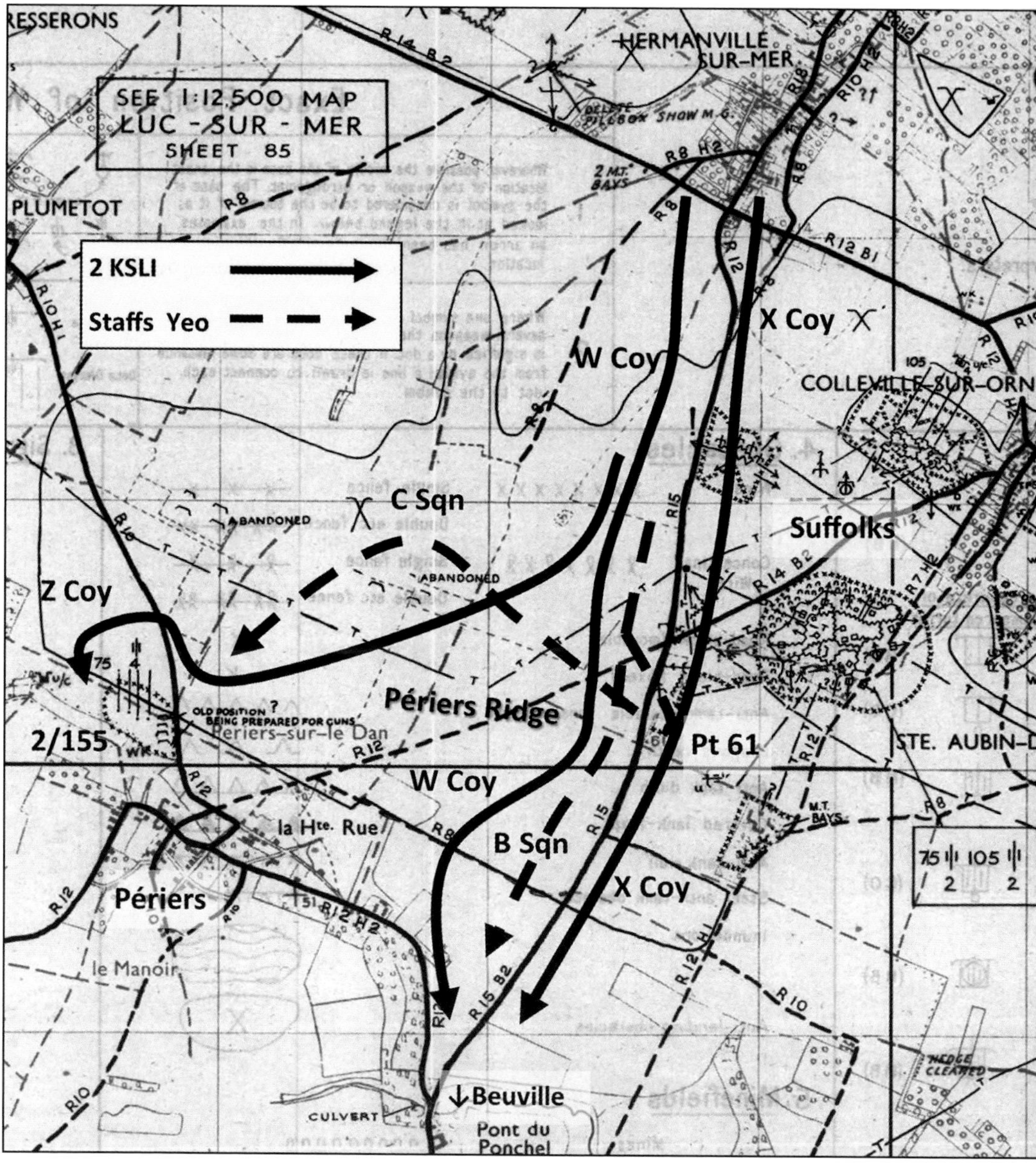

The tactical overprint map showing the defences through which 2 KSLI and the Staffs Yeo passed in the initial phase of the advance on Caen.

PERIERS SUR-LE-DAN, FOO sent forward to X Coy who take LE HOMME.' Corporal Littlar adds: 'We eventually made it over the ridge and onto the southern slope, where the fire eased off a bit' – temporarily!

Captain Ryland described a fine example of leadership under fire that kept the leading companies moving forward across the crest of the Périers Ridge in open country very similar to that the east of HILLMAN:

> It was typical of the complete disregard of enemy fire which Colonel Maurice always showed that when the battalion first came under fire on this

> slope everyone instinctively went to ground. A brother officer has related to me how, looking round and feeling extremely frightened, he saw the Colonel walking up the centre of the road, playing with the chinstrap of his helmet as he always did. He thought, 'Well – if he is all right, I suppose I shall be too,' and got up. The example spread, and in a few minutes the men were moving forward steadily.[18]

Meanwhile, C Squadron had arrived, secured Point 61 on the ridge without opposition and engaged German guns and transport beyond; but shortly after their arrival, accurate shelling forced the tanks into the cover of the northern slope, where they remained supporting the advance. B Squadron, redeployed on the right flank, came under effective fire from an anti-tank gun in area of Périers-sur-le-Dan on the route that 2 Warwicks would have taken, vindicating Brigadier Smith's decision to send them to the left. Three Shermans were knocked out, along with a pair of AVREs, presumably by one of the three 88mm guns left behind during the earlier redeployment of *Panzerjäger* Battalion 200. Facing the remaining tanks of the squadron, the enemy anti-tank gun was knocked out. The AVREs carried fascines that were to have been dropped in the pre-dug anti-tank ditches that bisected the route to the ridge above Caen.

From the same area the enemy's Russian 122mm guns were shelling the main axis and the tanks. Colonel Eadie requested the assistance of infantry to clear the battery, which was located in the orchards, woods and hedges west of Périers. At 1425 hours Brigadier Smith ordered Colonel Maurice to send a company to deal with the gun position, Major Wheelock's Z Company, which had hitherto been in reserve, was duly dispatched with an FOO.

Sherman Crabs were attached to the KSLI/Staffs Yeo battlegroup for the advance on Caen.

The enemy battery, 2 Battery of 1st Battalion 155 Artillery Regiment, consisting of four towed 122mm guns, was dug in in open field positions surrounded by barbed wire, with three machine guns covering the approaches. There is no mention of mines, but as they were likely to have been laid, the tanks were not prepared to lead the infantry onto the battery position.

The enemy battery was reported as being subdued at 1500 hours by a 'Mike' regimental target fired by 7 Field Regiment and by Z Company's small arms fire. The fire was controlled by Colonel Eddie as the FOO's tank was one of those knocked out. Several times when fire was lifted, the German gunners returned to their pits and had to be driven off again. Without engineers or flail tanks, the company was tied down, neutralising the enemy here for five vital hours. Eventually, a *Beutedeutsch* Polish soldier deserted and led Major Wheelock to a path used by the German gunners through the barbed-wire at the rear of the battery position. In the resulting attack, the German gunners ran, pursued through the woods by the KSLI, while back in the battery the guns were disabled by a Sapper NCO. Z Company consolidated in the area at nightfall.

Throughout the attack a platoon of 4.2-inch mortars from 2 Middlesex provided fire. Their war diary recorded that 'During this action Lieutenant Dixon successfully supported an attack by an infantry company on a four-gun battery in the PERIERS-SUR-DAN area which was holding up the advance.'[19]

Crucially, dealing with this battery took a tank squadron and one of the four rifle companies out of the KSLI's already very thinly-resourced drive on Caen. Z Company was only able to rejoin the battalion the following day, having lost nine men killed and twenty-three wounded. B Squadron remained in the area with Z Company neutralising the battery and covering the open right flank.

A 4.2-inch mortar of the 2nd Middlesex in action in Normandy.

By mid-afternoon it was already apparent that there were too few troops available to the 3rd Division, who were up against more Germans deployed in depth that elsewhere on the Second Army front. Also, a comparison of the difficulties faced by the under-resourced Z Company at Périers and A Company of the Suffolks at HILLMAN is obvious.

It is also worth noting that once the Staffs Yeo caught up with the KSLI, and with significant enemy opposition, the concept of a dash to Caen with the infantry mounted on tanks did not materialize. Such an operation supposes negligible resistance, as infantry crowded on tanks make very vulnerable targets. The tanks and infantry were, however, working together to overcome numerous enemy posts. Whether a similar delay would have been inflicted on the Warwicks, had they been deployed on this flank, is debatable, but they were hard up against the divisional boundary and any authorized bypassing west would have run into other enemy positions.

Beuville and Biéville

The road across the Périers Ridge to Caen took the KSLI down into a valley where the hamlet of Le Homme and the villages of Beuville and Biéville formed an almost continuous ribbon for a mile along the valley bottom. As 2 KSLI and C Squadron crossed the high ground and descended into the valley, they came under small arms and machine-gun fire as they approached Beuville. Around 1430 hours they were reported as being 'held up', but with the arrival of the first carriers of the KSLI's Support Company at 1450 hours, the battalion had greater punch. Colonel Maurice ordered W and Y companies to bypass the village to the left and right, respectively, and head down the flanks of the valley for Biéville. Meanwhile, X Company, along with a troop of C Squadron's tanks, was to clear Beuville. The 3-inch guns of 41 Anti-Tank Battery, along with the KSLI's 6-pounder guns and the remainder of B Squadron's Shermans, were deployed on the Périers Ridge and its southerly extensions in positions from which they could observe and provide fire support. Corporal Littlar, with Major Thornycroft's X Company, was still out in front:

> We carried on towards Beuville and decided that we would cross the [Le Dan] stream at a bridge. We could see the village on the other side but as we rounded a corner near the bridge, BAM! A chap from W Company was hit by an incendiary and killed instantly as the bandoliers of ammunition around his waist exploded.
>
> I thought the fire had come from a farm on my left, so I turned around and started shooting at the farmhouse. Took all the windows out. But of course, they fire from ground level. I wasn't to know that – these things you learn on the job. I saw another company commander taking a hit in his shoulder, then tossing a grenade over a wall because he thought the fire had come from there, but in truth none of us had any idea where it had come from.

A contour layered map of the ground from Beuville and Biéville, via the 'Anti-Tank obstacle' to the high ground of Objectives WINE and STOUT in the bottom left corner.

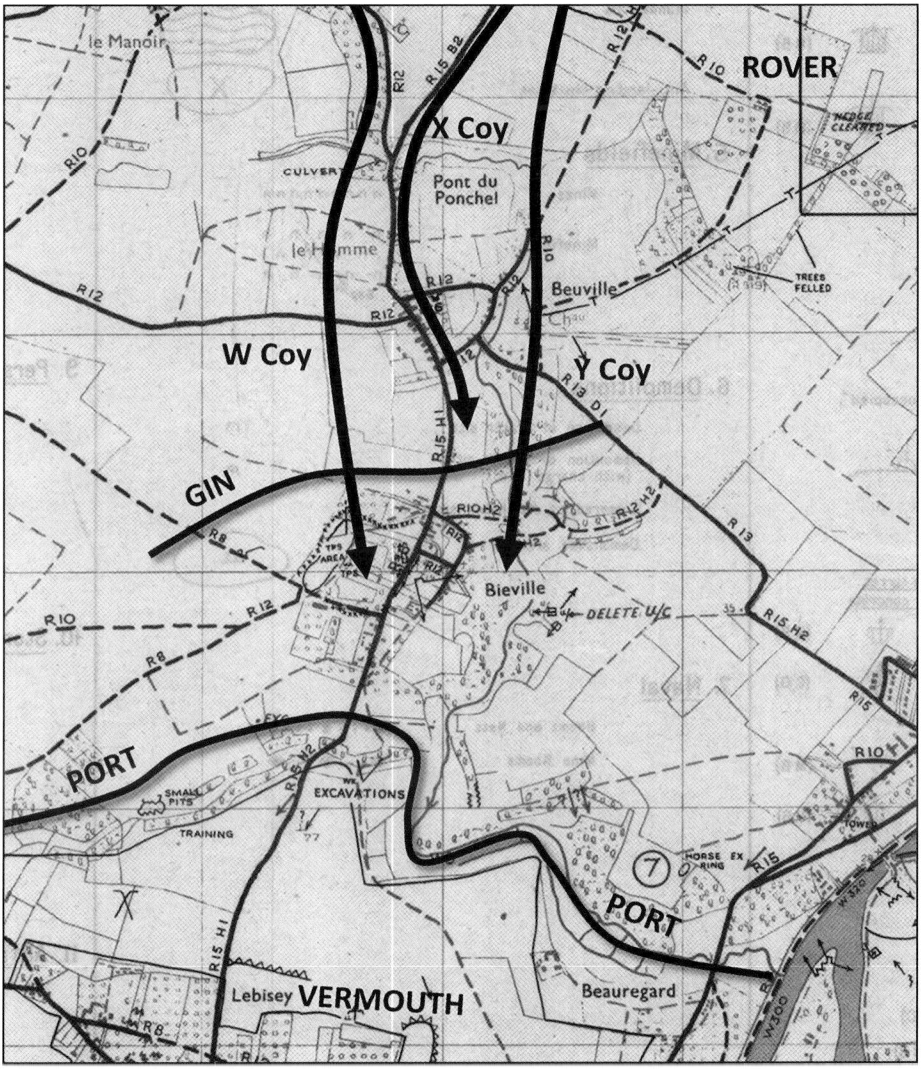

The attack of 2 KLSI on Beauville and Biéville. Line PORT runs along the bottom of the 'Anti-Tank Obstacle.

This was Major Slater of W Company, hit on the western flank of the village. His second-in-command, Captain Rylands, explains:

> X Company were meeting serious trouble from snipers in the north end of the village of Beuville. This consisted of strong stone buildings, interspersed with walled orchards – a paradise for determined marksmen fighting a delaying action. And delay us they did, so Major Slater, impatient because X Company seemed to be held up, walked up the road to the centre of the bother.

> Here he fought a private battle with some snipers and was seriously wounded in the arm. Nevertheless, he managed to give us a picture of the situation before he collapsed and was evacuated protesting.[20]

Corporal Littlar continued:

> By this time three tanks had caught up with us ... My platoon commander ordered me to go across the road and around the right-hand flank of the village, to the meadows at the back of the buildings. We scrambled up the banks, heading for the back of the village. All the while we were being fired on by snipers ... A corporal in charge of one of the other sections came up to me and told me who had been hit by snipers, and most of them were other NCOs. We both got our jack knives out and removed the stripes from our uniforms and put them in our pockets. We rubbed some dirt onto our uniforms where the stripes had been. We never wore our stripes again during that campaign.

Lieutenant Jones commanding 10 Platoon of Y Company described his part in the fighting on the eastern outskirts of Beuville:

> I called up my Company Commander on the radio to advise him of my whereabouts, and he informed me he was 'holed up' by snipers, behind a wall just inside the village, and would I please get him out! I zig-zagged down the road with two of my men and they threw smoke grenades to cover the escape

Château de Biéville and its grounds were used by German logistic support units.

> of the Major. As we rushed back to the platoon, a sniper, whom I suspected was in the belfry of the village church, fired one shot and the soldier to my right was hit in the head. Within a second or two, the soldier on my left was also hit.[21]

Beuville was reported as taken, and at 1545 hours and approaching from the flanks, 'W and Y Coys reach forward edge of BIÉVILLE.' Y Company reported 'no opposition during advance on left', while 'W Coy having received some casualties on the way proceeded to "mop up" area of Chateau.' Second Lieutenant Murray of 8 Platoon later described what happened:

> Before us was Biéville, a group of houses, a shop or two and a farm. A nest [of enemy troops] had been left there and had to be cleaned up. There I saw my first woman sniper, dressed in a German camouflage outfit. She seemed not the slightest perturbed when finally brought out. This resistance was not heavy, but it was taking time and men neither of which we could spare.[22]

Operations in an urban environment are notoriously slow, and in this case it had taken a precious hour and a half to advance a mile through the two villages.

Counter-Attack of 21st Panzer Division

At 1615 hours 2 KSLI's adjutant noted in the battalion's war diary: 'German tanks seen approaching from the west.' The expected counter-attack was on its way. The Staffs Yeo's war diary records:

> Recce Tp [already across PORT, the valley/'anti-tank obstacle'] now reported enemy tanks advancing North from the direction of CAEN. CO asked for the immediate release of 'A' Sqn who arrived just in time to take up battle positions to the West of Biéville.

This was the result of Colonel Eadie's concern that the brigade's 6-mile western flank he was covering was too thinly held, and his request for the return of A Squadron from HILLMAN, where it had just arrived. The squadron returned to the flank in time to confront 21st Panzer Division's counter-attack.

For *Gefreiter* Peterson, the driver of a Panzer IV in 22 Panzer Regiment, it had been a slow start to the day:

> We were alerted early on 6 June and manned our vehicles. I had fought in Russia and after receiving a wound in the thigh was sent to the 21st Panzer in France which was being rebuilt. I was quite happy there, though by 1944 things had deteriorated for various reasons: the imminent threat of invasion, our lack of proper training and the air raids.
>
> For some time on that day we received no orders. Then, at long last, late in the morning we were ordered into column on the road where our panzers were camouflaged to some degree, and we moved off with orders to break through to the sea and wipe out any Allied troops we encountered. We went some way with no problems. In my position I could see little and hear

The 21st Panzer Division's counter-attack and the line of defence adopted by the British and Canadian division.

> nothing but the engine and my commander's orders. He was a veteran *Feldwebel* who had fought in Africa, and like the rest of our crew a good friend.

On his return from Paris, *Generalmajor* Feuchtinger's focus was on preparing to launch an attack on the airborne landing east of the River Orne; but at 1130 hours (Allied time), just as his attack was developing, orders came from General Marcks that the action against the paratroopers was to be broken off. Instead, leaving behind 125 *Panzergrenadiers*, the division was to launch an immediate counter-attack against the British landing north of Caen. As in the case of the *Hitlerjugend* the change of mission required a complete rearrangement of orders and redirection from the routes that the division's units were already on. This, of course, caused additional difficulties and delays.

The shortest route for that part of the division to the east of the Orne was through Caen, but the only bridges still intact were those in the city centre and a railway bridge south-west of Colombelles, and these were under regular fire. Lighter vehicles were able to dash across the central bridge and then make slow progress through the increasing amounts of rubble. The commander of 22 Panzer Regiment, *Oberst* von Oppeln-Bronikowski, realized, however, that his tanks could not get through the city. According to the divisional history:

> The commander of *Panzerregiment* 22, who drove past his stationary armoured companies in his command car, ordered them to bypass Caen to the east and to the west. He ordered the companies that were in the rear to bypass via the railroad bridge at Colombelles, and several elements to use the longer route along the western part of Caen. All radio traffic was strictly forbidden. Von Oppeln-Bronikowski could no longer keep his companies together. *Panzerregiment* 22 was broken up.[23]

With the change of orders and routes, the last tanks to leave the Falaise area, *Hauptman* Herr's No. 5 Company, thanks to making their own way across country, were the first to arrive in the assembly area in the woods around Lebisey to the north-east of Caen.

At 1507 hours, OKW formally regrouped formations to the Seventh Army. SS *Gruppenführer* Dietrich's I SS Panzer Corps came under General Dollmann's command, consisting of 21st Panzer, 12th SS *Hitlerjugend*, Panzer *Lehr* and the 716th divisions. However, at this stage General Marcks' LXXXIV Corps remained in command of the entire invasion area until such time as Dietrich could establish his headquarters and take over the delivery of the counter-stroke. The 22nd Panzer Regiment and the *Hitlerjugend* were on the road, but with the weather clearing they were under constant attack by Allied fighter-bombers and consequently would be unable to arrive for the concentrated and decisive attack Rommel planned. The divisional history recorded that 'On the western edge of Caen, eight Typhoons delivered a low-level attack and damaged six panzers. All five command panzers [Mk III] were eliminated, and an additional panzer dropped out with mechanical problems.'

Oberst von Oppeln-Bronikowski, the commander of 22 Panzer Regiment.

The situation was in fact worse than shown on higher headquarters' map boards. As a result of the forward deployment of 21st Panzer Division, its units had been positioned to add depth behind the 716th Division's coastal defences. Consequently, these companies were drawn into the fighting, and it was impossible to disengage most of them. *Oberschütze* Kortenhaus, a driver of a panzer IV, concluded that 'The 21.Panzer Division was no longer a cohesive formation. The elements that could be assembled for the decisive counter-attack in the afternoon of 6 June 1944 amounted to less than half a panzer division.' It can be argued that this was the inevitable effect of Rommel's 'string of pearls' policy. In short, the 21st Panzer Division was neither an effective operational nor a strategic reserve, as a result of Hitler's compromise.

The obvious and well-studied orders given to *Generalmajor* Feuchtinger by General Marcks were to 'cross the Orne north and south of Caen, with elements in Caen, advance on both sides of Hill 61, to attack the enemy forces that have landed between the mouth of the Orne and Luc-sur-Mer and hurl them back into the sea.'

Another veteran of the *Afrikakorps*, *Leutnant* Grabmann, commanded a reconnaissance platoon in *Panzer-Aufklärungs Abteilung* 21:

> We were to make a strong thrust directly to the coast and west of the Orne, wipe out the enemy and take over the beaches to prevent further landings. By then we were in a state of some excitement, but the enemy planes were overhead and we knew we had been spotted. We had heard the great bombardment on the shore and as we went along the road, we heard the sounds of battle.

Warned of the approach of tanks, Corporal Littlar and X Company were halted in the southern outskirts of Biéville:

> After we crossed the road to the village of Epron, our deployment was halted, and the order came to dig in. Some anti-tank guns were moved into the area, so we were expecting German tanks, but I hadn't seen any of them at that point. We had 20 minutes to dig in, so we paired up and got our shovels and picks out. We were in an orchard so the soil wasn't too bad. You dig in roughly to shoulder-height. By about 5pm we were properly dug in.

Feuchtinger's plan was to attack with two *Kampfgruppen*, one based on 22 Panzer Regiment and the other on *Oberst* Rauch's 192 *Panzergrenadier* Regiment. There was limited regrouping of infantry and companies of Panzer IVs between the two commands. *Oberst* von Oppeln-Bronikowski's armour-heavy *Kampfgruppe* on the right was to swing around the wood at the end of the Anti-Tank Obstacle and head north-east via Point 61 towards SWORD Beach. Rauch's *Kampfgruppe*, which was infantry-heavy, was to strike north via Mathieu and Cressons to the sea between Lion and Luc-sur-Mer.

The 'Anti-Tank Obstacle' and the 'Anti-Tank Ditch'

Barring the way to Lebisey and Caen were two obstacles, one natural and one man-made. The first was a steep-sided valley running east-west that extended from halfway to Epron, across the front of 185 Brigade's advance, which was referred to as the 'Anti-tank Obstacle' and nicknamed 'PORT'. Although crossed by the road from Biéville to Lebisey, along its length its precipitous sides were wooded and represented an obstacle to armour. The other obstacle took the form of the 'Anti-tank ditches', dug by the Germans, presumably in expectation that engineers would sooner or later find their way across the Obstacle. The largest ditch extended from the Canal de Caen, north of the Lebisey Wood, and thereafter in shorter stretches for some three miles to the west to Buron, protecting roads and defensive features and no doubt designed to channel the enemy into potential killing areas. The line of the ditches was approximately coincident with report line ALE.

There was clearly confusion between 'obstacle' and 'ditch' at the time. Corporal Davies of C Squadron Staffs Yeo recalled, 'We thought the anti-tank ditch was the little valley itself, but in fact I don't think what we hit was specifically an anti-tank defence.[24]

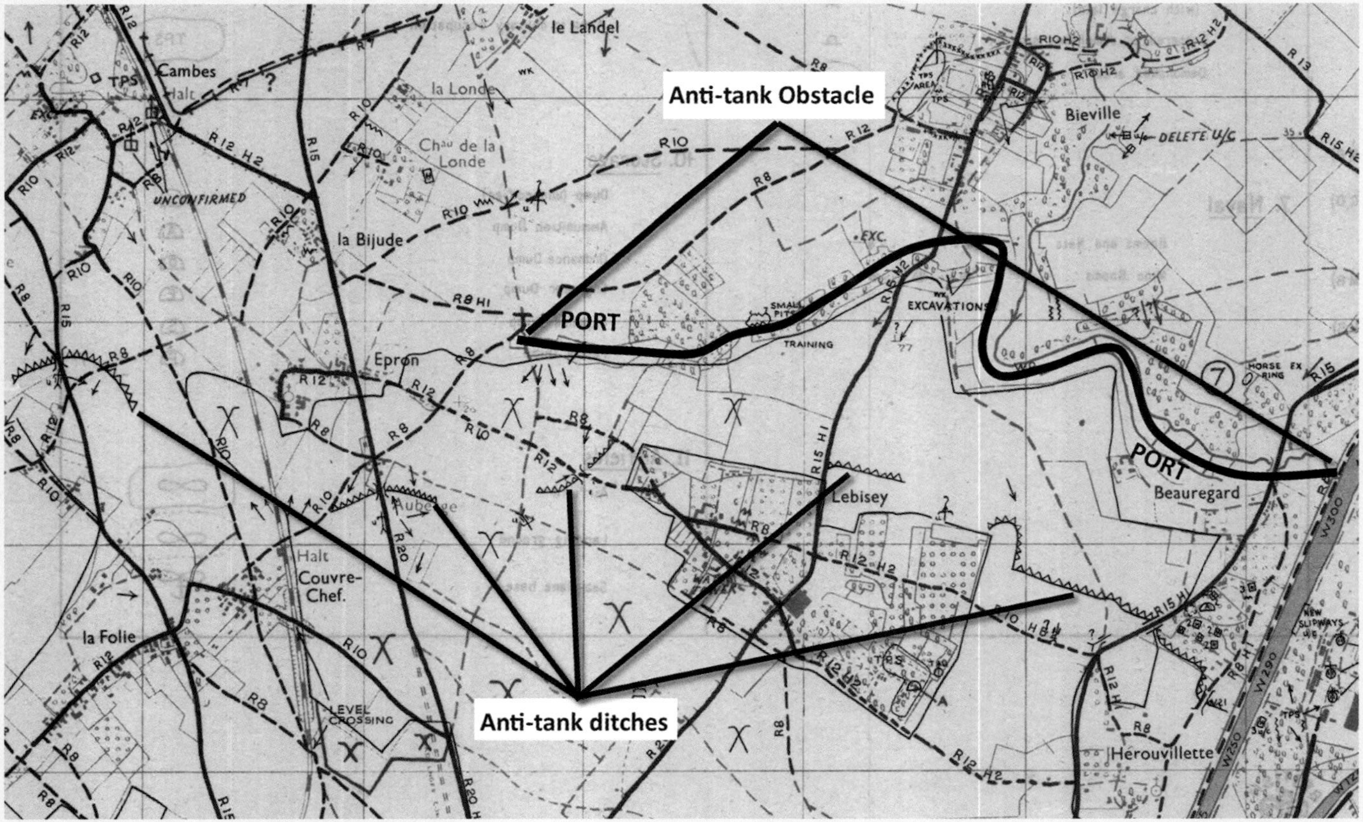

The tactical overprint showing the anti-tank ditches and annotated to show the Anti-Tank Obstacle (PORT).

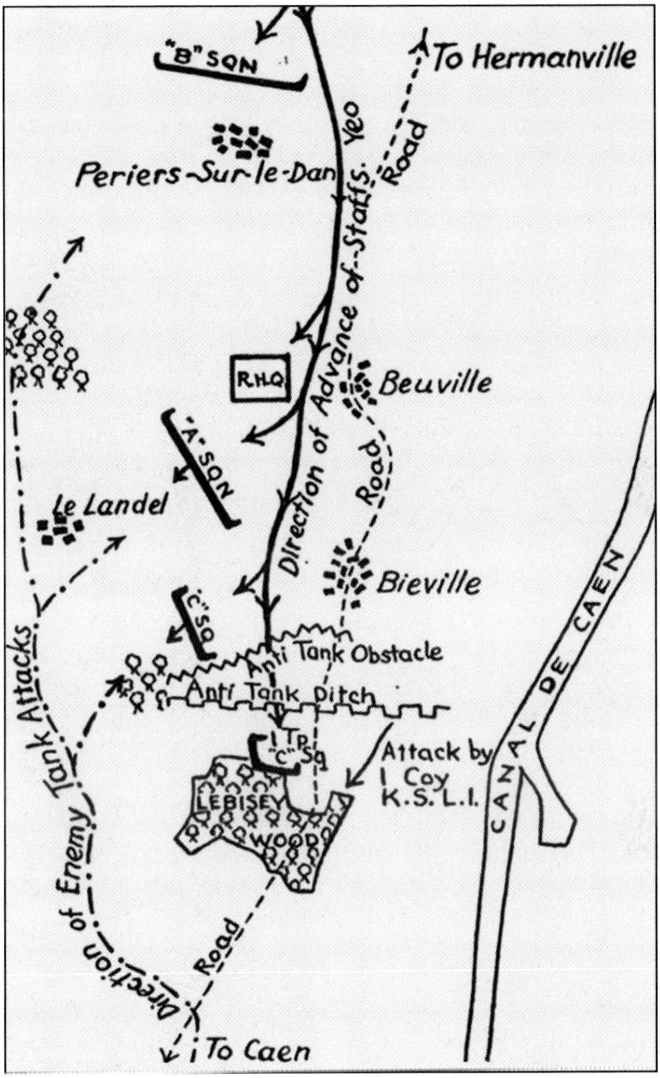

A map from the Staffordshire Yeomanry's regimental history showing the deployment of the squadrons on the western flank of 185 Brigade's advance.

As was German commanders' practice, General Marcks was at the *Schwerpunkt* (crucial point) ready to direct operations. Kortenhaus recalled:

> Greatly aroused, Marcks held Feuchtinger responsible for the delayed commitment of the 21.Panzer Division and objected strongly to the division's approach march and the manner in which the division had been commanded in battle up to this point. This was a painful scene for others to witness as one general shouted at another red-faced general.

> General Marcks took the leadership of the attack in his own hands and, thereupon, told *Oberst* von Oppeln-Bronikowski that the war would be lost if he did not succeed in hurling the British back into the sea.

With the British infantry halted in the valley obstacle, *Hauptman* Herr's No. 5 Company, along with the tanks of von Oppeln-Bronikowski's regimental headquarters, twenty-four Panzer IVs in total, appeared from behind the wood into view of the British light tanks. Of this attack *Oberschütze* Pearson, the driver of a Panzer IV, wrote:

> At last, I learned the enemy were near and I should be ready to drive across the fields if necessary. I saw smoke ahead and the *Feldwebel* told us our own infantry were in action. We halted several times and I had no idea what was happening until I suddenly heard bangs and our *Feldwebel* dropped down into the panzer and began using his periscope, warning us to get off the road at a second's notice. Because of the obstructing hedges and ditches this would not be easy.

C Squadron Staffs Yeo and the guns of 41 Anti-Tank Battery's troop on the Périers Ridge started to fire as the panzers came into range at somewhat over 1,000 yards.

> The enemy tanks advanced very fast and were engaged when they reached the Western end of the A/Tk obstacle. Two were K.O.'d and the remainder moved West into the wooded country in the direction of LE LANDEL. Two troops A Sqn moved across to our right flank and when the German tanks emerged No. 1 Tp engaged and destroyed four. Other enemy tanks swung still more to the West and moved fast for the high ground above PÉRIERS-SUR-LE-DAN. 'B' Sqn. ordered three 17-pdr tanks and one Sherman III to engage and three more German tanks were destroyed. No other enemy tanks then [advanced] from the woods.

Oberschütze Pearson continued:

> Then I heard greater explosions and saw one of our panzers firing ahead of us. It stopped, but I could not see any targets at all. The road was now blocked, but I saw one of our panzers go through the hedge and I was ordered to follow it. I drove on and went through the hedge with difficulty, and at once saw the tank ahead blow up in flames. The *Feldwebel* shouted orders and the gun crew went into action. I had my visor closed as there were now bullets pinging over the tank and I could hardly see through my periscope because of the smoke. Our seventy-five was banging away, even though I myself had only the vaguest idea where the enemy was. Then the *Feldwebel* shouted, 'Go left! Go left!'

The engagement had been somewhat one-sided, with C Squadron's 17-pounder Fireflies claiming seven targets, in exchange for two Shermans damaged and an

An image that shows the source of confusion resulting from the fitting of additional *Schürzen* armour around the turret of a Panzer IV. When combined with their long barrel and muzzle break, there was plenty of scope for misidentification.

M10 knocked out. The regimental history noted that 'Some of [the targets] were wrongly described as Mk. VI tanks owing to the additional armour plates fitted.'

Panzer radio operator Werner Kortenhaus recalled:

> The British fire was accurate and came from a number of directions. Four Panzer IVs were immediately lost. At this range, German fire was generally ineffective.[25] *Hauptmann* Herr led his company back to a reverse slope position and attempted to do a 'horizon crawl' to the west to find another jump-off point.[26]

This first attack by *Kampfgruppe* von Oppeln-Bronikowski had failed, but they would try again as they advanced deeper into the gap between 3rd British and 3rd Canadian divisions.

Lebisey (VERMOUTH) – The High-Water Mark

With the departure of the panzers, Lieutenant Colonel Maurice kept trying to advance and brought forward his only uncommitted company from the east of Biéville, Major Steel's Y Company. Their task was to cross the Anti-Tank Obstacle and secure the village of Lebisey, with two troops of tanks from C Squadron and sections of the Staffs Yeo's Recce Troop that raced across the open to the Obstacle. Corporal Davies, the commander of a Sherman Mk III of C Squadron, recalled the report of a predictable anti-tank gun covering the road across the defile:

> They'd found this gun up on the hill, so the squadron leader told me I'd got to go up the road, which was the quickest way up to this gun ... In our regiment, they always sent one tank in front, commanded by the Corporal,

> so that if he got knocked out, the tanks behind were supposed to be able to see from where he'd got hit. You weren't supposed to rush in, three tanks together.
>
> When I drove up to the road, the gun started firing along the road again. There was just no way I could get the tank up the ridge from there ... I reported this to the squadron leader, so what we did was to go up [the slope] and round, coming towards the side of the gun position. We were pressing on when three Germans, the picket for the guns, popped up. I automatically said 'Driver, Right' to miss them, and of course they started shooting at us. I learnt my lesson: you get blood on the tracks, if necessary. As soon as the gun crews on the hill caught sight of us – we were that close we could see the gun-crews, we were covering them with machine-gun fire – they hopped it.

Having cleared the anti-tank gun, the Recce Troop and Shermans pressed on across open country, reaching the northern outskirts of Lebisey at 1730 hours. The Shermans were not stopped by either of the obstacles as the enemy had not cratered and mined the road. On arrival they reported, 'No. 1 Troop found very few enemy in Lebisey ... only a few disorganised infantry.' These were probably support troops, but before long *Kampfgruppe* von Opplen was arriving, so the British tanks and infantry were under pressure and unable to penetrate deeply into the orchards and the village. The KSLI's war diary recorded at 1800 hours:

> Y Coy report held up by crossfire from enemy MG in woods and snipers amongst trees also enemy of approx. forty trying to get round their flank.

The M3 Stuart Light Tank that equipped British armoured regiment's recce troops. In British service it was known as the Honey.

> Situation reported back [to 185 Brigade]. Decision made to establish firm base in BEUVILLE and withdraw Y Coy after dark.

Some of the Germans that Y Company reported were infiltrating along the Anti-Tank Obstacle from the east but they were dealt with by artillery and mortar DFs. Y Company held firm in Lebisey, despite the loss of Major Steel, who was killed by machine-gun fire while up with his forward platoons in the village. With panzers 'somewhere out to the west', the brigade war diary summarized the situation:

> About 1800 hrs CO 2 KSLI re-established communication with company which had reached outskirts of LEBISEY. He was informed that casualties were heavy, that the company commander was killed and that they were unable to penetrate the wood owing to the thick nature, concealed MGs and snipers and that a party of the enemy were in process of encircling them. The CO considered that to commit his two available companies (already considerably depleted by casualties) into this extensive and obscure objective and without a firm base behind them was unwise.

With the sound of armour to the west, Colonel Maurice had a real fear that if he consolidated his battalion in the as yet unsecured Lebisey Wood,[27] the enemy panzers could cut him off and their infantry finish the job.

> This was passed back to the Brigade Commander who agreed to the withdrawal of the company from LEBISEY and ordered 2 KSLI to establish a firm base SOUTH of BIEVILLE. This withdrawal was carried out after dark without undue loss. Situation at nightfall therefore was three companies 2 KSLI digging in at BIEVILLE.

At 2315 hours battalion headquarters of 2 KSLI noted, 'Y Coy withdraw successfully without further casualties.' The Staffs Yeo also pulled back. 'At last light the regiment rallied and leaguered west of Biéville, but in spite of innumerable snipers in the adjacent woods we were not seriously disturbed in the 3½ hours in leaguer.'

Sundry delays and too little combat power had brought the Intermediate Brigade's advance on Caen to a halt, and they fell back to positions that were 2½ miles from the Orne bridges in the city. On their right, the option of an advance by 9 Brigade, the Reserve Brigade, had not materialized, an advance that would have taken them to Cambes and Galmanche and into line with 185 Brigade. Instead, 9 Brigade less 2 Lincolns were transferred to an eastern axis. The Warwicks, already having been so diverted, inevitably became involved in the battles around Objective RUGGER. Their war diary recorded:

> The German Strong Point SOUTH of COLLEVILLE-SUR-ORNE [HILLMAN] was still holding out and 2 KSLI and 1 NORFOLK, who were advancing by the original axis, had suffered casualties from this position. For this reason the Battalion was ordered to advance along the axis

> COLLEVILLE-SUR-ORNE–BENOUVILLE–BLAINVILLE. BENOUVILLE was found to be held and 'A' Coy put in a successful attack on this position at about 1830 hours. 'D' Coy was now ordered to take over the defence of the bridges over the ORNE from the Airborne Division. The rest of the Battalion continued on towards BLAINVILLE, meeting opposition the whole way from a German Mobile Delaying Force armed with MGs and A-tk Guns. The Battalion halted for the night on the outskirts of BLAINVILLE at midnight, having had four killed and thirty-five wounded.

The Warwicks had been fighting 8 Company of 192 *Panzergrenadiers*. This company, along with troops of the 716th Division, had been attempting to recapture Objective RUGGER from 7 Para for most of the day, but with the arrival the Warwicks they conducted a fighting withdrawal. Blainville was out on a limb, 2½ miles from Lebisey. Meanwhile, the third battalion of 185 Brigade, 1 Norfolks were, following the same delays and fire from HILLMAN, at 1930 hours 2½ miles to the KSLI's right rear approaching objective ROVER, where they were ordered to halt and consolidate for the night rather than press on to the high ground above Biéville.

Amongst the other criticisms of 185 Brigade already mentioned are unfavourable comparisons drawn between the considerable drive and leadership of 2 KSLI shown by Colonel Maurice and that of the commanders in the Warwicks and the Norfolks. The capture of Caen by the Intermediate Brigade on D Day was, following the German reinforcement during April, always going to be unlikely. However, if the whole of 185 Brigade had got across the Anti-Tank Obstacle onto Objectives WINE and STOUT astride Ring Contour 60 on the ridge above the city, its further defence would have been compromised and it could have been captured, as expected, 'within days'.

Chapter Eight

The Reserve Brigade

The main body of 3rd Division's 9 Brigade started landing on the narrow strip of sand, mainly from LCIs, at 1145 hours, some forty-five minutes late. At this point most of the obstacles were under water, but enemy response by this time largely took the form of intermittent mortar and shell fire. The war diarist of 2nd Battalion, The Royal Ulster Rifles (2 RUR) wrote:

> Here the Battalion caught first sight of the enemy as batches of snipers with hands over their heads were being rounded up from the houses and sand dunes lining the beach. By this time the sea had developed a considerable swell. The Battalion was well used to wet landings when carrying out exercises, but this was without doubt the wettest on record, most people landing in at least 4 feet of water and many in as much as 5½ feet. The majority became soaking wet from the top of their heads.[1]

In most cases the larger LCIs used by the brigade's infantry grounded further from the beach than the LCAs. The RUR account continued:

> Although the beaches had been almost cleared of the enemy, hostile shells and mortar bombs were falling in fair quantities. Consequently, even though the Battalion formed part of the reserve brigade in the Assault Division, the landing was made very difficult and uncomfortable. Many of the Riflemen being small in size were finding it difficult to get ashore, particularly in view of the fact that over and above their normal kit – heavy enough – they were each carrying a bicycle.[2] Few casualties only were experienced on the beach, those there being from shell and mortar fire.

SWORD Beach remained under German mortar and artillery fire throughout D Day and thereafter. Much of it originated from as yet uncleared battery positions sited inland, but it also came from batteries as far east as the 380mm guns at Le Havre. Whether or not the four 100mm Skoda guns that had not been properly put out of action at Merville by 9 Para opened fire during D Day on their pre-registered target areas on SWORD Beach is debated.[3] However, periodic shelling of the beach from the east contributed to slowing the disembarkation of the 3rd Division and consequently contributed to the failure to generate the planned tempo of operations. A key factor in the subsequent action of 9 Brigade is recorded in the headquarters' war diary:

> At 1300 hrs the party landed and in a very short time HQ was established in the Assembly Area NORTH of HERMANVILLE-SUR-MER. It was here

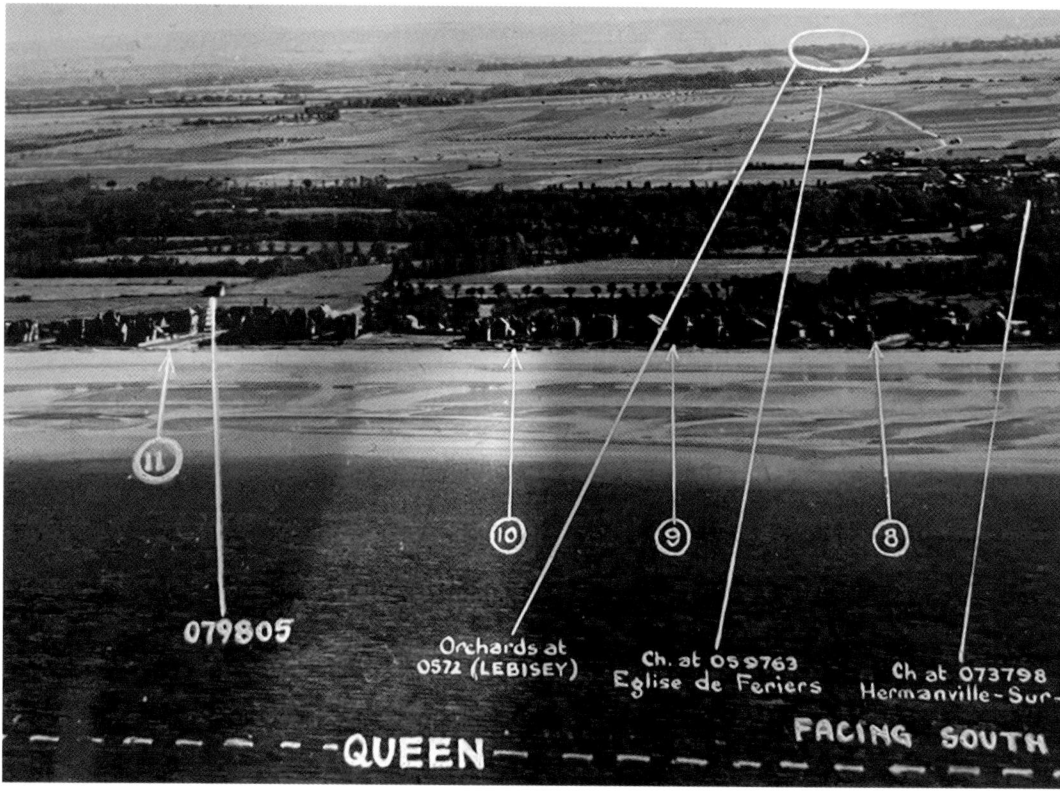

One of the oblique air photos illustrating the open ground south of Colleville and Hermanville rising to the Périers Ridge and Lebisey beyond.

> that the enemy struck a severe blow. A mortar bomb falling in the HQ severely wounded Brig. JC CUNNINGHAM, MC, the G. III, the IO and one LO, and killed the I [Int] Sjt . . . HQ was moved about ¾ mile inland.[4]

These casualties produced a hiatus at a critical moment, and it took some time for a functioning headquarters to be reconstituted. Colonel Orr, the deputy commander, was still afloat in a landing craft not due to touch down for some hours. In the meantime, Lieutenant Colonel Harris was summoned from 2 RUR to take command of the brigade, but it meant that 9 Brigade was effectively stalled at a crucial point in the operation.

Unlike the beach, the assembly areas were under fire from small arms as well as artillery and mortars, and the 2nd Battalion, The Lincolnshire Regiment (2 Lincolns) was soon in serious contact with the enemy in its assembly area. Arriving in this uncomfortable situation south-east of the outskirts of Lion-sur-Mer, the battalion came under fire from the houses and 'the enemy [who] were established in some strength in a strongpoint'. The Lincolns became more fully involved than planned in 41 Commando's fight for TROUT (WN-21) and a château 500 yards inland from coast. The resistance, despite the help of Landing Craft Flack shooting up the seafront, plus A Company 1 South Lancs, had been too strong for the small number of lightly armed commandos. The enemy in the château were quickly neutralized by fire with the help of the Lincolns' A and

B companies, but the garrison of TROUT, knocking out supporting AVREs with a 50mm gun at 100 yards range, held out.

At this point, with further information arriving in the divisional headquarters regarding the move of 21st Panzer Division around Caen and the deduction that the main enemy counter-attack was likely to develop on the division's right flank, the plan was changed. As a result, 2 RUR was to advance just one bound forward to Point 61 on the ridge between Beauville and Périers and dig in, in order to thicken up the defences on the right flank. The 1st Battalion, The King's Own Scottish Borderers (1 KOSB) were to join 2 Warwick in an advance on the left flank. 2 Lincolns, under command of 8 Brigade, would remain in the Lion-sur-Mer area holding ground alongside 41 Commando.

Meanwhile, 27 Armoured Brigade's third regiment to land, the East Riding Yeomanry (ERY), was approaching the beach. Their task was to support 9 Brigade and they were to have landed at H+5½ hours (1230) along with many of 9 Brigade's vehicles, but the landing programme was by now running approximately one hour behind schedule. There was, however, to be another delay caused by one of the bouts of German coastal artillery fire.

> At 1.15 p.m. we were going well and were about 2,000 yards from the shore when shells began bursting all around us; some fragments hit the crafts, and a few minor injuries were received. The Navy then had orders to take us back out of the shelled area whilst H.M.S. *Warspite* opened up on the coastal batteries, some of which were as far away as LE HAVRE. Meanwhile, our infantry had landed and were asking for us to join up with them . . . We could not, for security reasons, say too much to our infantry on the wireless, but indicated we might be a little late for our appointment. It was one of the less pleasant moments in the landing, having to turn tail, however temporarily, when in sight of land, but there is no doubt that had the Navy not taken the step they did, many craft would have been lost, and some of us with them. However, thanks to H.M.S. *Warspite*, the coastal guns decided they were no match for the Royal Navy, and at approximately 2.10 p.m. on 6th June 1944, the regiment set foot again in France, from where it was almost the last to leave on 1st June, 1940.

Trooper Farrell, a Sherman driver of the regiment, described his disembarkation:

> The crossing was really rough and everybody felt that bad, they were all glad to get landed. They couldn't get landed quick enough to get off the sea, that's how bad it was. Obviously with the Tank Landing Craft, they couldn't go right into the beach, but they went in as near as they could. Then, they dropped the ramp, and then first thing that I saw was the water coming up to meet us through the periscope! Then, we went down into the water. I don't know how deep it was, but as soon as you hit the bottom you put your foot down and got out as quick as you could. Obviously, some of them didn't get out at all and didn't make it . . .[5]

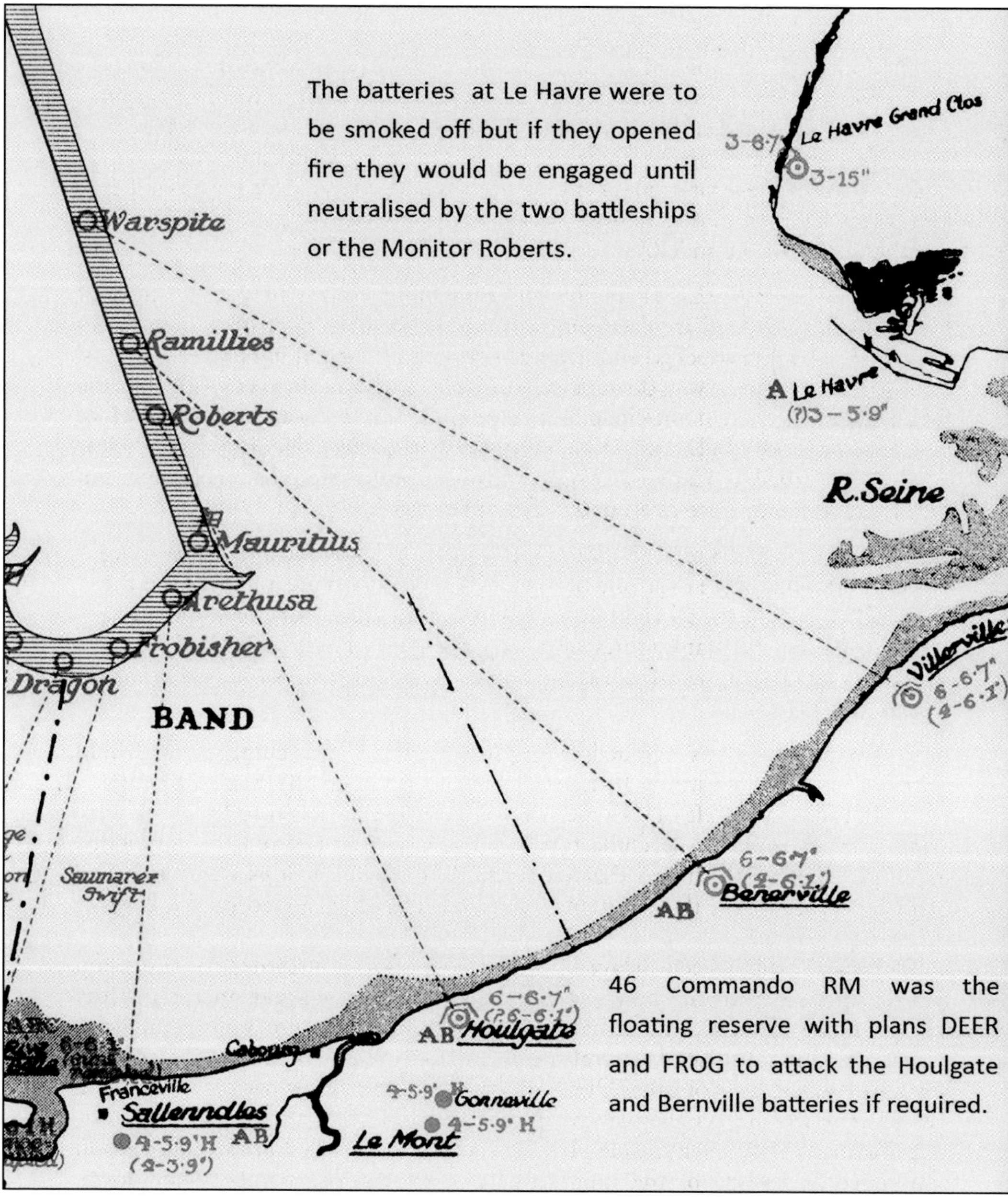

The German batteries astride the mouth of the Seine were to be neutralised by the ships of Bombardment Force D. The enemy fire from this quarter eventually led to the abandonment of BMA MOON behind SWORD, following the loss of 100,000 gallons of fuel and 400 tons of ammunition.

The ERY's Shermans drove ashore from their landing craft 50 to 150 yards from the beach through water 2–5 feet deep. Farrell continued:

> The Luftwaffe paid one of its visits and bombed the place where our Infantry Brigade, the 9th, were collecting for a conference on their immediate action in view of the fact that the Canadians had been unable to take a very strongly fortified place, a radar station on our right [Douvres]. Unfortunately, one of the enemy planes got a direct hit on the Brigade conference; the Brigadier was very badly wounded, and all the staff, except for the Brigade Major, were either killed or wounded.[6]

By the time the ERY's LCTs finally approached the beach at 1412 hours, most of the obstacles were still in place, and as the tide fell they were beginning to re-appear. Add to this wrecked and damaged craft, and the landing craft coxswains' task of threading their way through the obstacles to get as close as possible to the beach took longer than anticipated. The plan to clear 225 yards of the beach of obstacles on both RED and WHITE would have given landing craft a clear run in. As recalled by Captain Choate, the obstacles presented a real danger, but the situation could have been disastrous for his LCT:

> As we approached the beach there was a lurch followed by a nasty scraping sound. We had gone over one of the steel-tipped obstacles and wrecked the propellers. We were all right as the LCT drifted in ... Fortunately most of the shells and anti-tank mines on top of the steel tripods had already been defused by the Sappers before the tide came up. Otherwise it would have been much worse.

Particularly delayed was A Squadron, landing from LSTs via cumbersome Rhino ferries, quite a few of which had been lost during the cross-Channel passage.

Inevitably, some craft of all types and contents were forced to beach or were ordered in by assistant beachmasters to sectors well away from their intended touch-down. The result was that sections, platoons and troops were unable to easily locate the rest of their unit on the beach, all of which added another level of 'friction'.

The ERY, having been delayed landing, were now confronted by confusion and queues to get off the beach, with enemy mortar, shell and small arms fire, though much reduced, still a hazard. While the tanks were waiting to drive through the gaps, Luftwaffe aircraft made another of their appearances overhead, having managed to avoid the Allied air forces' fighter cover patrols thanks to a low-level intrusion. As they swept in to bomb they ran the gauntlet of anti-aircraft fire. There are multiple claims of kills by naval and ground forces and contradictory reports of the number of aircraft and the number shot down. Suffice to say, several enemy aircraft were lost. A fair proportion of the 300-plus sorties were made by FW-109 aircraft over SWORD during the course of the day.

The ERY squadrons, amidst conflicting priorities, took their turn in getting off the beach, but in exiting via the as yet narrow and imperfectly cleared lanes

Light anti-aircraft guns were amongst the early landers on SWORD. They were deployed to cover the beach exits and the assembly areas.

through minefields there were vehicle casualties. Trooper Buckingham recalled the situation:

> Passing between the houses on an exit from the beach we hit a mine that broke a track and we were stuck there for hours. We could not repair it where we were because of other mines, so we had to wait until another vehicle could pull us back and we could do the repair. While we were there we shelled [with 75mm main armament] a nearby house to dispose of a sniper causing casualties.[7]

The majority of tanks, having landed between COD and SKATE, had to turn west along PIKE towards their assembly area, which was reached around 1440 hours, almost two hours late. The field chosen turned out to have been marked as a minefield, and a Sherman Crab was called up to clear it. There were, however, no mines, and not until much later was it realized that those minefields marked with '*Achtung Minen*' signs in white lettering were real, while those marked in yellow were dummies.

With B and C squadrons having motored the short distance inland, their Shermans had to be de-waterproofed as soon as they reached the assembly areas, to avoid overheating and thus serious damage to engine and running gear. In the case of the Shermans this included air vents and hatches that had been sealed to 7 feet, to permit them to drive ashore, if necessary, through sea water to a depth of 6 feet. Much of the waterproofing material could be blown off by electrically initiated detonating cord set in the Bostic sealant.[8]

In the open ground below the Périers Ridge, the ERY in their assembly area were liberally shelled while waiting for orders and the arrival of A Squadron. Much of the enemy fire seemed to be coming from the west. Out in that direction, the 13/18 H's A Squadron had been reduced to little more than troop strength while alongside A Company 1 South Lancs since landing. Consequently, Major Matthew's B Squadron ERY was deployed a short distance towards Lion-sur-Mer to cover the brigade's flank. On their arrival from the beach at 1730 hours, A Squadron ERY was sent out to relieve B Squadron.

Other than the squadron deployed to the right flank, the ERY remained in its assembly area all afternoon; but with 21st Panzer Division well on its way, General Rennie would have needed to maintain a potent divisional reserve. An uncommitted armoured regiment was ideal for this purpose, and this is almost certainly why the ERY were held in their assembly area rather than being committed to supporting the Warwicks and KOSB to the left, where the strength of the 13/18 H's squadrons was much reduced. C Company 2 Middlesex (Machine-Gun) were also in reserve, along with two 4.2-inch mortar platoons. In terms of the division's D Day tasks, 'getting ashore and staying ashore' by retaining a reserve in the face of a counter-attack by a panzer division was clearly more important than the early capture of Caen.

Tactical Headquarters and General Rennie had been ashore since 1030 hours, with a slimmed down Main Headquarters being operational in the northern part of Hermanville by 1300 hours; but at 1600 hours the war diary records: 'Div HQ shelled – Div Comd ordered move to alternative HQ at COLLEVILLE-SUR-ORNE. Div G1 and remainder of party on HQ ship and standby ship came

Grouping of 21st Panzer Division for their Counter-Attack

As already highlighted, the dispersal of the division to add depth to the defences of Caen astride the Orne meant that the counter-attack was launched by only half the division.

Kg von Opplen – west of Hérouville	Kg Rauch – St Contest/Cussy
II Bn Pz Regt 22	I Bn 192 Pz Gr Regt
I Bn Pz Regt 22 (–4 Coy)	8 & 10 Coy III Bn 192 Pz Gr Regt
I Bn Pz Gr Regt 125 (–3 Coy)	III Bn Pz Arty Regt
1 Coy Pz Pioneer Bn	
III Bn Pz Arty Regt	

The remainder of the division, under *Oberst* von Luck, was deployed east of the Orne to contain 6th Airborne Division.

Tanks de-waterproofing in a D Day assembly area.

ashore.' At a crucial moment in the battle, the staff of divisional headquarters were changing location, which was also bound to have an impact on the conduct of the battle.

The Counter-Attack Continues

With the advance of the leading elements of II/22 Panzer Regiment around the western end of the Anti-Tank Obstacle having been checked by the combined efforts of the KSLI and Staffs Yeo, the German commanders awaited the arrival of further panzers from their Battalion I. Meanwhile, No. 5 Company continued north on their 'horizon crawl', looking for a weak spot in the 3rd Division's flank. *Oberst* Oppeln-Bronikowski, having appreciated the strength of the British on the ridge above Biéville on their arrival, ordered his I Battalion to advance on an axis a little further west via Château la Londe. Having covered a mile from Epron and reached the area of the Le Landel hamlet, the panzers came into the arc of fire of A Squadron of the Staffs Yeo, which had been rushed back onto the high ground west of Beauville. Kortenhaus wrote:

> *Gruppe von Gottberg* came under heavy artillery fire as it advanced. In the thick hedgerow terrain near Le Landel, the *Panzergruppe* came under fire from A Squadron, Staffordshire Yeomanry and fire from 17-pounder anti-tank guns. Radio contact failed to function and was also subject to enemy interference. In short order, six tanks were lost.[9]

Oberst Rauch (*left*) and *Oberst* von Oppeln-Bronikowski (*right*).

Of these six tanks, the Staffs Yeo claimed four in their war diary: 'Two troops "A" Sqn moved across to our right flank and when the German tanks emerged No. 1 Tp engaged and destroyed four.' Kortenhaus continued: 'As the group attempted to shift further to the west, it came under fire from B Squadron, Staffordshire Yeomanry and lost three more tanks.' B Squadron's action is described thus:

> Other enemy tanks swung still more to the West and moved fast for the high ground above PÉRIERS-SUR-LE-DAN. 'B' Sqn. ordered three 17-pdr tanks and one Sherman III to engage and three more German tanks were destroyed. No other enemy tanks then [advanced] from the woods.[10]

For British losses of a handful of tanks and M10s, Kortenhaus concluded:

> The regiment had lost thirteen tanks. The attack by *Panzerregiment* 22 failed in the face of the superior firepower of a resolute enemy, who shot better from favorable positions at long range. The attempt to take the Périers hill, which was the prerequisite for a breakthrough to the coast at this point, failed.
>
> It proved critical that the attacker had been able to capture and secure the commanding Périers hill in the early afternoon of 6 June 1944. Certainly, the withdrawal of *Panzerjäger Abteilung* 200 in the morning of that day was a contributing factor, but the most important reason was the delayed start of

Werner Kortenhaus, a crewman in a Panzer IV of 22 Panzer Regiment.

The 88mm PaK 43 of the type issued to *Panzerjäger Abteilung* 200. In comparison to the dual-purpose version it had a relatively low profile when fully dug in. It was normally towed by a Somua half-track.

> the counterattack by *Panzerregiment* 22, which did not arrive until 14 hours after the regiment had attained readiness for march in the early hours of this 6 June 1944. One can only imagine what the outcome could have been if *Panzerjäger Abteilung* 200 had dominated the Périers hill in the morning with its 24 heavy 8.8cm anti-tank guns.

Further west, however, *Oberst* Rauch's 192 *Panzergrenadier* Regiment was making better progress, with the corps commander General Marcks personally leading *Hauptman* Rätzer's *Kampfgruppe* made up of his I Battalion's *Panzergrenadiers* and elements of 736 Infantry Regiment. Being further west, they advanced steadily into the void between the British and the Canadians, who were advancing from JUNO Beach. By 2000 hours Rätzer had reached the coast and was advancing east and west to make contact with the garrison of TROUT WN-21 and WN-24 at Luc-sur-Mer. In this area to the west of Lion-sur-Mer, the ERY squadron came forward to assist the Lincolns and knocked out a half-track and another light armoured vehicle for the loss of one of their tanks.

At 1920 hours, C Squadron was ordered forward from reserve 4 miles south to thicken up the Staffs Yeo's defensive flank between Périers and Beauville. Here they were engaged by a Marder I 75mm anti-tank gun mounted on a Lorraine Schlepper chassis. Opening fire, the enemy missed with their first round, but the next two hit a Sherman, killing two of its crew. The gun had, however, been seen and it was quickly knocked out, along with two anti-aircraft guns, in an exchange of fire.

At this point the deep throbbing sound of massed aircraft could be heard approaching from the north. Landing astride the River Orne, these were the glider and tug combinations of 6 Airlanding Brigade (Operation MALARD) and a re-supply drop for 6th Airborne Division (Operation ROB ROY). Kortenhaus recalled:

> The sight of this mighty airborne armada had unsuspected and unforeseen consequences on the German side. For the men of the 21.*Panzer Division* and 716.*Infanterie Division*, this incoming flight was an immense demonstration of the Allied control of the air. Not a single German aeroplane contested the approach. All the grenadiers could do was lie on their backs and fire on the aircraft with their rifles. The lack of suitable means to defend against the incoming flight was shattering and had significant psychological effects. Many now realized that the war was lost.
>
> For *Gruppe* Rauch, at the coast, the incoming aircraft created a false impression that the enemy was in the process of committing airborne troops in its rear. At the same time as the airborne landings, an enemy [Canadian] armoured attack from the Cresserons area was threatening *Gruppe* Rauch, and a German advance on the Caen–Courseulles Road was thwarted by a Canadian ambush.

Shermans, infantry and an M10 Tank Destroyer in the Assembly Area inland from SWORD.

It was not only the fighting soldiers who believed they were being cut off to the south by the airborne landings just 3 miles distant:

> The command of the 21.*Panzer Division* was also deceived. *Generalmajor* Feuchtinger had been driving behind the attacking groups of his division in a command car and, due to the lack of functioning communications, had little influence on events. Impressed by the incoming flight of gliders, he ordered *Gruppe* Rauch to call off its attack and withdraw to its starting positions.

In a post-war interview with Major Schulman, *Generalmajor* Feuchtinger summed up his counter-attack:

> Once over the River Orne I drove north to the coast. By this time the enemy, consisting of three British and three Canadian Infantry divisions, had made astonishing progress and had occupied a strip of high ground about 10km from the sea. From here the excellent anti-tank gunfire of the Allies knocked out eleven of my tanks before I had hardly started. However, one *Kampfgruppe* did manage to bypass these guns and actually reached the coast at Lion-sur-Mer at about seven in the evening . . . I retired to take up a line just north of Caen. By the end of that first day my division had lost almost 25 per cent of its tanks.[11]

As the enemy began to disengage, the ERY squadron was ordered to pull back, presumably to reconstitute a strong divisional reserve, and at 2245 hours, the squadrons all having been in action to some extent, were back in a leaguer south of Colleville. The Norfolks, who had been halted at ROVER as the counter-attack developed, were spared attack, as were the Warwicks who, having left D Company to secure RUGGER, reached the northern outskirts of Blainville with three rifle companies and dug in, molested only by small arms and mortar fire.

Across 3rd Division there was a general feeling of relief and in some passing moments surprise amongst individuals that they had survived. However, with a panzer division lately in contact, being under fire principally from the east and in still doubtful weather, there was no room for complacency. An indication of the 3rd Division's view of its situation overnight on 6/7 June is contained in an entry in 20th Anti-Tank Regiment's war diary. With the CO having coordinated the anti-tank defence of the beachhead, the Adjutant noted at 2345 hours: 'RHQ settle down for a little rest, but it is necessary to maintain a strict watch owing to the instability of the situation.'

For the Germans, with the orders for a coordinated counter-attack to throw the Allies back into the sea by nightfall on 6 June being given far too late, the following situation report was recorded in Seventh Army's *Kriegbuch*:

> 24.00 hours. 716 Infantry Division is still defending itself at strong points. Communications between division, regimental and battalion headquarters, however, no longer exist, so that nothing is known as to the number of

Soldiers of 2 RUR assembling on the lateral road (PIKE) behind the beach.

> strongpoints still holding out or of those liquidated ... The Chief-of-Staff of Seventh Army gives the order that the counter-attack of 7 June must reach the coast without fail, since the strongpoint defenders expect it of us.

The 716th Division had been directly in the path of Second Army's attack. It was not yet clear to the Germans that other than a few *Wiederstandneste*, all that remained of the division were scattered detachments holding villages or making their way south under their own commander's initiative. The 21st Panzer Division would, however, be deployed into defence overnight.

Leutnant Schaaf, who had been in action on the Périers Ridge until the arrival of the Staffs Yeo, was one of many without orders. At one point he came across an infantry battalion headquarters, with which he exchanged information. The infantry had been told to withdraw south, so without being able to contact his battalion headquarters, Schaaf decided to join them; but whilst they were making their way back, one of the Lorraine Schleppers threw a track and became stranded in a ditch. Heading towards Point 64, he spotted a hastily assembled roadblock of farm machinery and the distinctive outline of British helmets. Scharff instructed his gunners to remove their helmets and had them drape a canvas sheet over the *Balkenkreuz* (Wehrmacht emblem) on the vehicle's hull. Brazenly, the guns then drove through the roadblock; even though the British soldiers saw them for what they were, they seemed too surprised to open fire before the guns were gone. As the battery reached the outskirts of Caen they joined a stream of straggling men and vehicles making their way back towards the city.

When Schaaf reported to the divisional artillery headquarters, he was told that his was the only battery, among eleven in the regiment, to make contact since

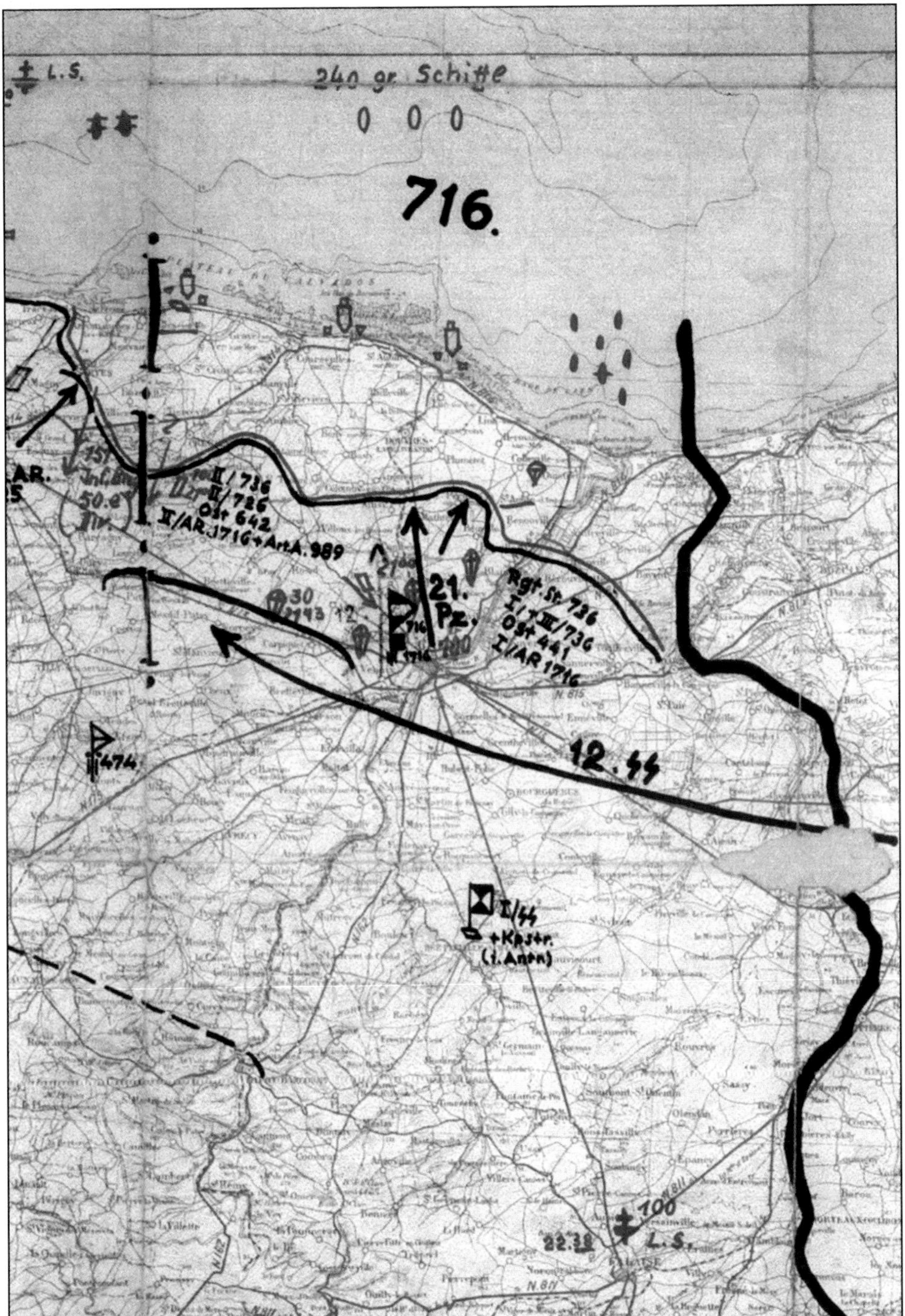

An extract from the German situation map issued overnight by von Rundstedt's headquarters, showing their understanding of events inland from SWORD.

morning. They pressed him for information about the situation forward, about which there was still a terrible confusion. Then he was ordered to take up position near Epron, just north of the city.

* * *

For the reasons covered in this and the preceding chapters, it was always unlikely that Caen could be captured on D Day. Only if the Germans in the SWORD area had collapsed could the city have been taken; but if sundry factors had been more favourable for the 3rd Division, they might well have advanced beyond Lebisey to the Ring Contour 60, denying the enemy an opportunity to mount a defence to the north of the city. Equally, if the German chain of command had reacted more quickly with the only panzer division in the invasion area, things could have been very much worse for the 3rd Division. Captain Scarffe summed up the Division's achievements on D Day when he wrote, 'The 3rd Division had done more than all that was expected of them once details of enemy disposition were known.'[12]

III Flak Corps

It is customary to calculate the strength of the German forces facing the two armies of 21st Army Group based solely on the number of panzer divisions they were confronted by. This, however, was just a part of the equation. Amongst others such as *werfer* brigades, the powerful III Flak Corps was deployed to contain the Second British Army and became particularly strong around Caen. Its commander, *General der Flakartillerie* Pickert, recalled being given orders to move to join the Seventh Army on D Day:

> In the afternoon of 6 June 1944 there arrived the preliminary order to get ready to move off in the direction of Normandy via Paris. In the evening of 6 June 1944 the Commanding General verbally received more detailed information regarding the landing in Normandy, as well as the order to go into action: III AA Corps is assigned to *Panzer Gruppe* West and ordered to cooperate with this Panzer Group. The Corps [typically] remains directly subordinate to the Luftwaffe Administrative Command (*Luftflotte* 3) in every respect. It is to move, with all dispatch, into the area west and south-west of Caen, and to support the Army in combat, drastically concentrating its forces. The main mission remains anti-aircraft defence, but the Army is to be aided in its ground combat as much as possible. Connections are to be taken up immediately with *Panzer Gruppe* West (Gen d Panzer Tr Geyr von Schweppenburg) in the area west of Thury-Harcourt (exact locality no longer recalled). The fourth regiment (1st *Flaksturm-Regiment*), committed in the region of Isigny [between OMAHA and UTAH beaches], is to be extracted as soon as possible.[13]

Fully motorized, the Corps consisted of twenty-seven heavy batteries and twenty-six lighter batteries, manned and supported by around 12,000 men. Some elements

General der Flakartillerie Pickert, commander of the powerful III Flak Corps.

A Flak 36 88mm triple-purpose gun, the workhorse of III Flak Corps' major units. In Normandy it proved to be too large and cumbersome to survive in the front line.

of the Corps were already in the invasion area, while the rest marched across northern France and were concentrated in Normandy by 8 June.[14]

The 88mm guns of the Corps were a potentially powerful addition, having not only the dual capability of anti-aircraft and anti-tank but also possessing a very effective HE round, a useful addition which made up to an extent for the lack of artillery in German formations. The suitability of the 88mm flak with its high silhouette for front-line anti-tank use is commonly overstated. There were, however, organizational issues. With Allied air supremacy, the Corps' prime interest was providing anti-aircraft fire, which led *Gruppenführer* Dietrich, commander of I SS Panzer Corps, to complain that 'Every time I position guns [to assist the ground battle], someone moves them.' Even though the guns were supposed to be only under administrative command to *Luftflotte* 3, Luftwaffe influence remained over the way they were used.

Chapter Nine

Lebisey – 185 Infantry Brigade's Battle

> Dempsey to proceed relentlessly with original plan. He will hold a flank on the River ORNE and capture CAEN and BAYEUX. He will then pivot on CAEN and bring his right forward. Likely that 51 Div will come in behind CAEN moving east of River ORNE. The two Armies to join up at PORT EN BESSIN. Do not want US troops brought in through 2 Army beaches.
>
> [Montgomery – signal to 21 AG Main HQ, AM 7 June 1944]

General Crocker's three divisions of I Corps had conducted the assault landing on the coast of North-West Europe by sea and air and were ashore with a decent if not yet secure lodgement. The Corps had, however, fallen short of its D Day objectives. On the right flank, 3rd Canadian Division had not reached Line OAK, the Caen–Bayeux railway, and to the east of the River Orne, while 6th Airborne Division had secured a buffer to protect that flank, it was significantly smaller than planned. In the centre, 3rd Division, having advanced over 5 miles inland, had been halted short of Caen. The Corps' orders for D+1 were for the infantry divisions to continue the advance, closing up to their D Day objectives.

For the Germans, the impact of the sundry deception measures had been to delay the timely issuing of orders for Rommel's counter-attack. In addition to delaying 21st Panzer's deployment, OKW initially directed one of the strongest formations in France away from the battle area. Thanks to 12th *Hitlerjugend* SS Panzer Division not being redirectedby OKW to deploy for an attack west of Caen until the afternoon of D Day, a division that could have been in action on 6 June was badly delayed. What happened was that, having stood to hours earlier, at 0700 hours on 6 June *Hitlerjugend*'s staff had received orders from Fifteenth Army to support 711th Division against an assumed Allied landing on the beaches east of the Orne. They were to use pre-recced routes for the second of their three possible deployments, Option B. First to march to the concentration area at 1000 hours were *Standartenführer* Kurt 'Panzer' Meyer's 25 *Panzergrenadier* Regiment, but with the situation in 711th Division's area being clarified and the scale of the threat north and north-west of Caen becoming more than apparent, they were halted. At midday *Generafeldmarschall* von Rundstedt requested the transfer of the *Hitlerjugend* to Seventh Army around Caen for action in the sector of 716th Coastal Division, i.e. Option C.[1]

A column of *Hitlerjugend* vehicles on the march in Normandy including a Panther, half-track motor cyclists and a *Kubelwagen*.

An immediate redirection was not possible as the division had been marching for some hours towards Option B. Therefore, the routes to the new deployment to the south-west of Caen needed extensive re-planning. In addition, it was not until 1432 hours that OKW in Berchtesgaden finally released the *Hitlerjugend* to Seventh Army. The mission they were given followed at 1700 hours:

> The 12 SS Pz Div and the Panzer *Lehr* Div are attached to the AOK [Seventh Army] with immediate effect for action against the bridgehead in the sector of 716 Inf Div. The AOK issues the following order through Panzer Group West:
>
> The 12 SS Pz Div is to deploy immediately northward … in the area on both sides of Evrecy … and is initially attached to LXXXIV AK. Its mission is to drive the enemy who has broken through, adjacent to the 21 Pz Div on the west, back into the sea and destroy him.

The other armoured formation allocated to Army Group B was 130th Panzer *Lehr* Division, which had also been released from the area of Chartres and was directed to come into the line to the west of the *Hitlerjugend*.

However, it was not until 1800 hours on 6 June that the *Hitlerjugend*'s divisional Tactical HQ set out to drive to 716th Division's headquarters, but the low cloud that had helped cover movement during the morning had now given way to clear skies and fighter-bombers. Reports of the torrid time that 21st Panzer had experienced transiting west around Caen during the afternoon resulted in the bulk of the *Hitlerjugend* being initially ordered not to march until 2000 hours; but

General Speidel, in an attempt to make up for lost time, ordered an immediate move. With the roads crammed with German transport, the Allied fighter-bombers struck. Riding in a truck, *Sturmmann* Pock of 25 SS *Panzergrenadiers*, which was leading the division's main body 75 miles west, recorded in his diary:

> The number of our vehicles knocked out keeps growing. They are sitting where they were hit, burnt out. Grenades are scattered about, shells, all types of ammunition, amongst them dead soldiers.
>
> The march this day becomes more dangerous. The pastures and fields are ploughed by bomb craters. We realize more and more that the enemy, as far as materiel is concerned, does not seem to be inferior to us.

As in the case of *Generalmajor* Feuchtinger's division, once the *Hitlerjugend* was on the move air interdiction played a vital role in further delaying the division's deployment. The failure to bring a second panzer division into action on 6 June is widely regarded as a success for FORTITUDE and a vital lost opportunity for the Germans at the opening of the invasion.

One of the *Hitlerjugend*'s soft-skin vehicles knocked out during the march to the front. Throughout the battle only 6 per cent of armoured vehicle casualties were caused by Allied aircraft, but that is not to underestimate their significant impact on German operational movement, logistics and morale.[2]

Travelling ahead of his regiment, it took *Standartenführer* Meyer eight hours to reach 716th Division's headquarters in a cave in the quarries on the northern outskirts of Caen. He told *Generalmajor* Richter that 'I lay for a good four hours in roadside ditches because of air attack.' It was apparent that Richter's [716th] division had all but ceased to exist, and that 21st Panzer Division's afternoon counter-attack had failed and its units were falling back to the high ground covering Caen. Around midnight, Meyer was summoned back to the caves, this time for a briefing by I SS Panzer Corps, who had arrived and taken command of the sector as far west as Asnelles, behind GOLD Beach. The *Hitlerjugend*'s task for 7 June was to operate on the left flank of 21st Panzer in a coordinated counter-attack, beginning at 1200 hours, which was to thrust north to the coast aimed at driving the Allies back to the beaches. The panzer grenadiers would initially be advancing through the scattered detachments of 716th Division, which still occupied some of the villages north-west of Caen. According to Feuchtinger, who was also present at the conference, Kurt Meyer 'studied the map, turned to me with a confident air and said, "Little fish! We'll throw them back into the sea."'

The long route from their assembly area, slow night movement, and shortly after the return of daylight the resumption of Allied fighter-bomber interdiction sorties, all these meant that only 25 SS *Panzegrenadiers* were in cover west of Caen preparing to attack. Delays to H Hour multiplied, with the loss of bowsers and the resulting difficulties of getting fuel forward to replenish the ninety Panzer IVs of II/12 SS Panzer Regiment. This eventually resulted in agreement that the advance would begin at 1600 hours.

The 3rd Division's intelligence assessment was that barring their way into Caen were the disparate remains of 716th Division. Overnight, however, Feuchtinger had deployed the troops he had assembled for the previous afternoon's counter-attack in positions north of Caen. He was under orders to join the *Hitlerjugend* in the drive to the coast, but 192 *Panzergrenadier* Regiment remained in place to the east of the Caen–Douvres railway line. For reasons never satisfactorily explained, Feuchtinger did not order the half of his division west of the Orne to attack.

3rd Division's Plans – D+1

The original instruction was: 'Should the enemy forestall us in Caen, 3rd British Division will contain the enemy in Caen and retain the bulk of its own forces disposed for mobile ops in the covering position.' However, with the British and Canadian divisions stalled north of Caen, nowhere near the envisaged covering position, a new plan was required, one that would concentrate on the capture of city. Following a comparatively quiet night, broken only by sniping, shelling, some mortaring and nighttime Luftwaffe bombing raids, the orders issued to the brigades were as follows: 185 Brigade was to continue the advance south with the immediate object of securing the important tactical area of Lebisey, the wooded area surrounding it and Ring Contour 60 (Objectives STOUT and WINE). This was an important objective as, once it was in British hands, direct observation

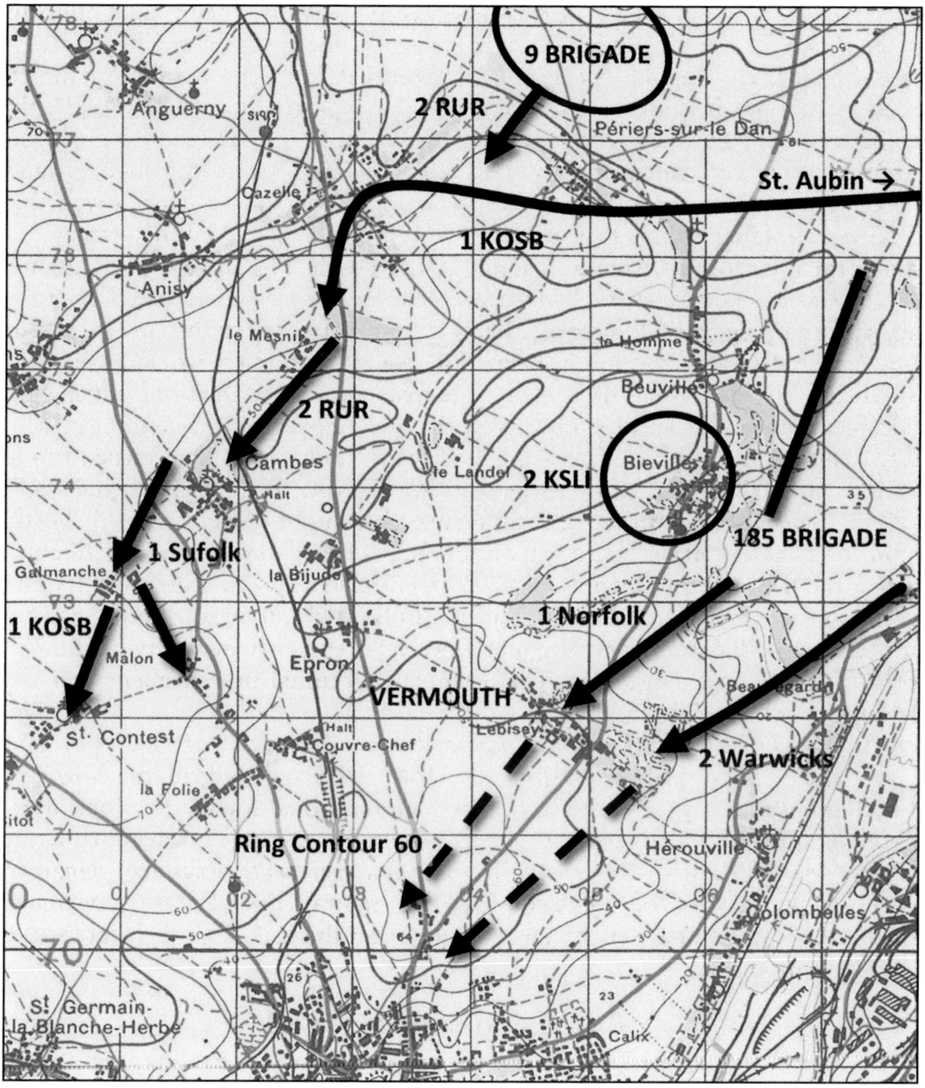

3rd Division's plans for the advance on Caen during D+1.

over the city would be secured, and it would also deny the enemy views of the country north to SWORD Beach. 9 Brigade was to advance south-west and capture first Cazelle and then St Contest, where it was intended to link up with 3 Canadian Infantry Division. 8 Brigade, depleted as a result of its assault role on the previous day, was to secure Cressons and Plumetot, take over the defence of the Périers Ridge from 9 Brigade and mop up the rear areas where a number of Germans had been bypassed. This latter task included the château in Lion-sur-Mer and TROUT WN-21, both of which were still holding out.

Lebisey Woods and Village

Unaware of the full extent of 21st Panzer Division's deployment at Lebisey and on the ridge during the night of 6/7 June, 185 Brigade issued a warning order for the resumption of the attack on Objective VERMOUTH, Lebisey Wood and the village. It was only after dawn that Brigadier Smith's Orders Group assembled for 2 Warwicks and 1 R Norfolks to receive their instructions on wood and village, respectively. They were planned to be supported by A Squadron of the Staffs Yeo, with fire provided by the three field regiments of the divisional artillery on the wood and a Royal Navy cruiser on the village. As the infantry approached, the guns were to switch their fire in order to isolate the objective, with the 105mm Priests targeting the southern edge of the area and the cruiser engaging Ring Contour 60. In the exploitation phase the two battalions would move onto this high ground. 2 KSLI was to provide a firm base in the area of Beuville and form the brigade's reserve for the attack.

A Squadron had been expected to provide close support to the advance of two battalions, but there were two problems. Firstly, with the left wing of the 21st Panzer Division concentrated overnight north of Caen and their panzers and anti-tank guns deployed in defence, any advance into and across the Anti-Tank Obstacle was met with such a fusillade of solid shot that they were driven back into cover. Secondly, approaching the obstacle from the north-east, the tanks could not easily find a way across the steep-sided valley. Captain Talbot, an FOO of 16 Battery mounted in a Sherman, added that 'Vehicles were unable to negotiate the swampy ground at the bottom of the gully.' The squadron was consequently ordered to remain where they were and to attempt to shoot the Warwicks into Lebisey Wood … 'but the tanks spent most of the day in over-watch [positions from which they could observe and provide fire support].' The regimental history, however, records that:

> The ground to the East of Biéville was unsuitable for the purpose of the required support and it was found that there were no possible crossing places of the natural A/Tk obstacle between the main axis and the road BLAINVILLE–CAEN.

Since the Warwicks had been halted to the north of Blainville at dusk the previous evening, a preliminary operation to clear this village was necessary. As the battalion moved forward to the start line on the Le Dan stream, A Company on the left came under fire from Beauregard, and this, along with swampy ground, resulted in a delay of the original 0845 H Hour to 0945.[3] During this time they were shelled and mortared while waiting in their FUP and, due to the delay, lost the planned artillery bombardment. Despite this, and still unaware of the strength of the enemy in Lebisey, they were urged to 'get on with it' by the chain of command.[4] The risk was appreciated, but in the belief that they could still capture Caen before the Germans occupied it in strength, it was one that needed to be taken.

The battalion plan was to advance with two companies forward, A left and B right, towards the eastern end of Lebisey Wood where, once it was secured, C Company would pass through to clear the western half. At this time D Company was still performing its defensive role at objectives RUGGER and CRICKET but when relieved was to follow up as the battalion's reserve.

The delay of the attack was passed to the gunners, but owing to poor VHF communications the message did not reach B or C companies, who crossed the start line at the original time without a fire plan in support. The Commanding Officer, seeing two of his companies advancing steadily through the corn, apparently unopposed, at 1100 hours ordered A Company forward along with his tactical headquarters. The Germans allowed the Warwicks' companies to advance across 1,000 yards of open ground towards the wood before springing their trap, waiting until the leading platoons were within 200 yards before

185 Brigade's plan.

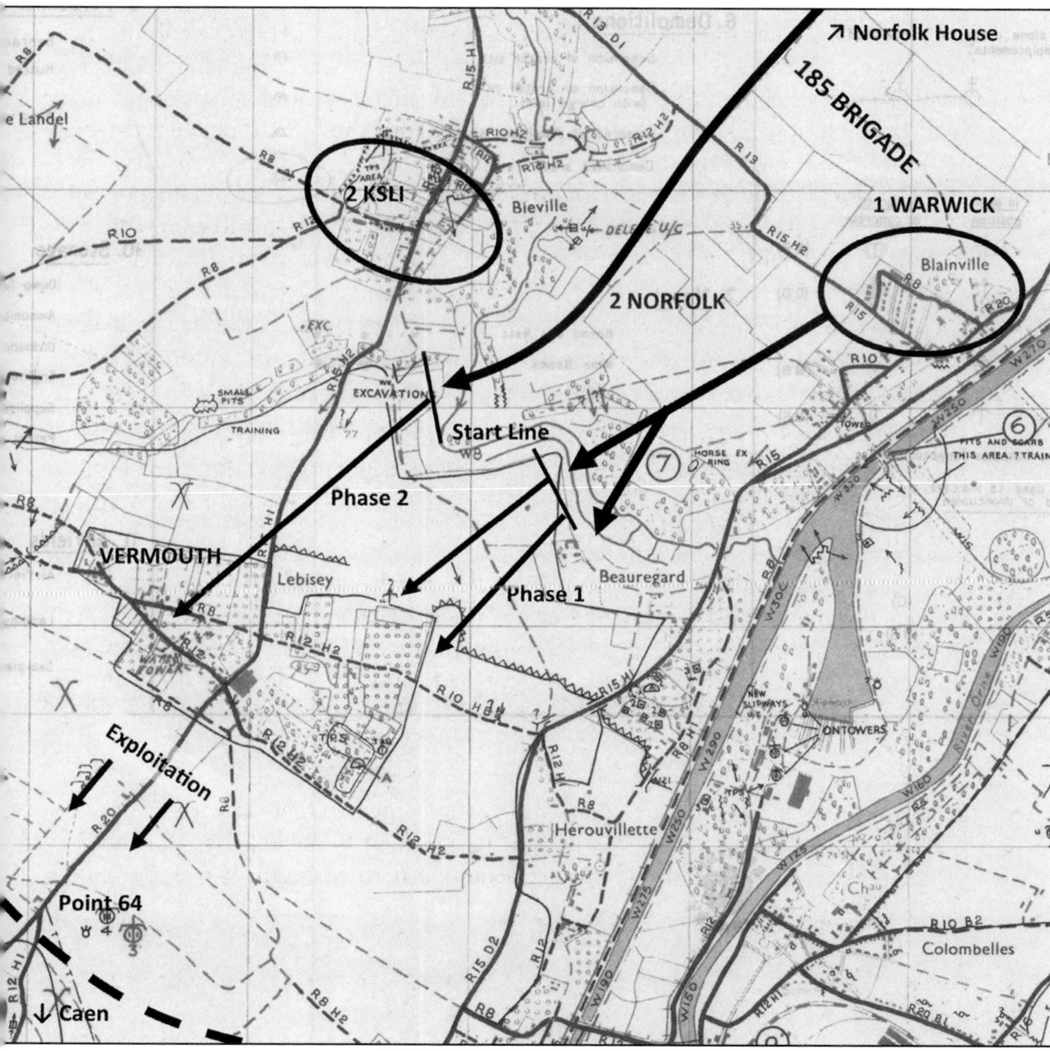

opening fire. Helped, however, by two SP guns firing smoke and HE, both companies reached the edge of the wood. With commendable dash, they

> gained a foothold on the northern edge of the WOOD and were pinned down by very heavy German MG fire from inside the WOOD from well-prepared positions, receiving heavy casualties, particularly to one platoon of B Co led by Lt A DOCHERTY, who penetrated into the WOOD. All his platoon is missing and it is not known what happened to them.[5]

Despite coming under indirect fire, 'B Company and battalion headquarters also reached the wood in a mad rush for cover', where Colonel Harden was killed whilst moving in the open in an attempt to co-ordinate a resumption of the attack.

As the more powerful vehicle radio sets could not be brought across the Anti-Tank Obstacle there was a consequent reliance on man-pack sets. However, the transmissions of these low-power VHF sets of the day were easily screened by obstructions such as the valley of the Dan and the trees of the Lebisey Wood. Consequently, the passage of information within battalions and the brigade was poor, and situational awareness was based on often third-hand messages, most originally passed via FOOs' 18 Sets. For example, significant artillery fire could not be brought down on the wood, as it was not known how far into it the Warwicks had penetrated. Consequently, fire was concentrated on the southern edge of the wood in the hope of preventing German reinforcement. In this situation it is not surprising that several crucial decision were made in 185 Brigade during 7 June amidst a very thick fog of war, and calls for fire were responded to far less quickly than normal.

Major Illing, whose A Company came up to join B and C Companies on the left, remembered:

> I recall advancing up the convex slope through high corn. This provided good cover and it was not until the crest was reached that one came into view of the enemy lined up along the ridge on the edge of the wood. Once we came under fire at very close range the forward platoons tried to work forward by fire and movement in the classic pattern and the reserve platoon to work round the flank. However, being pinned by fire was a reality and without tank or artillery fire support, progress was impracticable. The battle became a small arms fire fight at close range ... Although it led to a serious setback it taught some very salutary lessons.

Three companies were now 'pinned down along the fringes of the wood by concentrated enemy fire that rendered individual movement extremely difficult. The German position along the ridge proved too extensive to be outflanked.' Lacking fire support from tanks and their own support weapons, which were waiting to cross the Anti-Tank Obstacle, 2 Warwicks, according to the brigade war diary,

> remained on the edge of the wood under continuous heavy and accurate machine gun and mortar fire from about 1200 hours to 1500 hours. At this

The German view of the open ground from the north-east corner of Lebisey Wood across the site of the anti-tank ditch to the ground across which the Warwicks advanced.

> time the fourth company [D Company], which had been relieved of its duties on the Benouville bridge ... joined the rest of the battalion and were put into a left flank attack.[6]

D Company's attack at 1500 hours from the left flank 'wiped out the German position that had been holding [up] A Company', who were preparing to advance further into the wood. The division's digest continued:

> This eased the situation slightly and was about to be exploited when the Germans counter-attacked with tanks. 2 Warwick then managed to get themselves into a tank-proof locality in the thickest part of the wood where they remained pinned under continuous heavy fire until 2230 hours when orders to withdraw were received.

During the course of the afternoon, with reports that the battalion had taken the wood, the Warwicks' main headquarters vehicles, plus those of the Carrier, Mortar and Anti-Tank platoons, drove along the main Biéville–Lebisey road to join the rest of the battalion. This road had been used by the KSLI the previous day, but now the 21st Panzer Division had it properly covered by fire and 'ambushed the lot with machine guns and tanks'. Virtually all the vehicles were hit and, laden with ammunition, they burned fiercely, but most of their crews escaped into the standing crops, where they lay up until after dark and then exfiltrated back to their own lines. The Adjutant and all three support platoon commanders, however, were numbered amongst the missing.

The incorrect supposition that the Warwicks controlled the wood was followed by another at 1340 hours, when Brigadier Smith finally received a message that three companies of Warwicks were established on their objective and that D Company was following up. Based on this information, he issued a warning order for 1 R Norfolks to be prepared to advance through the Warwicks,

A wounded soldier of the 3rd Division being carried from a Jeep ambulance into a damaged building being used as an RAP in Biéville,

clear the village and exploit to Ring Contour 60 south of Lebisey. An O Group, previously ordered for the north edge of Lebisey Wood at 1600 hours and which would have revealed the true situation, was cancelled, and unfortunately the headquarters of 2 KSLI near Biéville was used instead. Any attempt to approach Lebisey would have instantly told commanders that the reports were false, or at least less than fully accurate, but at 1400 hours another message was received, again stating that the Warwicks had captured their objective. At 1545 hours, the Norfolks left ROVER on the high ground near Beuville to move to their FUP in the dead ground to the east of the Lebisey road, from where they were to advance and exploit the apparent success of the Warwicks. They had, however, been seen and were heavily shelled and mortared. 'About this time disquieting reports began to filter back about the true state of events in Lebisey Wood which were only too happily confirmed by returning wounded … there seemed little doubt that the situation was critical.' The Norfolks' historian wrote:

> Unfortunately plans went astray and the attack went off at half-cock, with the result that the Warwicks found themselves in a very difficult position, being unable to move forward without heavy casualties or backwards without exposing themselves and giving the initiative to the enemy. There was nothing for it, and we had to go and restore the situation.[7]

After some discussion at HQ 2 KSLI, the Brigade Commander ordered the Norfolks forward to Lebisey Wood and left it to the discretion of Lieutenant Colonel Bellamy whether to consolidate prior to further exploitation or to cover the withdrawal of 2 Warwicks and then extract his battalion after dark. Only speculative artillery could be arranged since the location of 2 Warwicks in the wood was still unclear. The fire available was a series of DFs that could be called for and adjusted by observers. The Norfolks' H Hour for the advance was set for 1800 hours, and 'these decisions were referred to the Divisional Commander who approved.' At first, all seemed well, but according to Major Wilson, 'In the afternoon we moved well away from the road down to the stream facing the Lebisey feature some 1,000 yards ahead. All sorts of rumours were going around of massed tanks and enemy counter-attacks but to us everything seemed fairly quiet.' However, once they were in the wood, the battalion's history recorded:

> It was not easy going, but we managed to get our anti-tank guns and mortars to a position from which they could give us some form of support. The forward companies were having a bad time and we suffered quite a number of casualties. Enemy tanks were also reported and altogether it was most unhealthy.

The War Office report noted that 1 R Norfolk 'arrived in Lebisey wood in good order' and eventually fought their way to the first lateral track. The war diary, however, recorded that 'This Bn intended to attack in front of VERMOUTH and found it to be well prepared defensive posn, contrary to expectations.'

> Here they came under heavy machine-gun and sniper fire which it was found impossible to locate or on which to bring down supporting artillery fire. One company was caught in an enemy minefield and casualties started to mount up.

The decision was, of course, taken by Colonel Bellamy to withdraw both battalions from Lebisey Wood at last light. This was successfully achieved, and the battalions of 185 Brigade were back in their starting positions by 2300 hours.

For taking over command of the Warwicks, fighting in the wood and for the skilful withdrawal, Major Kreyer was awarded the DSO, but in the fighting in Lebisey Wood the losses to the Warwicks were serious. After men returned from the wood over the following days, casualties totalled ten officers and 144 other ranks; in the Norfolks, nineteen were killed and an estimated sixty wounded.

The QF 6-pounder gun was the standard equipment of British infantry battalions. Its performance matched or exceeded the German PaK 40 once an armour-piercing discarding sabot (APDS) round came into general issue at the end of June 1944.

One of the battalion's casualties, Corporal Ashdown of D Company, who was wounded in Lebisey Wood,

> has written to his Company Commander from a hospital in ENGLAND saying that when his Company withdrew his injuries prevented him accompanying it. Two Germans attended to his wounds and left him lying near the enemy position. He managed to crawl towards the English Lines where he fainted. He next remembers waking up in a Base Hospital.

The presence of a large proportion of the 21st Panzer Division that had gone over to the defensive in a strong position on the high ground east of the Caen–Douvres railway had decisively checked 185 Brigade on D+1. The first part of what was to be the German line for the next month had solidified. To the west of the railway line, facing 9 Brigade, the opposition had also been assessed as the remnants of 716th Division.

In the aftermath of the fighting the Warwicks dug in behind the KSLI, reorganized and took in replacements. Their war diary noted:

> The Brigade was ordered to form a firm base around the area BIEVILLE–BEUVILLE and the day was spent in digging in and re-organising under spasmodic shelling and one air bombing attack. The Battalion had a few casualties during the day. Reinforcements came up in the evening composed of five officers and one hundred and twenty-three other ranks [mainly] from our own First Line Reinforcements.[8]

So heavy had the battalion's casualties been that twenty-seven soldiers from the Worcesters and a handful of Dorsets found themselves allocated from the casualty replacement system and rebadged as Warwicks.

The failed counter-attack by elements of 21st Panzer Division had brought the D-Day advance on Caen to a halt by late afternoon. It was, however, the remarkably competent overnight regrouping and redeployment of forces that was overseen by *Generalmajor* Feuchtinger's veteran commanders that decisively halted

British and Canadian Medium Artillery

Due to land during D Day, 53rd (London) Medium Regiment Royal Artillery was amongst those units delayed aboard ship by the loss of Rhino Ferries during the crossing of the Channel. Other than the recce parties, the regiment was the first unit of 4 AGRA to land in Normandy and come into action in support of the 6th Airborne and the 3rd Division at Lebisey and Cambes.

British and Canadian medium regiments were grouped into Army Groups Royal Artillery (AGRA) along with sundry other field, heavy and anti-aircraft regiments. AGRAs were normally affiliated to a corps but could be grouped as required to support major offensives.

The workhorses of the medium regiment were the 5.5-inch and 4.5-inch guns. They were superficially similar (the carriage of the two guns was almost exactly the same, for example), but their different calibres gave the guns overlapping but complementary capabilities.

BL-5.5-inch Gun. The gun was provided with 82lb high-explosive shells, which with Charge Super gave it a maximum muzzle velocity of 1,950 feet per second and a range of 18,100 yards. This meant that from gun positions between Hermanville and Colleville, Caen and its environs were well within range. The other ammunition used extensively during offensive operations was the 100lb smoke shell. In addition to high explosive and smoke ammunition there were illuminating rounds and several types of chemical shell. The normal HE fuse for the shell was the

A British BL-5.5-inch gun in action.

5.5-inch shells dumped ready for use.

pre-war percussion impact No. 117 fuse, but by the end of 1944 the T100 proximity fuse was becoming available.

BL-4.5-inch Gun. This gun specialized in counter-battery work, having a longer barrel, which gave greater accuracy and a range of 20,400 yards using Charge Super for its 55lb shell. Its nickname was 'The 10-mile sniper'. The overuse of Charge Super was avoided because it caused excessive barrel wear.

The prime mover for both guns was the 4 × 4 AEC Matador truck.

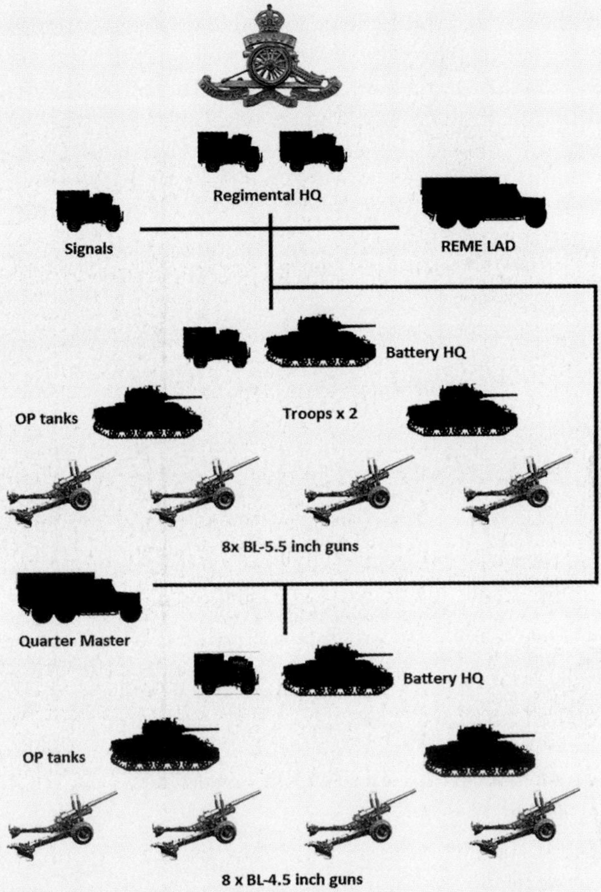

The regimental historian described their first few day in action:

> Throughout this time we gave direct support to the forward brigades of 3rd Division. 210 Battery on the left, with 1,500 yards of open valley between 185th Brigade and the invisible Germans in Lebisey Wood, had a straightforward job plastering the wood daily with predicted fire in concert with 7th Field Regiment and the machine guns and mortars of 2nd Middlesex. 209th Battery on the right had the tricky task of helping 8th and 9th Brigades to edge forward in some nasty fighting through the close country from Cazelle through Cambes to Epron ... In addition, we fired steadily in support of the flanking divisions – 3rd Canadian attacking Carpiquet on the left and the Highlanders in St Honorine across the Orne – and spare time was fully occupied with counter-battery shooting, much of it with air OP, and with attempts to knock out the massive chimneys of Colombelles factory which gave the Germans a commanding view of the whole beachhead.

the drive on the direct route to Caen. The deployment of the panzers and anti-tank guns along the edge of the Lebisey Wood and village condemned the British infantry to fighting unsupported by either the tanks of the Staffs Yeo or their own heavy weapons. In addition, the companies that attacked at the original H Hour, thanks to a communication failure, did so without a fire plan; this condemned them to fighting an infantry battle, something that days later would not be countenanced, but at the beginning of a campaign training counted for more.

Further west, 9 Brigade were in action but they, too, were brought to a halt, albeit for different reasons in a distinctly different battle.

I Corps' plans for operations around Caen on D+1.

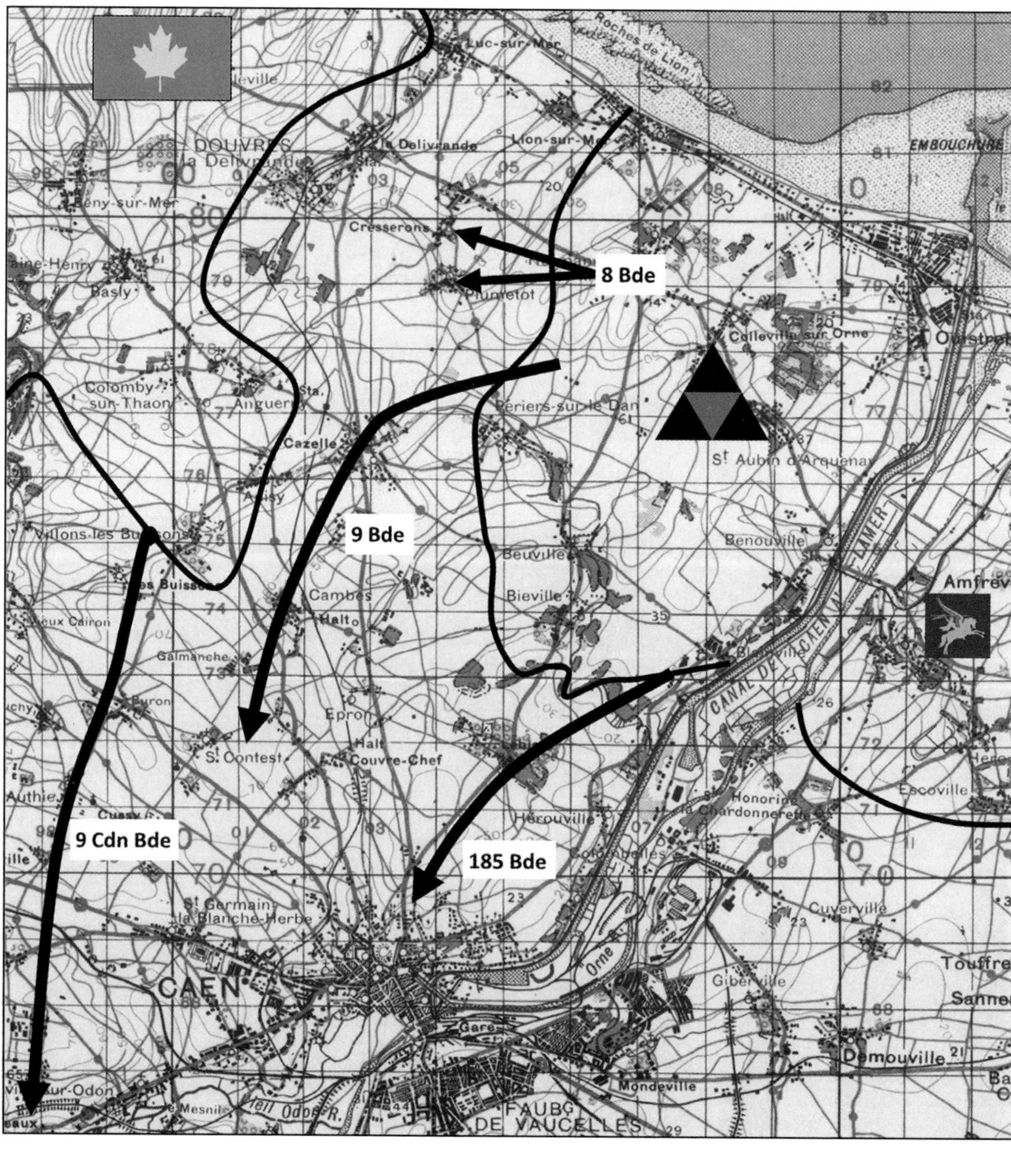

Chapter Ten

Cambes-en-Plaine – 9 Infantry Brigade's Battle

The drive on Caen, delays getting ashore and the presence of elements of 21st Panzer Division had resulted in 3rd Division forming a distinct and potentially vulnerable salient during D Day, which continued efforts to reach Caen would only extend. While 185 Brigade resumed its fight to reach the city from the north, on the division's right flank, 9 Brigade was to advance some 6 miles from their overnight positions, south-west via Périers-sur-le-Dan and via Cambes-en-Plaine to the area north-west of St Contest. For 9 Brigade:

> The Intention remains as before, to establish the Brigade in the St. Contest-Melon area. The attack is to be in four phases:
> (a) Cambes by 2 R.U.R.
> (b) Galmanche by 1 Suffolk.
> (c) Contest by 1 K. 0. S. B.
> (d) Melon [Mâlon] by 1 Suffolk.

The brigade's battalions were to attack in succession (see map, opposite and page 183). These operations would bring the division's forward positions on the right flank alongside 185 Brigade's on the high ground above Caen and eliminate the salient the KSLI had formed the previous day. Further west, 3rd Canadian Division was to advance to the Caen–Bayeux railway line, totally reducing the salient.

The 2nd Royal Ulster Rifles (2 RUR) led 9 Brigade's initial advance from the high ground south-west of Hermanville through the village of Périers against opposition provided by Germans who had been left behind and sniped at passers-by. At 0830 hours, the 1st King's Own Scottish Borderers (1 KOSB) were brought back to the division's right flank from their overnight position at St Auban d'Arquenay and took over the advance south from Périers. Their initial objective was Cazelle (today Mathieu), but at 1210 hours while they prepared to launch an attack, the village was found to be undefended. Thus, C Company led the battalion through Cazelle to some substantial woods south-east of Le Mesnil. The KOSB's padre, Iain Wilson, recalled that during the advance:

> Six Heinkels suddenly appeared out of the clouds prepared to attack us, but a swarm of our fighters quickly engaged them and drove them off. Half a mile further on we reached a fairly large wood – Le Mesnil – where we were ordered to halt and dig in, much to Colonel WFR Turner's chagrin. As

> we were digging, a heavy and accurate mortar concentration came down inflicting eight casualties on B and C Companies.[1]

While 1 KOSB were deploying into defence, 2 RUR had 'leap-frogged through' to resume the lead and prepared to attack Cambes, which was thought to be 'lightly held'. However, by mid-afternoon the *Hitlerjugend* had begun its part of Rommel's counter-attack around the western side of the city. Only 25 SS *Panzergrenadier* Regiment had arrived and begun its advance north when approached by 9 Canadian Brigade. On their way to the coast, their initial objective was a line through Anguerny, 6 miles north of Caen. On the regiment's left flank, the III/25 SS *Panzergrenadiers* and five companies of Panzer IVs had immediately

The attack of 25 SS *Panzergrenadiers*, 7 June 1944.

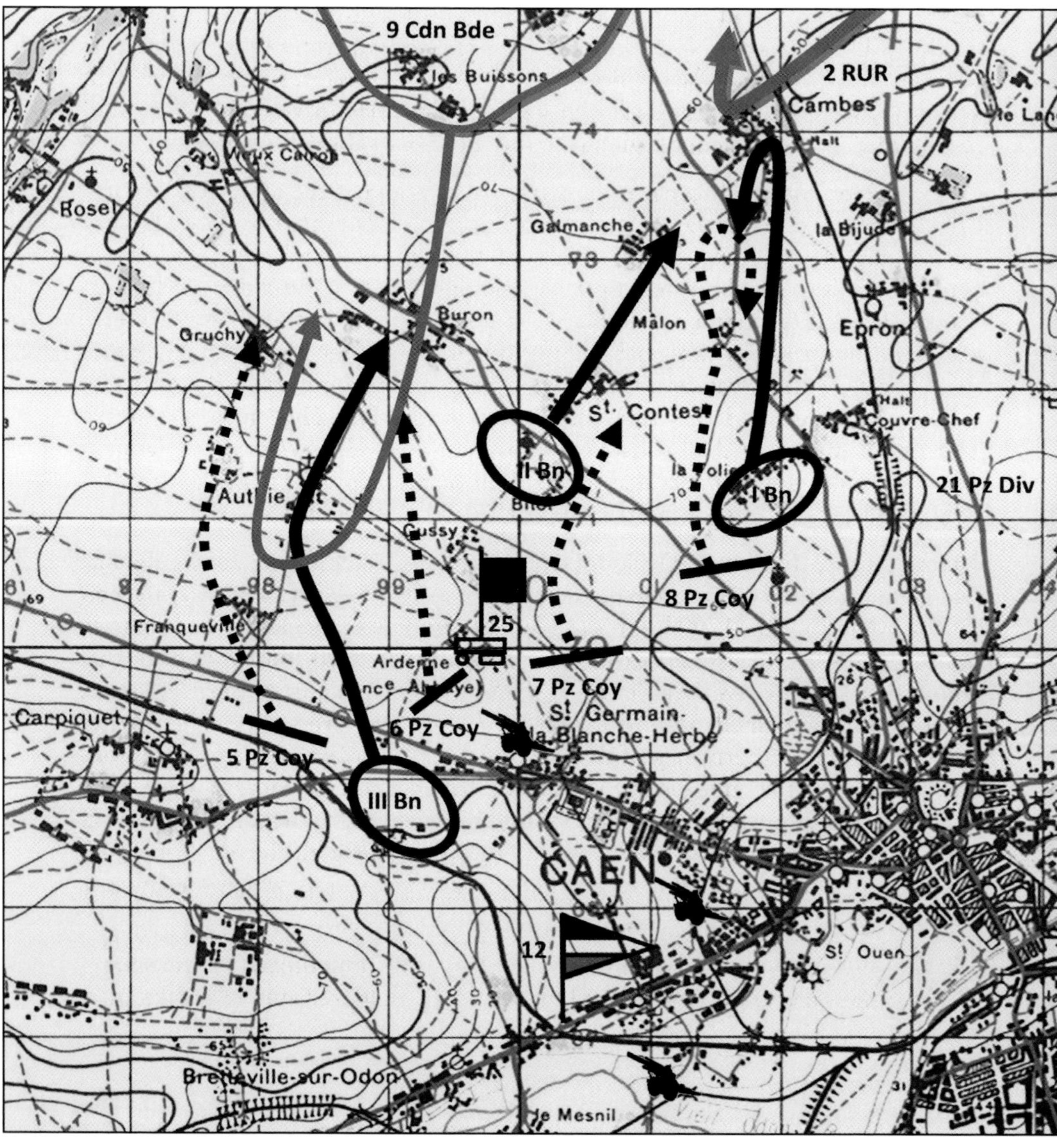

become entangled with the Canadian 9 Brigade, which was advancing south through Buron and Authie. In the panzer grenadiers' centre, II/Battalion and a company of tanks had reached the farming hamlet of Galmanche largely unopposed, while *Sturmbannführer* Waldmüller's I Battalion was advancing north on Cambes and its woods. The result was that 2 RUR and I/25 SS *Panzergrenadiers* were going to fight an engagement in Cambes and the wooded parkland.

As there was still a gap between 3rd Division and the Canadians to the west, Colonel Harris's plan for the advance on Cambes was to cover the open right flank with a squadron of the East Riding Yeomanry's Shermans. The other available squadron was deployed in the centre in close support of Captain Aldworth's D Company, which was to deliver the assault. Providing artillery fire support were the 105mm Priests of 33 Field Regiment with their FOOs mounted in Sherman OP tanks; but once they had worked through the fire plan, the guns were called to support 1 Norfolk in Lebisey, and consequently little support was available to D Company later on in the attack. The RUR's other three rifle companies were halted alongside the Le Mesnil woods in reserve, where they were strafed by four enemy fighters. Major Ellison of the ERY wrote:

> The Colonel decided to use two squadrons to support the attack. 'A' went out to the right to form a protective screen and to shoot into the village from the flank; 'B' Squadron were to support from the left and go in with the infantry. We were all formed up along a wood ready to move when the Luftwaffe decided to intervene. Fighters came in very low and very fast and let go with their cannon and machine guns; fortunately they hit hardly anyone, and were off and away in a flash. They or some more returned in another twenty minutes, and this time the tanks managed to give them a better reception with their AA .5 machine guns, and there were vernacular claims by some crew commanders that they had smartened up their tails, though all appeared to be going on pretty well for their bases just the same.[2]

Captain Aldworth formed D Company up for the attack in the cover of some dead ground behind a low ridge between Le Mesnil and Anisy. They began their 1,500-yard advance at 1700 hours, still largely ignorant of what awaited them in Cambes thanks to the château's wooded grounds and a 10-foot stone wall that surrounded the park. As they were still a full 1,000 yards short of their objective, mortar bombs and shells started to burst. D Company pressed on, and as they approached the northern apex of the woods Captain Aldworth took two platoons towards the left face and his second-in-command, Captain Montgomery, took the third platoon, plus the men of company headquarters, to the right. Arriving at the wood they faced the problem of breaking into it through the tall stone wall. Lieutenant Jenkin, the commander of B Squadron's 3 Troop, which was in close support, recalled:

> At the start we were back behind the infantry, but sometime after the start I had a message to go forward and help them as they were pinned down by

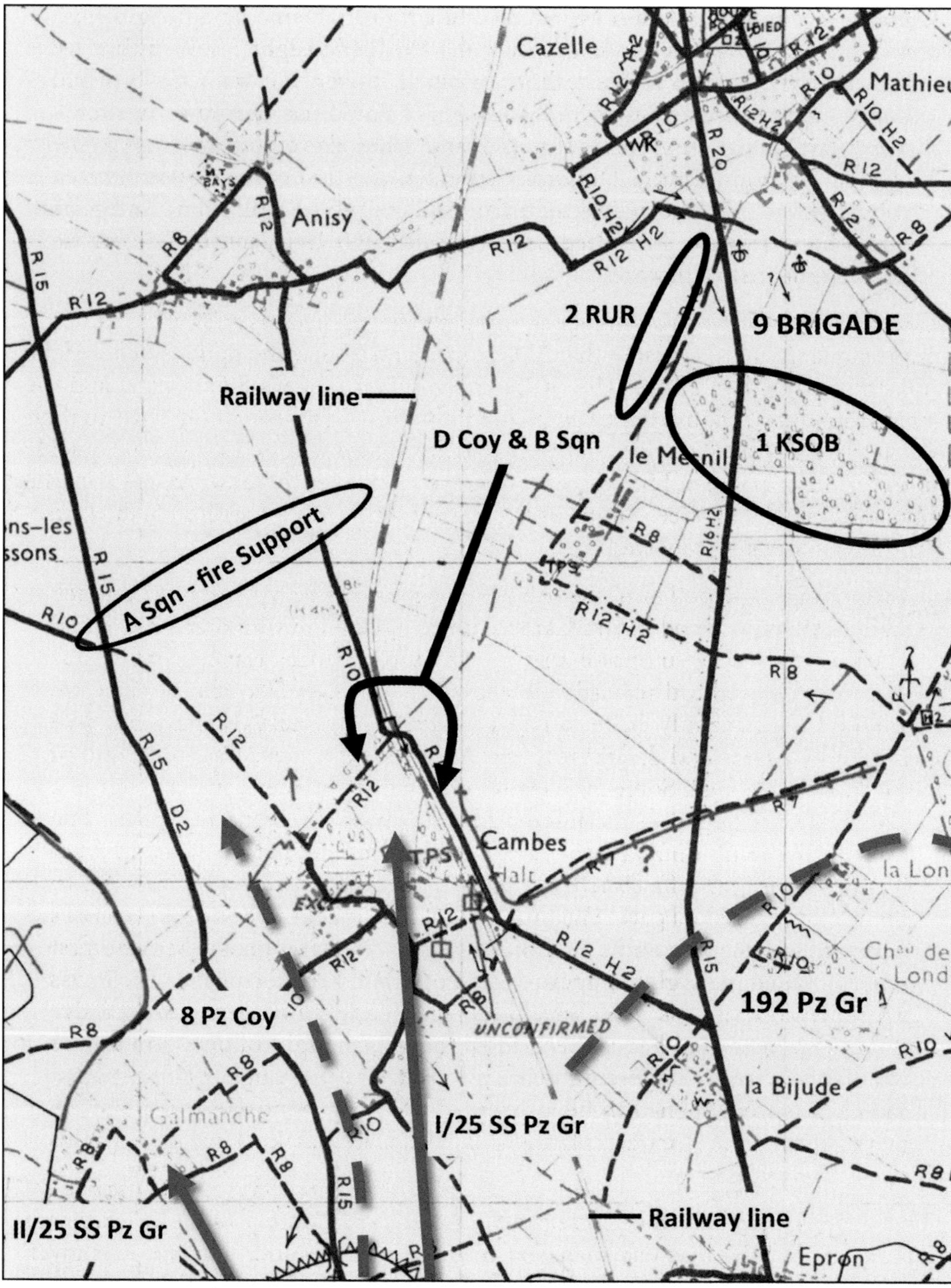

The attack of D Company 2 RUR, mid-afternoon of 7 June 1944. The railway line that ran north across the RUR's axis of advance was the boundary between the 21st and *Hitlerjugend* panzer divisions. Being a light railway, it was not an obstacle to manoeuvre. The 'wood' at Cambes referred to in the accounts was, in fact, parkland surrounded by a wall and belt of trees.

> machine-gun fire. We went forward as a troop and came up against a high wall. It was not possible to get over it. (With hindsight I realise that we should have gone up to the wall and pushed it over, but we had never had much built-up area training nor guessed we could use our tanks in such a way.) My next reaction was 'get round' and ordered everyone to circle to the right. Sergeant Tommy Dukes was point tank ... Tommy found a track which took us into the main street of the village and we realized we had gone into a hornets' nest. The place was swarming with Germans, but clearly we had caught them unawares.

It would appear that Waldmüller's young panzer grenadiers reached Cambes at approximately the same time that D Company arrived at the opposite end of the objective, while five Panzer IVs of *Obersturmführer* Siegel's 8 Company and the supporting Sig 150mm infantry guns fought with A Squadron of the ERY to their flanks. Inside Cambes, one of the panzers broke down and two were quickly knocked out, another bogged, and Siegel's own tank became trapped in the branches of a fallen tree. South of the village an SS NCO artilleryman, *Unterscharführer* Stöcker, reported:

> Everything went well until the infantry encountered heavy fire and the attack stalled. We now stood before Cambes on an open plain with our vehicles and guns. Under the assumption that the infantry would advance further, our platoon pulled ahead towards Cambes. We really had no choice since we would have probably been wiped out within the next 10 minutes. We reached Cambes and dived into a ravine. Suddenly, there was the sound of tracks in the village. Some 50 metres in front of us, a Sherman came out of a side road. It stopped in the intersection and spotted us and our guns. The turret of the tank immediately swung towards us and before we knew what was happening, the first shell was fired. We saved ourselves by jumping to the left over a locked gate. We found ourselves in a farm. Some of the crews were only about one and a half metres away from the guns when the first shell slammed through the tractors and guns. We were fortunate since it was probably an anti-tank shell which kept going. If it had been an explosive shell, we would have had it. Because of the great weight of our supplies, we did not carry armour-piercing weapons. Fortunately, a single infantryman of the I./25 who happened to be lost joined us at the front. He had a *Panzerfaust*. After some accurate planning, a Sherman was knocked out by this single *Panzerfaust*.

The tank engaged by the *Panzerfaust* was almost certainly one of Lieutenant Jenkin's Shermans that had managed to get into the wood. The account given by the regimental historian correlates with that of *Unterscharführer* Stöcker. Lieutenant Jenkin 'went straight up to the village with them [D Company], and when the infantry were held up by machine gun fire [they] went to ground with many casualties.' It not having occurred to him in his first battle that he could

The 150mm sIG 33 infantry gun and its Sd.kfz.10 tractor of the type used by the 25 SS *Panzer-grenadiers'* 13th Infantry Gun Company and knocked out by 3 Troop.

simply drive through the wall, Jenkin had driven around looking for a gap. Major Ellison wrote:

> He took his tanks into the village alone. They were shot at by three long-barrelled German Mk. IV tanks; they set the first on fire and disposed of another. In this very close and quick fighting the troop lost one of its tanks, and the whole crew except two, who were also unfortunately killed later.
>
> Lieutenant Jenkin still went on; he himself dismounted and manned an infantry anti-tank gun to dispose of the third German tank. In this engagement, for the loss of one tank his troop of four destroyed three enemy tanks, one armoured half-track, four ammunition lorries and a motorcycle.

Of the infantry's fight, Private Keenan of D Company later recorded:

> There was a 10-foot high wall around Cambes Wood and there wasn't a hole in that wall except for a hole in the corner and we had to go through that hole … We'd just got in and we could see anti-personnel mines hung up in the trees and mines on the ground. Machine gun fire opened up on us from the left and we were pinned down. The company commander, Major [*sic*] Aldworth, was up leading the men to the left and was killed. My platoon officer told me to tell Captain Montgomery, who was leading the other two platoons, that the company commander was dead and that we were pinned down and we were going to pull out. So I crawled the whole way back through the wood and up the other side to where the Captain was and told him. He agreed and I went back and told the platoon officer.
>
> We had to leave the wounded behind because the trees were that close together that you would only have killed them trying to drag them through so the idea was to leave them there and let the Germans look after them … but they did it the dirty way.

Later, 2 RUR found the soldiers of D Company, who they presumed to have been wounded in the D+1 action, shot in the head. If this unconfirmed report is correct, Cambes joins the list of war crimes committed by the *Hitlerjugend* in their first days in action, alongside those at Abbey Ardenne and Audrieu.

Captain Aldworth's body was later found inside the wood, confirming that the RUR infantry had broken through the wall on the left flank before the company was ordered back having lost thirty men. *Sturmbannführer* Waldmüller also ordered I/25 *Panzergrenadiers* to withdraw to positions 150 yards south of La Cambe. He argued that he was out on his own without contact with 21st Panzer Division to the east and II/Battalion had not yet come up on the opposite flank around Galmanche. *Oberleutnant* Fusten, the commander of No. 1 Company, recalled the difficulty he experienced in persuading his fanatically motivated *Hitlerjugend* soldiers to withdraw:

> The drive and determination of the attack were so great that disengagement from Cambes caused problems. Individual groups had doggedly worked their way forward. In some cases, and depending on the terrain, they had advanced significantly in the broken terrain – the village and the woods. They all had the will to reach the sea. It was difficult to enforce the order to withdraw. It encountered disbelief and was carried out only with hesitation. Still, the withdrawal movement did not have a negative impact on the superb fighting spirit.[3]

The soldiers of the two armies, less a handful of veterans, were in their first battle and had suffered equally heavy losses. They both recoiled, leaving La Cambe

Sturmbannführer Waldmüller, the commander of I/25 SS *Panzergrenadiers*.

General Sir Miles Dempsey, the commander of the British Second Army.

loosely in the hands of the *Hitlerjugend*'s outposts. Further casualties were suffered from increased mortar and artillery fire across 9 Brigade as they dug in around Anisy and Le Mesnil.

During the course of D+1, 9 Brigade had made over 2 miles of ground on the division's right flank before the engagement with the SS at Cambes brought the advance to a halt. They had, however, significantly closed the gap between themselves and the Canadians to their right, whose advance had similarly been halted in an encounter with the *Hitlerjugend* around the villages of Authie, Buron and St Contest.

The second of 3rd Division's D+1 advances on Caen had been halted, and more widely, I Corps, with the failure of 3rd Canadian Division to reach the Carpiquet area, had not enveloped the western side of the city. The Germans had succeeded in holding Caen against the first Allied onslaught, but General Dempsey was not yet ready to concede the prize.

The Second Battle of Cambes

With the arrival of the *Hitlerjugend* and their link-up with 21st Panzer to produce a strong front north and round to the west of Caen, 3rd Division was temporarily standing on the defensive, expecting a counter-attack that never came. The

Germans had realized that they needed to build up combat power before repeating the attack, and both 21st Panzer and 25 SS *Panzergrenadiers* were deployed holding ground. With I/25 SS *Panzergrenadiers* digging in just a few hundred yards south of Cambes, *Standartenführer* Meyer noted:

> During the night 7/8 June, I/25. Reinforced positions since a renewal of the enemy's attack was expected the next day. Scouting parties reconnoitred towards Cambes and determined that only the woods north of the village were in enemy hands.[4]

To the west, 26 SS *Panzergrenadiers* had arrived during the night of 7/8 June and were struggling for position with the Canadians and with the left flank of 50th Division east of Point 103.

But what of the intent to capture Caen? The 21st Army Group Narrative, quoting the G log of Headquarters Second Army for 8 June, states the intention of I Corps to have been:

> (a) to maintain the present position and contain the enemy in front of Caen in order to give a further 24 hours' build up for 51 H div.
> (b) the next phase to be a corps plan for the capture of Caen.

The author of the narrative concluded:

> There can be little doubt that the above intention, coupled with the necessity to ensure the security of the lodgement area established on D Day, which was subject of intense enemy reaction particularly to the bridgehead west of the Orne, were the main concern of the Headquarters during this period under review. It must have been a period of some anxiety since the reserves available not already committed never amounted to more than one division and one armd bde (51 H div and 4 Armd Bde); yet it was of the utmost importance to retain the initiative and as conceived in the original OVERLORD plan seize Caen and the ground to its south for the construction of airfields as quickly as possible.[5]

During the course of 8 June, the RUR's commanding officer and gunners of 33 Field Regiment conducted a series of recces for a deliberate battalion attack on Cambes from Anisy, for which Colonel Harris his gave orders at 1630 hours. These were lacking much detail on the enemy, since the wall around the château grounds and tree cover at the northern end of the village prevented effective recce by the company commanders. It was correctly thought that Cambes was lightly held by SS outposts. It was, however, apparent that I/25 SS *Panzergrenadiers* now had the support of their II/Battalion in Galmanche, 500 yards to the south-west of Cambes, and of 192 *Panzergrenadiers* in La Bijude, a similar distance to the south-east.

During the short hours of darkness on 8/9 June, no-man's-land was busy. After dark, C Company carried out a nuisance raid on the German positions, and for their pains were promptly counter-raided in Le Mesnil. So as not to concede the moral high ground, the Germans were raided again before dawn.

To ensure maximum fire support from the divisional gun group, the first medium guns ashore and the ships' artillery, their availability had to be coordinated for the renewed attack on Cambes. Hence, 'Zero Hour' was to be 1500 on 9 June, with the leading companies crossing their start line at 1515 hours.[6] The 6-inch guns of a HMS *Dane* of Bombardment Force E engaged the village and woods for five minutes, while the divisional artillery took on Galmanche. The 2nd Middlesex added the fire of 4.2-inch mortars and Vickers machine guns to the bombardment. *Standartenführer* Meyer observed that most of the British fire fell in Cambes, which was, unknown to the RUR, largely no-man's-land. Neutralization of the flanking German positions of Galmanche and La Bijude was, however, more effective.

Colonel Harris gave his mission as: '2nd Bn The Royal Ulster Rifles will capture and consolidate Cambes.' They were to form up south of Anisy for an attack from the north beneath a low but distinct ridge 1,000 yards from Cambes, with A Squadron of the East Riding Yeomanry (ERY) in support on the immediate right. Already tactics were developing away from the doctrine preached on the training areas of the UK.

> This involved the tanks moving independently and selecting positions from which they could 'shoot in the infantry' with observed fire from their 75mm guns and Browning machine guns. It proved most effective and was warmly appreciated by the infantry whom the ERY supported. This was partly because the tanks were not so close to them as to draw enemy fire. This became their standard tactic with both the 3rd British and later the 51st Highland Divisions.[7]

The aim was that the tanks, approaching from a different direction, would arrive on the enemy position at the same time as the infantry to provide close support. Of the ERY's other two sub-units, C Squadron was covering the left flank, particularly La Bijude, while B Squadron remained in reserve at Le Mesnil. Additional armour support was provided by a troop of five AVREs, which with their petard mortars were to fire demolition rounds at the wall and into the village houses during their clearance. As mines had been encountered during the attack on 7 June, Royal Engineer mine-clearance teams accompanied the infantry.

With Brigadier Smith on the ground mounted in a carrier, Colonel Harris would command the infantry concentrating on the assault on Cambes, and the CO of the ERY would oversee the armoured fight, particularly on the flanks. With his adjutant acting as gunner, and going forward in his Sherman to a position where he could exercise command most effectively, the colonel was greeted by enemy AP fire. Discretion was required, and he pulled back to a position from where he could command effectively, rather than be distracted by having to exchange fire with the enemy.

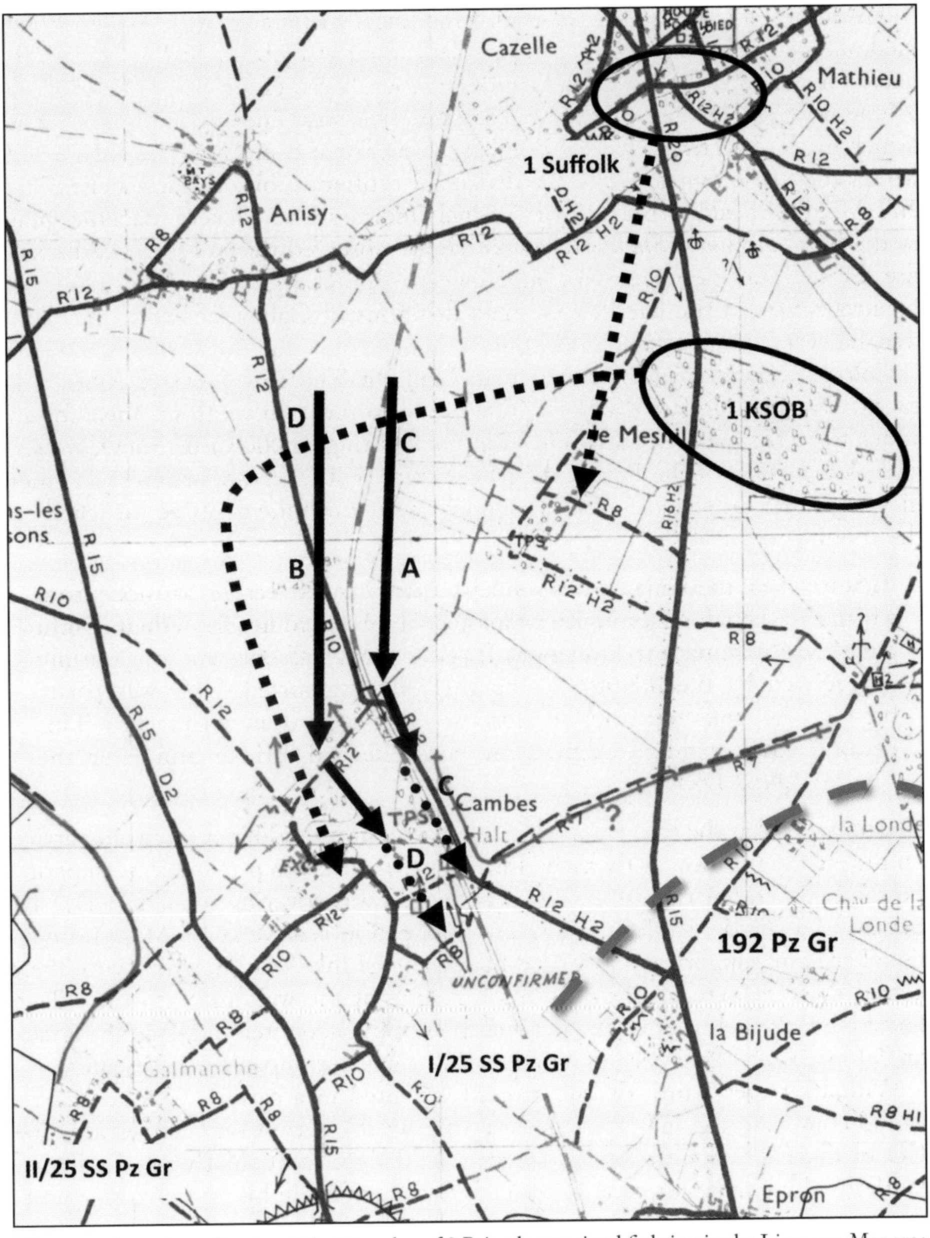

The second attack on Cambes. The Lincolns of 9 Brigade remained fighting in the Lion-sur-Mer area with 8 Brigade, so the Sufolks joined 9 Brigade for the attack on Cambes and the projected exploitation.

Meanwhile, at 1445 hours the Suffolks marched for their assembly area around the Le Mesnil château, ready to take over the advance and attack Galmanche in the second phase of the attack. Their regimental history records:

> The track was littered with the folding bikes brought ashore by the battalions of 9 Brigade three days before. They had ceased to be of any use as they had been run over by tracked vehicles. The Battalion reached its Assembly Area around Le Mesnil farm as the barrage supporting 2 RUR began. The sound was enormous, both terrifying and impressive in its effect. The occupants of the farm suddenly realised that perhaps it would no longer be advisable to remain there. They started to pack up some belongings and moved out in a great hurry, leaving a farmyard with a lot of animals still in it.

The RUR's attack began at 1515 hours with two companies forward, B Company right and A Company left, and D and C following.

> The advance having commenced, the first objective was reached at 1630 hrs. The men advanced in good order and were well spaced out, direction being steadied by the Commanding Officer from the left. On reaching the ridge some 1,100 yards from the objective, whence they could be permanently observed by the enemy, they advanced under a heavy barrage of mortar and shell fire accompanied by machine gun fire. In spite of this, the Battalion continued the advance in open order keeping perfect distance with the same concern as that shown on a company field firing exercise.

The Commanding Officer of the East Riding Yeomanry was watching the advance from the start line, and later confessed that he had said to himself, 'This is where they get to ground, and the attack is held up.' However, to his surprise, the RUR continued, although Rifleman Keenan was wounded during the advance:

> In that second attack we came under heavy shelling from the Germans and about 150 yards from the edge of the wood an 88 dropped close to me injuring my side and that was my war finished. There was heavy shelling that day and when I got hit, I was glad that it hadn't been a bigger one.
>
> I made my way back through the corn field and came across two stretcher bearers from our unit who had both been shot in the knee by machine gun or sniper fire. We did first aid on each other and eventually were moved back to our own medical post and I was moved back then down to the beach into a big tent and then shipped back to England.

Under flanking fire from Galmanche and La Bijude, B and A companies advanced, but anti-tank guns in La Bijude knocked out three of the AVREs. However, two troops of A Squadron heading for Cambes had 'dashed forward through the infantry with their guns blazing, subduing the Germans temporarily' – but long enough for B Company break through the wall and into the

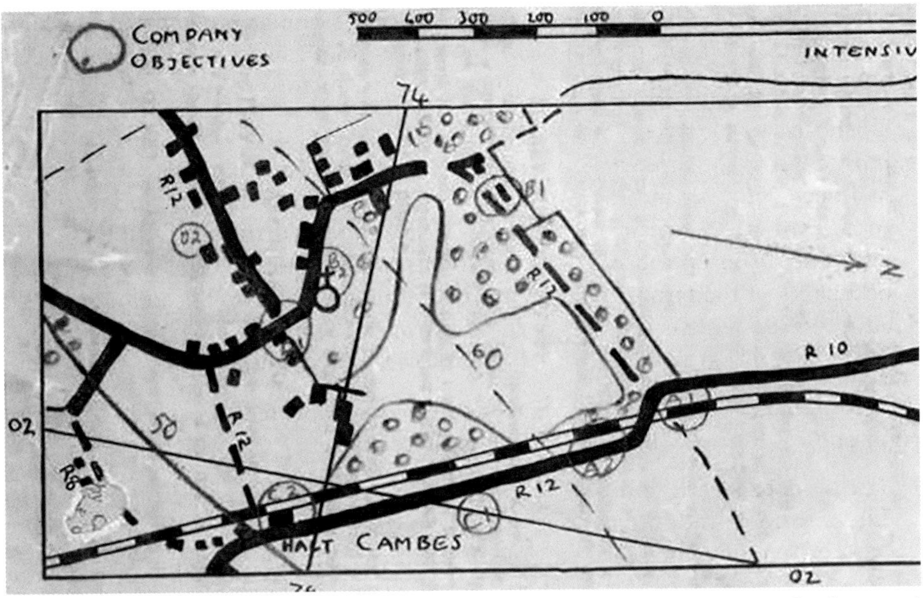

A section of a sketch map from 2 RUR's war diary showing the company objectives for the second attack on Cambes. The attack was from the north i.e. right to left on the map above.

wood on its north-western face. Rifleman Dorsey was with B Company on the right:

> We got into the wood; it was more like a park really, with grass areas that we feared to cross but for the size of the tanks. I didn't see any live Germans but the noise was tremendous, mortars and bullets were flying everywhere, multi-coloured tracer ricocheting off the tanks and the walls of the houses. We knew where we were heading as we could see the battered church tower through the trees ahead of us. We lost one man hit from our section on the way through the corn but by the time we were told to 'reorg' [halt, deploy for immediate defence and reorganize] there was only the corporal and three of us.

Meanwhile, A Company, having secured the northerly point of the wood, advanced down the north-eastern face of Cambes to their objective, where C Company took over the advance to the railway halt. With B Company having reached the area of the church, the significantly reduced D Company passed through them to clear the remainder of the village. The Shermans were joined by the two surviving AVREs in helping the infantry of C and D companies to clear the already largely destroyed houses, some of which were burning. Only one of the five AVREs that started out survived the battle. Once the rifle companies were in Cambes, the battalion's anti-tank guns were on the move forward. 'In the face of accurate 88mm and mortar fire they succeeded in being manhandled into position, with the exception of one detachment, which had received a direct hit from an 88mm shell. The gun was later recovered.'

The AVREs were not alone amongst the British armour in taking casualties; out in the open the ERY were fighting their own battle. The *Hitlerjugend*'s 7 Company II/25 SS *Panzergrenadiers*, with *Obersturmführer* Havermeister commanding No. 1 Platoon (*Zug*), was dug in at Galmanche facing north. He recalled his battle with the ERY squadrons:

> When the commander of the *Pakzug* [anti-tank platoon] reported to me at the command post of I.*Zug*, a tank assembly at Buissons, I was initially sceptical but then believed his assertions. We quickly brought the three PaKs, under cover of the south-west park wall in the orchard, behind I.*Zug* into the prepared open firing positions. We had barely taken cover when ten panzers started to move out of Buissons. I was so startled that I did not immediately recognize the direction of their movement.
>
> The attack was obviously not meant for us, but for I.*Bataillon* on our right. The Canadians [*sic*] had apparently no knowledge of the protrusion of our front line, almost abreast of the north-western edge of Cambes. In any case, their commanders led the attack from open hatches with visual contact, in the direction of Cambes. I held back the *Pak* commander until the ideal distance existed and ordered I.*Zug* to join in with machine guns and sharpshooters as soon as the first *Pak* shell was fired. The *Pak* commander opened the fireworks at his discretion almost immediately from all three guns simultaneously on the enemy flank. Within a few minutes, six tanks were knocked out and the others were driving in wild curves, their commanders dead. Crews who bailed out suffered heavy losses from the fire of I.*Zug*. Only then did artillery fire on I. Battalion set in.

The ERY described this as 'withering fire', with Lieutenant Brokke's tank being one of those 'driven in wild curves' until it burst into flames. Nonetheless, the surviving tanks of the squadron stuck to their task, firing off all their ammunition.

Meanwhile, at Brigade Main HQ, where General Rennie was observing the attack, the situation was far from clear. The KOSB's war diary recorded:

> The situation of 2 R.U.R. in Combes was unknown at Headquarters 9 British Brigade. The battalion rear link had great difficulty in moving forward, and forward to rear communications [*sic*] had broken down. Although a success signal had been observed about 1615 hours it did not satisfy the Divisional Commander who was at Brigade Headquarters. The Brigadier had gone forward earlier in his carrier and nothing had been heard further from him. It later transpired that this carrier had been hit and set on fire, though Brigadier Orr escaped unhurt. The Divisional Commander placed the Commanding Officer 1 K.O.S.B., Lieut. Colonel Ronny, temporarily in command of the brigade and ordered 1 K.O.S.B. to attack and consolidate Cambes from the unit's existing position in Le Mesnil wood. The battalion

Rifleman Bailey, RUR, was killed in action during the attack on Cambes on 9 June 1944.

was temporarily commanded by the battalion second-in-command, Major Coverdale.

Two companies of the KOSB were immediately sent forward to assist and consolidate. They came under machine-gun fire from the left, but the advance continued thanks to a smokescreen laid by the battalion's 3-inch mortar platoon. Arrival on their objective to the right of 2 RUR 'was greeted by a further spasm of very heavy 88mm and mortar fire, but fortunately some cover was available in the form of motor transport bays and some trenches.' The leading companies were shortly joined by the remainder of the battalion fighting in the woods and village as darkness fell. One commentator noted: 'With two battalions in such a small area it is a wonder that they didn't fire on each other.' As dusk settled, and with the Germans' main positions south of the village intact, there was clearly not going to be any exploitation. There was no attempt to produce a coherent defence, and the KOSB's companies joined those of 2 RUR in digging in where they were for the night.

During the fighting, it had seemed for a while that the subsequent phases of the operation to advance on Galmanche and St Contest would be able to go ahead. The Suffolks' regimental historian recorded:

> Meanwhile the CO [Colonel Goodwin] had gone forward in his carrier to be with Brigade Headquarters to wait for the word for the start of Phase 2. The

> CO when he heard that the codeword for Phase 2 had come over the wireless went forward to make a reconnaissance. As the carrier moved forward it was hit by a shell from an 88mm gun. The Intelligence Officer Lieutenant Paddy Keville and the signaller Lance Corporal Stevens were killed and the CO badly wounded. Major Kit Gough as second in command back at the farm was informed and calmly took over command. It turned out that the code word received had been for Phase 2 of the RUR attack.

Consequently, the Suffolks remained in the area of Le Mesnil as the brigade's firm base. Despite the all too prevalent mistakes with code words, overall it had been a well-planned, coordinated and executed attack; but it had taken two battalions to secure a village that was held only by SS outposts. The casualties suffered during the attack largely resulted from mortar and flanking machine-gun fire, but as the advance progressed through the village they were also caused by I/25 *Pannzergrenadiers*' main positions to the south. As 9 Brigade's battalions began to dig in and consolidate their position, enemy mortar and artillery shell fire redoubled and continued for around five hours without intermission.

The RUR's casualties for 9 June were three officers and forty-one other ranks killed, ten officers and 134 ORs wounded, and one officer and ten ORs missing: a total of 196 casualties. German casualties were, considering the scale of the fighting, low: twenty-five reported for the day, and the I/25 SS *Panzergrenadiers* barely mention the attack in their war diary.

German sources record several attacks being launched on 192 *Panzergrenadiers* around La Bijude east of the German divisional boundary and claim that these were broken up by fire. There is, however, no record of such attacks being launched by 9 Brigade or 185 Brigade to the east. The timings are such that they were most probably the movement of the KOSB in Le Mesnil Wood just before the afternoon attack and the later arrival of the Suffolks to take over from the KOSB as the brigade's firm base. Either way, these movements attracted enemy attention away from Cambes during the evening and no doubt disrupted the expected counter-attack on 2 RUR and the KOSB.

The two battalions remained in Cambes, while the Suffolks dug in around Le Mesnil and its château. Following three full torrid days in defence at close quarters with the enemy, 2 RUR were relieved in their defensive positions as part of a rotation of battalions that lasted a month.

The report on D+3's fighting reads:

> The two main actions of Lebisey and Cambes end the major activities of 3 British Division for the period under review. Much had been accomplished and even if the primary task, the capture of Caen, or at least the insurance of securing observation on that town, still eluded this division, at least contact had been made with the Canadians on the right, an unbroken front with depth and solidarity had been built up in the face of bitter enemy opposition, and security of the vital beaches in rear had been assured.

By the end of the fighting, Cambes château was reduced to a ruin; it was never rebuilt.

> With the general stiffening of the enemy opposition it now became apparent that no breakout from the bridgehead could take place, and so far as 3 British Division was concerned Caen must remain a tantalising and unattainable prize until the build up over the beaches, in men and material, had been vastly increased. Inevitably this will take time, longer perhaps than the troops, still full of fight, could appreciate. A lengthy period of active defence followed which everyone throughout the division was to find most irksome.

The 3rd Division had suffered 630 casualties on D Day, and further heavy losses, particularly at Lebisey and Cambes, had exceeded these by D+3. As an example of the arrival of battle casualty replacements, the RUR's war diary noted that '1st line Reinforcements arrived consisting of 1 Captain, 6 Subalterns and 129 Other Ranks.' These were only partial replacements for the combined losses of over 225 men from the attacks on Cambes and attrition while in defence. It was apparent from the early days of the campaign that, thanks to the intensity of the fighting and the resulting high number of casualties, the 21st Army Group's estimate of the number of unit reinforcements required was inadequate. Consequently, the replacement depots were quickly emptying, and Second Army formations and units would soon be reduced in size. The fighting during the immediate post-D Day period by 3rd Division was an indication of a manpower crisis that would by the end of the campaign in Normandy see divisions, brigades and units being disbanded and their soldiers sent to others to maintain their fighting strength.[8]

Sappers with mine detectors pass a platoon of Universal Carriers and 6-pdr anti-tank guns in cover in a sunken road north of Lebisey Wood on 8 July.

How many of these men of 2 RUR photographed on D Day had become casualties by D+3?

Chapter Eleven

'The End of the First Phase'

With the failure to advance beyond Cambes, it was obvious to divisional, corps and army commanders that the German deployment across the north of Caen was solid. The decision was made that for the time being there were to be no further attempts by Second Army to capture the city by direct attack. The 21st Army Group Chief of Staff, Major General de Guingand, wrote:

> Montgomery had some very good reasons for not continually pressing the attack on Caen beyond the early stages. To start with, the enemy was there in considerable strength. Then a failure here might jeopardise the whole plan, for it should be remembered that an enemy success against our hinge would have meant the over-running of our beaches and of our supplies. The country was suitable for defence in the area which we held, and the Orne and Odon rivers supplied natural obstacles. Further to the East it was more open, and not so suitable. So once our initial efforts to rush Caen had proved unsuccessful and the enemy had reinforced that area, the whole aspect had changed.[1]

The War Office report provides further context:

> The Intelligence appreciation on the evening of 9th June was that the first phase of the battle was now over; the coastal crust had been broken. We were now involved in that second phase when the enemy's divisions west of the Seine, his tactical reserves for the NEPTUNE area, were assembling. The enemy build-up was increasing but not at the rate we had anticipated, thanks to the cutting of the Seine bridges and the mounting of the threat to the Pas de Calais.[2]

Another reason not to become overextended at Caen was the disappointing rate and quantity of the all-important Allied build-up, which would in itself constrain future operations, as explained in the 21st Army Group's Administrative history:

> The build-up was already showing signs of falling behind schedule. Discharges on D Day, particularly in the early part of the day, were slower than had been planned owing to lack of exits, congestion on the beaches, and rough weather. Damage and losses of small craft had been high. This all resulted in craft returning late to the United Kingdom and in lesser numbers than estimated.
>
> The situation as reported by BUCO (Build Up Control Organisation) at 1600 hours was that the craft build-up for D plus 2 and D plus 3 would,

Major General Freddie de Guingand.

therefore, be some 12 hours behind schedule and only about 40 per cent to 60 per cent of plan.[3]

With losses of landing craft and Rhino Ferries during the passage and on D Day, and stranded craft obstructing the beach, delays multiplied over the following days; and as a result stocking Beach Maintenance Area (BMA) Moon behind SWORD Beach, enemy artillery fire from the east exacerbated delays. However, a week after D Day, BMA Moon was abandoned following a German bombing and/or shelling of the rear area that destroyed 100,000 gallons of fuel and 400 tons of ammunition.

Throughout the period from D Day to 9 June, the German intention remained to launch a concerted counter-attack on the Allied lodgement. It was temporarily suspended following an air attack on the headquarters of Panzer Group West, but Hitler and OKW continued to harbour an intent to drive the Allies back into the sea long after Rommel and his commanders on the ground had seen that such a

The positions held by 25 SS Panzer Grenadiers from the end of the invasion's first phase until Operation CHARNWOOD.

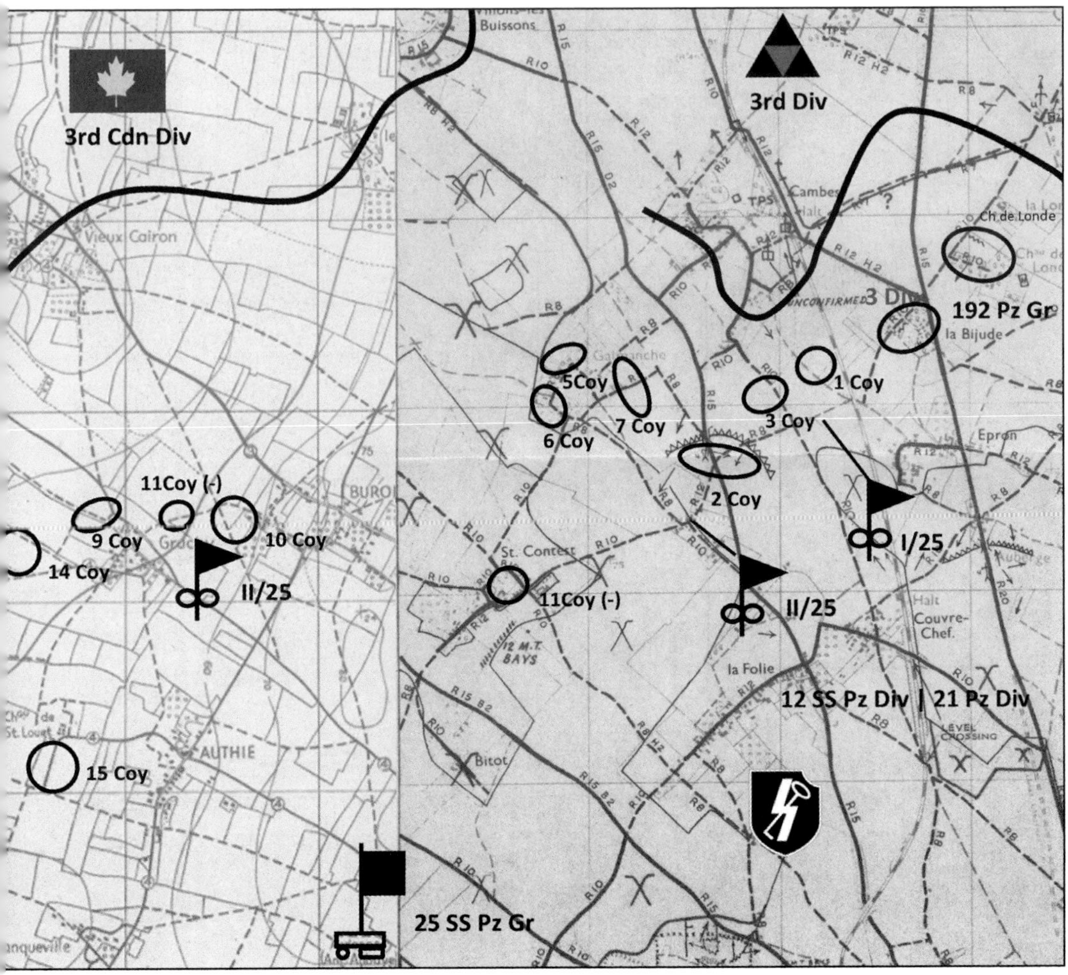

move was impossible. In the meantime, partly to buy time to gather strength for his counter-attack and partly because of Hitler's general refusal to countenance withdrawal, German forces were to rope off the Allied lodgement. The Führer's reaction to any withdrawal was that it moved the Allies and disaster one step closer to the Reich and Berlin. Consequently, even though his generals advocated withdrawing out of range of naval gunfire, OKW ordered them to stand and fight in the shadow of the Allied navies' big guns. This, of course, meant that Caen was to be held by I SS Panzer Corps, and OKW stuck to the last to its pre-invasion assessment of the city's importance, despite all the clearly emerging disadvantages of doing so.

In the short-term, expectation of significant German counter-attacks ran high in the Second Army, as this account of preparations in 3rd Division's area illustrates:

> On 11 June General Montgomery visited headquarters 3 British Division and outlined what might be expected. As a result the divisional commander informed all within his division of what was to be anticipated and stressed, particularly to administrative units, the necessity for all to stand firm should the eventuality arrive.This would allow already made countermeasures to be put into effect. Meanwhile the whole divisional area was prepared in detail to withstand the expected blow. Defence positions were dug deeper and improved, defensive fire plans were overhauled, and the field companies RE, assisted by large infantry working parties, laid down defensive minefields across the whole divisional front; these were effectively covered by the machine gun of 2 Middlesex or the anti-tank guns of 20 A Tk Regiment RA. The armoured units of 27 Armoured Brigade were also disposed in this counter-attack role and daily moved out from harbour areas to the then planned defence positions where constant watch was maintained.[4]

For General Dempsey's Second Army, with the way south through Caen to the airfield sites blocked by a pair of panzer divisions, the main effort was switched south on the axis Bayeux–Tilly-sur-Seulles–Villers-Bocage. Here XXX Corps met Panzer *Lehr* head-on as it arrived piecemeal in Normandy, and the belated committal of 7th Armoured Division into the Caumont Gap (Operation PERCH) was halted by I SS Panzer Corps' Tigers at Villers-Bocage. Elsewhere on its front, XXX Corps' fighting culminated in the capture of Tilly, but with its divisions exhausted.

For the Germans, with too few infantry divisions, the panzer divisions arriving piecemeal and the threat that developed south of Bayeux, which called for a shift and consequent dissipation of combat power to the west, General Geyr von Schweppenburg, Commander of Panzer Group West, commented in his post-war interview, 'Thus the fist was unclenched ...'

The tempo of the fighting in Normandy was greatly reduced by the north-easterly storm that brought the inload of supplies down to a trickle between 19 and 22 June. These few days not only gave the Germans the chance to reinforce

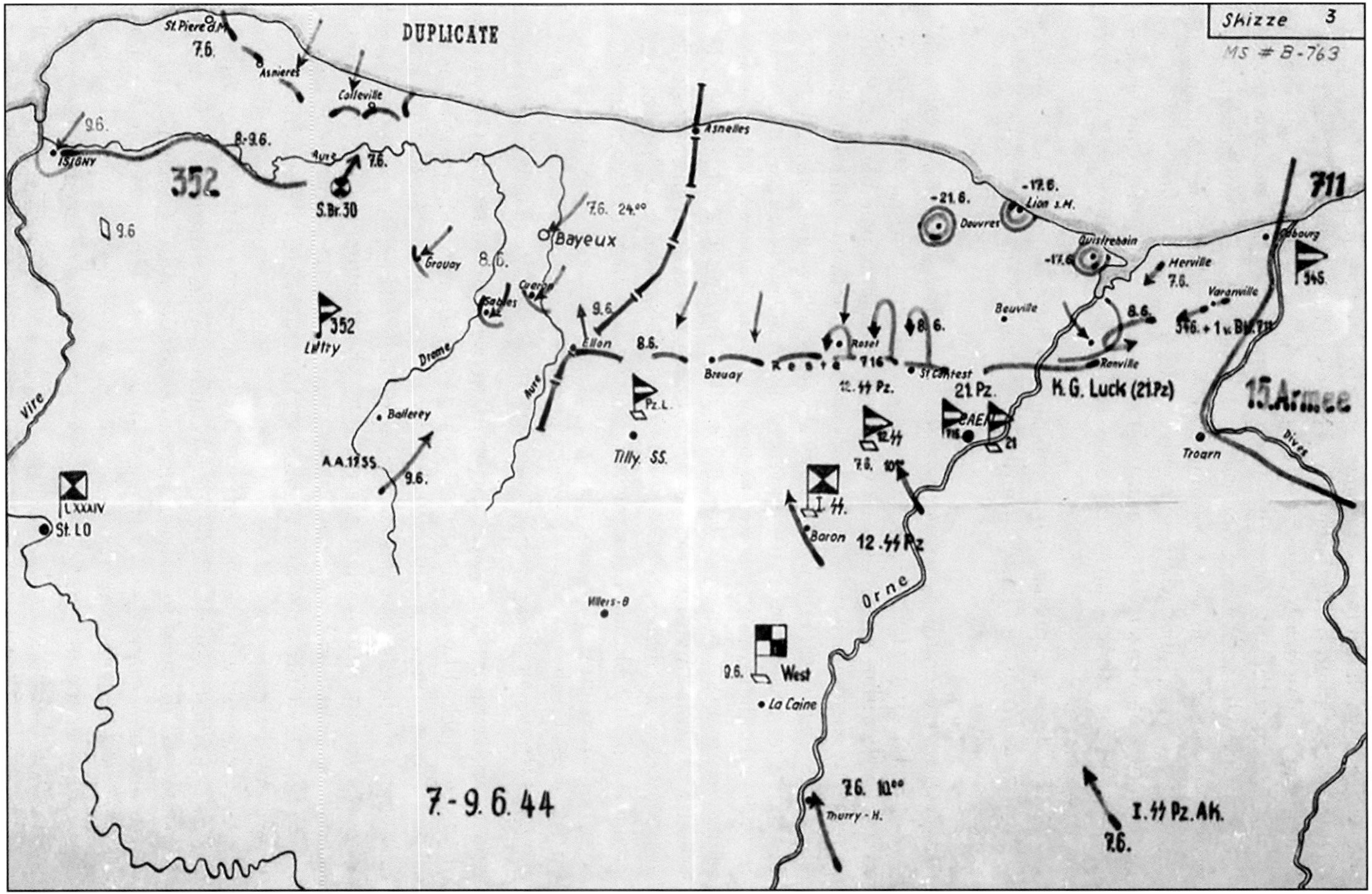

The German situation, 7–9 June.

and re-supply without the attentions of the Allied air forces, but reduced stocks of, for instance, 25-pounder artillery ammunition in the Allied rear areas to a critical level of just twenty-five rounds per gun. It took three days of frenetic labour to gather sufficient ammunition and complete (almost) the deployment of 43rd Wessex Division for Operation EPSOM, which was General Montgomery's next attempt to capture Caen, this time by envelopment.

The 3rd Division, meanwhile, remained in defence to the north of Caen, but they were to be by no means passive, although 'A lengthy period of active defence followed, which everyone throughout the division was to find most irksome.' Trenches had been dug and mines laid in anticipation of serious German counter-attack, and defences manned for days on end. Many of the division's war diaries emphasized the detrimental effect of enforced inactivity on morale. One stated:

> Men become more and more like vegetables, being forced to sit in one or two man slit trenches for long periods and how this vegetable growth is encouraged by enemy shelling and mortaring from which there is little relief . . . This atmosphere is encouraged most the further forward the troops are, being most noticeable in the forward infantry . . . The only means to counter boredom and maintain both morale and the fighting spirit of the forward infantry is to dominate no-man's-land by ceaseless and vigorous patrolling . . . For the next few weeks the infantry soldiers throughout the division were kept hard at this activity and the training gained was to prove inestimable value in the weeks of fighting that were to come. All units speak of the value of obtained by this period of activity during this period.

Mortar and machine-gun 'runs' by the Vickers platoons and 4.2-inch mortars of 2 Middlesex, and the 3-inch mortars of the infantry battalions, were a feature of this period. The aim was to disrupt German defences, particularly their re-supply, and cause attrition. These 'runs' were a deployment into positions, often in no-man's-land, followed by several minutes of fast and furious fire and then a hasty withdrawal, normally with German mortar bombs and shells falling as the platoons drove off in their carriers.

Even though the aim of taking Caen by direct assault from the north had for the time been abandoned, that is not to say that no attacks were mounted. During Operation EPSOM, I Corps was to conduct Operations MITTEN and ABERLOUR, two of a whole raft of attacks designed to conceal the true main effort, distract attention and tie down reserves. MITTEN proved to be an expensive partial success, but ABERLOUR was abandoned. The intent to take Caen by assault resumed in early July, with the Canadians closing in from the west in Operation WINDSOR, the attack on Carpiquet airfield, barracks and village. This was a necessary precursor to the main and successful assault on the city by three divisions of I Corps in Operation CHARNWOOD on 9 July 1944.

Appendix I

Führerbefehl No. 51

Führer Headquarters
3 November 1943

Top Secret

The Führer — 27 Copies
OKW/WFSt/Op.No. 662656/43 g.K. Chefs — Copy No ....

Directive No. 51

For the last 2½ years the bitter and costly struggle against Bolshevism has made the utmost demands upon the bulk of our military resources and energies. This commitment was in keeping with the seriousness of the danger, and the over-all situation. The situation has since changed. The threat from the East remains, but an even greater danger looms in the West: the Anglo-American landing! In the East, the vastness of the space will, as a last resort, permit a loss of territory even on a major scale, without suffering a mortal blow to Germany's chance for survival.

Not so in the West! If the enemy here succeeds in penetrating our defences on a wide front, consequences of staggering proportions will follow within a short time. All signs point to an offensive against the Western Front of Europe no later than spring, and perhaps earlier.

For that reason, I can no longer justify the further weakening of the West in favour of other theatres of war. I have therefore decided to strengthen the defences in the West, particularly at places from which we shall launch our long-range war against England. For those are the very points at which the enemy must and will attack; there – unless all indications are misleading – will be fought the decisive invasion battle.

Holding attacks and diversions on other fronts are to be expected. Not even the possibility of a large-scale offensive against Denmark may be excluded. It would pose greater nautical problems and could be less effectively supported from the air, but would nevertheless produce the greatest political and strategic impact if it were to succeed.

During the opening phase of the battle, the entire striking power of the enemy will of necessity be directed against our forces manning the coast. Only an all-out effort in the construction of fortifications, an unsurpassed effort that will enlist all available manpower and physical resources of Germany and the occupied areas, will be able to strengthen our defences along the coasts within the short time that still appears to be left to us.

Stationary weapons (heavy AT guns, immobile tanks to be dug in, coast artillery, shore-defence guns, mines, etc.) arriving in Denmark and the occupied West within the near future will be heavily concentrated in points of main defensive effort at the most vulnerable coastal sectors. At the same time, we must take the calculated risk that for the present we may be unable to improve our defences in less threatened sectors.

Should the enemy nevertheless force a landing by concentrating his armed might, he must be hit by the full fury of our counter-attack. For this mission ample and speedy reinforcements of men and materiel, as well as intensive training, must transform available larger units into first-rate, fully mobile general reserves suitable for offensive operations. The counter-attack of these units will prevent the enlargement of the beachhead, and throw the enemy back into the sea.

In addition, well-planned emergency measures, prepared down to the last detail, must enable us instantly to throw against the invader every fit man and machine from coastal sectors not under attack and from the home front.

The anticipated strong attacks by air and sea must be relentlessly countered by Air Force and Navy with all their available resources. I therefore order the following:

(A) Army:

(1) The Chief of the Army General Staff and the Inspector General of Panzer Troops will submit to me as soon as possible a schedule covering arms, tanks, assault guns, motor vehicles and ammunition to be allocated to the Western Front and Denmark within the next three months. That schedule will conform to the new situation. The following considerations will be basic:

(a) Sufficient mobility for all panzer and panzergrenadier divisions in the West, and equipment of each of those units by December 1943 with 93 Mark IV tanks or assault guns, as well as large numbers of anti-tank weapons.

Accelerated reorganization of the 20 Luftwaffe Field Divisions into an effective mobile reserve force by the end of 1943. This reorganization is to include the issue of assault guns.

Accelerated issue of all authorized weapons to the SS Panzer Grenadier Division Hitler Jugend, the 21st Panzer Division, and the infantry and reserve divisions stationed in Jutland.

(b) Additional shipments of Mark IV tanks, assault guns, and heavy AT guns to the reserve panzer divisions stationed in the West and in Denmark, as well as to the Assault Gun Training Battalion in Denmark.

(c) In November and December, monthly allotments of 100 heavy AT guns models 40 and 43 (half of these to be mobile) in addition to those required for newly activated units in the West and in Denmark.

(d) Allotment of large numbers of weapons (including about 1,000 machine guns) for augmenting the armament of those static divisions that are committed for coastal defence in the West and in Denmark, and for standardizing the equipment of elements that are to be withdrawn from sectors not under attack.

(e) Ample supply of close-combat AT weapons to units in vulnerable sectors.

(f) Improvement of artillery and AT defences in units stationed in Denmark, as well as those committed for coastal protection in the occupied West. Strengthening of GHQ artillery.

(2) The units and elements stationed in the West or in Denmark, as well as panzer, assault gun, and AT units to be activated in the West, must not be transferred to other fronts without my permission. The Chief of the Army General Staff or the Inspector General of Panzer Troops will submit to me a report through the Armed Forces Operations Staff as soon as the issue of equipment to the panzer and assault gun battalions, as well as to the AT battalions and companies, has been completed.

(3) Beyond similar measures taken in the past, the Commander in Chief West will establish timetables for, and conduct manoeuvres and command post exercises on, the procedure for bringing up units from sectors not under attack. These units will be made capable of performing offensive missions, however limited. In that connection I demand that sectors not threatened by the enemy be ruthlessly stripped of all forces except small guard detachments. For sectors from which reserves are withdrawn, security and guard detachments must be set aside from security and alarm units. Labour forces drawn largely from the native population must likewise be organized in those sectors, in order to keep open whatever roads might be destroyed by the enemy air force.

(4) The Commander of German troops in Denmark will take measures in the area under his control in compliance with paragraph 3 above.

(5) Pursuant to separate orders, the Chief of Army Equipment and Commander of the Replacement Army will form *Kampfgruppen* in regimental strength, security battalions and engineer construction battalions from training cadres, trainees, schools, and instruction and convalescent units in the Zone of the Interior. These troops must be ready for shipment at 48 hours' notice.

Furthermore, other available personnel are to be organized into battalions of replacements and equipped with the available weapons, so that the anticipated heavy losses can quickly be replaced.

(B) Luftwaffe:

The offensive and defensive effectiveness of Luftwaffe units in the West and in Denmark will be increased to meet the changed situation. To that end, preparations will be made for the release of units suited for commitment in the anti-invasion effort, that is, all flying units and mobile Flak artillery that can be spared from the air defences of the home front, and from schools and training units in the Zone of the Interior. All those units are to be earmarked for the West and possibly Denmark.

The Luftwaffe ground organization in southern Norway, Denmark, northwestern Germany and the West will be expanded and supplied in a way that will – by the most far-reaching decentralization of own forces – deny targets to the enemy bombers, and split the enemy's offensive effort in case of large-scale operations. Particularly important in that connection will be our fighter forces. Possibilities for their commitment must be increased by the establishment of numerous advance landing fields. Special emphasis is to be placed on good camouflage. I expect also that the Luftwaffe will unstintingly furnish all available forces, by stripping them from less threatened areas.

(C) Navy:

The Navy will prepare the strongest possible forces suitable for attacking the enemy landing fleets. Coastal defence installations in the process of construction will be completed with the utmost speed. The emplacing of additional coastal batteries and the possibility of laying further flanking mine fields should be investigated.

All school, training and other shore-based personnel fit for ground combat must be prepared for commitment so that, without undue delay, they can at least be employed as security forces within the zone of the enemy landing operations.

While preparing the reinforcement of the defences in the West, the Navy must keep in mind that it might be called upon to repulse simultaneous enemy landings in Norway and Denmark. In that connection, I attach particular importance to the assembly of numerous U-boats in the northern area. A temporary weakening of U-boat forces in the Atlantic must be risked.

(D) SS:

The *Reichsführer*-SS will determine what Waffen-SS and police forces he can release for combat, security and guard duty. He is to prepare to organize effective combat and security forces from training, replacement, and convalescent units, as well as schools and other home-front establishments.

(E) The commanders-in-chief of the services, the *Reichsführer*-SS, the Chief of the Army General Staff, the Commander in Chief West, the Chief of Army Equipment and Commander of the Replacement Army, the Inspector General of Panzer Troops, as well as the Commander of German Troops in Denmark will report to me by 15 November all measures taken or planned.

I expect that all agencies will make a supreme effort toward utilizing every moment of the remaining time in preparing for the decisive battle in the West.

All authorities will guard against wasting time and energy in useless jurisdictional squabbles, and will direct all their efforts toward strengthening our defensive and offensive power.

signed: *Adolf Hitler*

Appendix II

Extracts from 3rd Infantry Division's Op O No. 1

These paragraphs of the Op O cover the planned action of the 3rd Division's three brigades on D Day.[1]

Intention

12. The 3rd British Infantry Division will land on QUEEN RED and WHITE beaches and capture CAEN, and a bridgehead SOUTH of the R ORNE at that place.

Method

13. The Assault Brigade (8 British Infantry Brigade Group)

(a) 8 British Infantry Brigade Group with under command 13/18 H, 5 Assault Regt RE (less two squadrons) and 4 and 41 Commandos will carryout the assault on QUEEN RED and WHITE beaches and secure the beach head to include high ground about PERIERS-SUR-LE-DAN – ST AUBIN – D'AQUENAY 0976.

(b) Tasks in Detail
 (i) Assault and clear the beaches of aimed fire to enable 5 Assault Regt RE and Divisional RE to construct vehicle exits and clear beach obstacles (see para 26).
 (ii) Relieve 6 Airborne Division at BENOUVILLE and RANVILLE bridges as soon as possible or, should it be necessary, to attack and capture these bridges. The initial force for this task will consist of not less than one rifle company and one squadron of tanks.
 (iii) The destruction as soon as possible of the battery at 102780.
 (iv) The capture of high ground about PERIERS-SUR- LE-DAN and the battery at 0777.
 (v) The destruction of the Coast Defence battery at OUISTREHAM for which task 4 Commando is specifically allotted.
 (vi) The mopping up of the coastal area to LUC-SUR-MER for which task 41 RM Commando is specifically allotted.

(c) The aim of the Assault Brigade must be to establish a firm base quickly with one battalion on the PERIERS-SUR-LE-DAN feature so as to deny this ground to the enemy until the original assault battalions have completed their mopping up tasks and *are* available to reinforce that position.

(d) As soon as the situation on the Divisional front permits, the bridgehead at RANVILLE and BENOUVILLE will be taken over by a Battalion Group from the Assault Brigade. This decision will be made by the Divisional Commander.

15. The Intermediate Brigade (185 Infantry Brigade Group)

(a) 185 Infantry Brigade Group with Staffs Yeo in support will land at approximately H+2½ hours and will capture CAEN and a bridgehead SOUTH of the R ORNE at CAEN.
(b) This advance will be carried out with speed and boldness so that the enemy's local reserves can be overcome quickly and the Brigade established on its objective ready to meet counter attacks by reserve formations which may develop towards the evening of D Day.

Armour will be used boldly in this advance but when defences are encountered which cannot be overcome by the advanced guard a coordinated quick attack supported by all the available artillery will achieve the best results. It is very important in an advance of this nature that the commander should retain a reserve battalion in hand and keep control of his armour so that any weakening of the enemy can be immediately exploited.

16. Reserve Brigade (9 British Infantry Brigade).

(a) 9 British Infantry Brigade Group with the support of E Riding Yeo will land about H+5 1/2 and afterassembling SOUTH of the QUEEN Beach will move to PLUMEOT 0478 into Divisional Reserve,
(b) The Reserve Brigade is mobile and will be prepared:
   (i) To move rapidly to a forward concentration area on the axis CAZELLE 0276 – CAMBES ST. CONTEST with the eventual task of protecting the right flank of 185 Infantry Brigade and preventing infiltration between the 9 Canadian Infantry Brigade and 185 Infantry Brigade.
   (ii) In the event of 185 infantry Brigade failing to penetrate the northern defences of CAEN to attack CAEN from the WEST should that course appear to offer immediate prospects of success.
   (iii) Should the Canadian advance be held up, the reserve brigade will be prepared to drive the enemy from high ground about COLOMBY-SUR-THAON 0076.
   (iv) The enemy position now in preparation immediately NORTH of CRESSEROS may have to be mopped up if this has not already been done by the Assault Brigade.

Tasks (ii) and (iii) will be ordered by the Divisional Commander. Task (iv) will be carried out, should it be found necessary, by the Brigade Commander, but the two bicycle battalions of the Brigade and B Riding Yeo will be held immediately in readiness to move. A liaison officer will be sent to Divisional HQ immediately the Brigade has landed.

Appendix III

Order of Battle
3rd British Division

OVERLORD Assault Phase

(Major General Rennie)

8th Infantry Brigade (Brigadier Cass)
1st Battalion, The Suffolk Regiment
2nd Battalion, The East Yorkshire Regiment
1st Battalion, The South Lancashire Regiment

9th Infantry Brigade (Brigadier Cunningham/Colonel Orr)
2nd Battalion, The Lincolnshire Regiment
1st Battalion, The King's Own Scottish Borderers
2nd Battalion, The Royal Ulster Rifles

185th Infantry Brigade (Brigadier Smith)
2nd Battalion, The Royal Warwickshire Regiment
1st Battalion, The Royal Norfolk Regiment
2nd Battalion, The King's Shropshire Light Infantry

Divisional Troops

- Machine Gun and Heavy Mortar Battalion: 2nd Battalion, The Middlesex Regiment
- Royal Artillery (Brigadier Mers)
  7th Field Regiment (9th, 16th and 17th/43rd Field Batteries)
  33rd Field Regiment (101st, 109th and 113th/114th Field Batteries)
  76th Field Regiment (302nd, 303rd and 454th Field Batteries)
  20th Anti-tank Regiment (41st. 45th, 67th and 101st Anti-tank Batteries)
- Royal Engineers (Lieutenant Colonel Cocks)
  17th, 246th and 253rd Field Companies
- Medical
  8th, 9th and 223rd Field Ambulances
- Royal Signals
  3rd Division Signals
- Provost
  3rd Division Provost Company

27th Independent Armoured Brigade (Brigadier Prior-Palmer)
13th/18th Royal Hussars
1st East Riding Yeomanry
The Staffordshire Yeomanry

1st Special Service Brigade (Brigadier Lord Lovat)
No. 3 Commando
No. 4 Commando
No. 6 Commando
No. 45 (Royal Marine) Commando

4th Special Service Brigade
No. 41 (Royal Marine) Commando

Royal Marines
5th Independent Armoured Support Battery

79th Armoured Division detachments

Royal Armoured Corps
A Squadron, 22nd Dragoons

Royal Engineers
HQ 5th Engineer Assault Regiment
77th and 79th Assault Squadrons
71st and 263rd Field Companies
629th Field Squadron

Royal Artillery
HQ 53rd Medium Regiment
218th Battery, 73rd Light Anti-Aircraft Regiment
322nd Battery, 93rd Light Anti-Aircraft Regiment
B Flight, 652nd Air Observation Point Squadron RASC

RASC
106th Brigade Company
90th Armoured Brigade Company

'Phantom' Detachment
GHQ Liaison Regiment

101 Beach Sub-Area
5th King's Regiment and 1st Buckinghamshire Regiment
- Royal Engineers
  - 84th and 91st Field Companies
  - 8th and 9th Stores Sections
  - 50th Mechanised Equipment Section
  - 9th, 999th and 1028th Port Operation Companies
  - 940th Inland Water Transport Operating Company

- RASC
  21st Transport Column
  39th, 101st, 299th and 633rd Transport Companies
  96th and 138th Detail Issue Depots
  237th and 238th Petrol Depots
- Medical
  16th Casualty Clearing Station
  9th, 12th, 20th, 21st and 30th Field Dressing Stations
- Ordnance
  11th and 12th Ordnance Beach Detachments
  44th Ordnance Ammunition Company
- REME
  20th and 21st Beach Recovery Sections
- Provost
  241st and 245th Provost Companies
- Labour Pioneer Corps
  53rd, 85th, 102nd, 129th, 149th, 267th, 292nd and 303rd Companies

German PWs being marched back to be handed over to No. 6 Beach Group. During the afternoon of D Day a PW cage was established, but the drill for the first few days was to get PWs away on baord returning landing craft as soon as possible.

Appendix IV

Wehrmacht Ranks and their Allied Equivalents

Wehrmacht	Allied
Oberschutze	Private First Class
Gefrieter	Lance Corporal
Obergefrieter	Corporal
Obergefrieter	Senior Corporal
Stabsgefrieter	HQ Corporal (Admin)
Unteroffizier	
Unterfelwebel	Lance Sergeant
Felwebel	Sergeant
Oberfelwebel	Colour/Staff Sergeant
Stabsfelwebel	Sergeant Major
Leutnant	Second Lieutenant
Oberleutnant	Lieutenant
Hauptmann	Captain
Major	Major
Oberstleutnant	Lieutenant Colonel
Oberst	Colonel

Appendix V

SS Ranks and their Allied Equivalents

Waffen SS		British Army	US Army
SS-*Brigadeführer*		Brigadier	Brigadier General
SS-*Oberführer*		(not applicable)	Senior Colonel
SS-*Standartenführer*		Colonel	Colonel
SS-*Obersturmbannführer*		Lieutenant Colonel	Lieutenant Colonel
SS-*Sturmbannführer*		Major	Major
SS-*Hauptsturmführer*		Captain	Captain
SS-*Obersturmführer*		Lieutenant	1st Lieutenant
SS-*Untersturmführer*		2nd Lieutenant	2nd Lieutenant
SS-*Sturmscharführer*		Regimental Sergeant Major	Sergeant Major
SS-*Hauptscharführer*		Sergeant Major	Master Sergeant
SS-*Oberscharführer*		(not applicable)	Technical Sergeant
SS-*Scharführer*		Colour Sergeant	Staff Sergeant
SS-*Unterscharführer*		Sergeant	Sergeant
SS-*Rottenführer*		Corporal	Corporal
SS-*Sturmmann*		Lance Corporal	(not applicable)
SS-*Oberschütze*		(not applicable)	Private 1st Class
SS-*Mann*		Private	Private

Soldiers aboard a DUKW of one of No. 6 Beach Group's RASC companies off loading combat supplies as a part of the build-up.

Congestion on the beach during the late morning of D Day.

Appendix VI

The Effect of the D Day Fire Plan?

Over the years the apparent failure of the D Day fire plan to destroy more of the beach defences has been much criticised by veterans and historians alike. The integrated fire plan for landings on 6 June had not been tried before on such a scale and there was over optimism with of its effect that 'exceeded all contemporary expectations.' For instance, Brigadier Lord Lovat was assured that by the time his commandos reached Objective BASS on the coast near Ouistreham, the fire control bunker would be rubble – its still very much standing today. Brigadier Parham, the Second Army's Brigadier Royal Artillery had an altogether more realistic view of the effectiveness of the fire power being directed at the *Wiederstandneste* and inland objectives. He kept a diary that documented the planning over the four months prior to D Day and in an entry on 31 May he predicted the effect of the fire plan, crucially beginning with the statement 'As long as the cloud allows the fire plan, given perfect weather and freedom from cloud (which is essential) . . .'

1. A vast quantity of moderately aimed assorted missiles will fall on or near or not so near the beach localities from H–30 to H.
2. There will be a vast pall of smoke. As a result the very high proportion of the fire which is dependent on direct laying, will go haywire. But so will the Huns'.
3. Defiladed AT guns on beaches will cause a lot of trouble as many will survive. They will be hard to KO and will account for a lot of our own DDs and Centaurs on some beaches.
4. Counter battery and counter mortar will be our biggest headache.
5. The successful engagement of hull down tanks (Tigers and Panthers) lying back 3,000–4,000 yards from beaches and covering our painful progress through minefields will be difficult.
6. We shall be badly short of aerial observation early on.
7. The battle on D Day and for the next days will be a very rough house indeed. On it the war's result depends. BUT . . . we are absolutely certain to be ashore in enough places to stay there. Nothing else matters and we will then win the war, sooner or later & we hope soon. The Hun commanders on the spot are in for an interesting, exciting and highly depressing day.

Brigadier Parham knew that the allies had very little other than the DD tanks that could target an anti-tank gun in a concrete bunker sited to fire in enfilade across

While the guns of the allied fleet were able to neutralise German coastal gun batteries and defences, destruction of concrete positions was minimal, even for the 15-inch guns of HMS *Ramillies*, seen here in action off the Normandy coast.

the beach and his notes makes clear, the fire plan required good clear skies and visibility. Eisenhower's decision by to launch the invasion in marginal weather, for example, meant that the US medium bombers were ordered to add three seconds to their bomb run, which placed the bombs a half mile inland not on the bunkers, etc. at the back of the beach, while other targets like HILLMAN and MORRIS were either not bombed or received a fraction of what was due.

Appendix VII

Special Interrogation Report by First Canadian Army

Gentl Edgar Feuchtinger, Comd 21 Pz Div

In common with all senior officers who were prisoners of the Western Allies, at the end of the war *Generallutenant* Fuchtinger was interviewed by German speaking intelligence officers who later wrote up notes on the interview. An extract of that interview regarding his division's D Day action is reproduced below.

Preparations for the Invasion

13. 21 Panzer Div, along with 2 and 116 Panzer Divs, came under Army Gp B for tactical employment, although their training was directed by Panzer Gruppe West. Thus, on D-Day, 21 Panzer Div did not know which Army corps was to direct it the moment the battle was joined. Gentl FEUCHTINGER had been given definite instructions that, in the event of an invasion, he was not to make any move until he had been given his orders from Army Gp B. The delay that subsequently ensured 21 Panzer Div was committed against the Allied forces was due to this complicated and the cumbersome chain or comd. To further muddle the picture 47 Panzer Corps had arrived in VERNON about the 28th May with the object of controlling the Panzer formations of Army Gp B. As far as 21 Panzer Div was concerned, it never did come under comd of 47 Panzer Corps. The Inf Corps of Seventh Army consisted of 81 Corps at ROUEN [*sic*] and 84 Corps at ST LO.

14. The warning system in the event of invasion consisted of two alarms; Alarm 1 confined all ranks to their billets and Alarm 2 had them all actually sitting in their vehicles prepared to move. Neither of these alarms were used when the invasion took place. The disposition of 21 Panzer Div in NORMANDY extended from PERIERS 0576 as far South as FALAISE, and from THURY-HARCOURT 9446 as far East as MEZIDON 2756, an area of over three hundred square miles. Its tactical role was both to support 716 Inf Div defending the coast and to act as a tactical reserve in the rear areas. The need for playing this dual role resulted in neither one being done effectively.

15. HQ of the div was at ST PIERRE-SUR-DIVES 2749, with a tactical HQ at THEVILLE 2751. The Panzer Regt spread itself out in the area FALAISE-MORTHEAUX-COULIBOEUF 2439 – SASSY 1945 – JORT 2344. 125 Panzer Gr Regt had its I bn well south at MAGNY-LA-CAMPAGNE 2252 with its

II Bn almost on the coast at SANNERVILLE 1368. 192 Panzer Gr Regt was similarly disposed with the I Bn at CARPIQUET 9769 and II Bn at CAZELLE 0376. The anti/tk Bn was in a coastal defence role at PERIERS 0576 while the arty was well back in the area of THURY-HARCOURT 9446 and BRETTE-VILLE-SUR-LAIZE 0653. The wide dispersion of the units of the division was due to the thinness of German Troops on the ground, and the desire to defeat the invasion on the beaches and have a tactical reserve at one and the same time.

16. Not only was 21 Panzer Div dispersed on the ground so that a concentration of all its forces in a short time was virtually impossible, but it was practically emasculated of all its striking power to give effect to the Rundstedt–Rommel compromise plan. If the invasion came within the area or the Orne River the northernmost two Inf bns, one from each of the Panzer Grenadier Regts, were to immediately be put under comd of 716 Inf Div. The A Tk Bn of twenty four 8.8cm guns and the flak unit were also to be taken away from 21 Panzer Div, the former going to 716 Inf Div and the latter to the CAEN flak comd. By this order, any hope of 21 Panzer Div constituting an effective counter-attack force immediately following an Allied landing was irrevocably and effectively gone. It was a measure of the uncertainty of the High Command in the West that one of its most powerful armd formations was largely deprived of its offensive potentiality on 6 June.

D-Day and the day Following

17. It was between midnight and 0100 hours 6 June that Genlt FEUCHTINGER first heard the invasion had begun. Word was received from the forward bn of 125 Panzer Gr Regt that parachutists had begun to drop in the area TROARN 1667 - TOUFFREVILLE 1368. Although technically the unit had ceased to be under his comd the moment the Allies touched down in FRANCE, he nevertheless ordered them to engage the parachutists at once. Because communications were maintained with this bn of 125 Panzer Gr Regt, he held on to them in the following stages of the battle. The Bn of 192 Panzer Gr Regt West of the ORNE was, however, lost to him at that time. When it eventually returned it was worth little more than a company. The flak coy placed under comd of the CAEN flak staff was knocked out by ships' fire by noon of 6 June. Of the twenty four 8.8cm A Tk guns given to 716 Int Div, twenty one had been ordered West from the high ground upon which Genlt FEUCHTINGER had placed them and they did not fire a single shot all during D-Day. The three remaining 8.8s that had been unable to change their position as ordered by 716 Inf Div claimed no less than twelve Allied tks during the landing.

18. From the moment Genlt FEUGHTINGER heard the news of the landing just after midnight until 0700 hours on 6 June, not a single order was received by him from a higher formation. Thus, for six hours after our landing, the comd or the armd formation most immediate to the scene or operations was kept ineffectively and impatiently twiddling his thumbs. The order that he was not to make

any move until he had heard from Army Gp B had been most definite. Nevertheless, at 0630 hours, unable to stand the inaction any longer, the general ordered his div to attack the English 6th Airborne Div which had by now entrenched themselves in a bridgehead over the ORNE. To Genlt FEUCHTINGER, this threat seemed to be the most pressing or all and he felt that the best use or his one hundred and seventy armd vehicles could be made in the elimination of this airborne force. At 0700 hours his first intimation that the higher Comd still existed was given when he was informed that 21 Panzer Div was now under comd of Seventh Army. No order as to its role was issued. Between 0900 and 1000 hours he was placed under comd of 84 Corps which already was overburdened with the affairs of 719, 91, 242, 352 and 716 Inf Divs. 12 SS Panzer Div (*Hitlerjugend*) the only other armd formation immediately available. was in the area MORTAGNEDREUX and as far as Genlt FEUGHTINGER knew, still under the direct comd of Panzer Gruppe West.

19. It was close to 1000 hours on 6 June before 21 Panzer Div received its first operational order from a Higher comd. 84 Corps ordered the formation to stop its move against the 6th Airborne Div and turn West across the Orne where the forces protecting CAEN were rapidly disintegrating 22 Panzer Regt, the armd element, then moving North, had to suddenly change its direction with one battle gp crossing the ORNE at COLOMBELLES 0700 and another battle gp crossing the river at CAEN itself. In addition to 125 Panzer Gr Regt already inextricably committed, the heavy company of the reconnaissance regt, the assault company and some engineers were lopped from the div and left to fight the Allied airborne force. with the hope of containing the bridgehead and hoping the CAEN – TROARN road clear.

20. Once across the ORNE, the Panzer Regt, with about ninety effective tanks and two bns of Inf, attacked from CAEN towards LION-SUR-MER 0781, a village on the channel coast. The enemy, consisting of 3 British and 3 Canadian Inf Divs, had, by this time, made astonishing progress with forces as far South as LEBISEY 0572 and more important still had occupied the high ground (Point 61) at 0677. From this vantage point the Allied A/Tk guns opened fire at 2000 metres and in a short time had knocked out eleven tks of 21 Panzer Div. Genlt FEUCHTINGER became lyrical each time he referred to our A/Tk defences which he constantly described with the adjective "Ausgezeichnet" (excellent). Unable to reach the coast on this road one battle gp attempted to drive forward from PLUMETOT 0478 in the direction of HERMANVILLE-SUR-MER 0779. At 1900 hours one battle gp had actually reached the coast at LION-SUR-MER and the other gp was attempting to bypass the high ground dominated by our [3rd Division's] A/Tk guns.

21. It was at this moment, with the successful dash to the sea completed, that a reinforcement parachute landing of Allied forces took place on both sides of the ORNE. At the same time a sharp attack of English tks from the vicinity of

DOUVRES 0280 forced a withdrawal of the German Tps on the coast, and the div was taken back to a line running from 1470 East of the OREN – North West to ESCOVILLE 1071 – to the ORNE at BLAINVILLE 0873 – curving South to 065715 – and thence North West to 1,000 metres North of EPRON 0272. On his left flank 12 SS Panzer Div (*Hitlerjugend*) was to come in. By the end of this first day 21 Panzer Div had lost 25% of its str and had only seventy tks left to carry on the battle.

Appendix VIII

Generalfeldmarschall Rommel's Report to OKW

Generalfeldmarschall Rommel's weekly report from Army Group B to OKW provides an insight into the German perspective of the first few days of the campaign.

ESTIMATE OF THE SITUATION ON JUNE 11, 1944

The course of the fighting in Normandy so far clearly shows that the objectives of the enemy are:

(1) To establish a deep bridgehead between the Orne and the Vire as a base for a later attack with strong forces into central France, probably in the direction of Paris.
(2) To cut off the Cotentin Peninsula and to take Cherbourg as quickly as possible, in order to gain a large and serviceable harbour. It seems possible, however, as the situation is developing, that the enemy may abandon the occupation of the Cotentin Peninsula if fighting becomes too hard there, and make an early thrust into the interior of France, throwing in all of his resources.

Owing to the obstinate resistance of troops in the coastal defence sectors and the counter-attacks immediately undertaken by the major reserves available, the course of enemy operations has, in spite of the employment of most powerful means of warfare, taken appreciably longer than our adversary had hoped. The enemy also appears to be using more forces than originally intended.

The enemy is visibly reinforcing on land, under the cover of very strong aircraft formations. The Luftwaffe and our navy are not in a position to offer him appreciable opposition, especially by day. Thus the strength of the enemy on land is increasing more quickly than our reserves can reach the front.

Owing to the enemy's overwhelming air superiority it was not possible to bring up the 1st SS Panzer Corps, the 7th *Nebelwerfer* Brigade, III Flak Corps and II *Fallschirimjäger* Corps (Meindl) quickly into the area between the Orne and the Vire, or to make a counter-attack on the enemy forces which had landed. The 7th *Nebelwerfer* Brigade, III Flak Corps and II *Fallschirimjäger* Corps (Meindl) are still on the way up to the front, the I SS Panzer Corps has been forced on to the defensive in hard fighting and is being attacked on its open left flank by superior armoured formations.

The Army Group must content itself for the present with forming a cohesive front between the Orne and the Vire with the forces which are gradually coming up, and allowing the enemy to advance. In these circumstances it is unfortunately not possible to relieve troops still resisting in many coastal positions [on the Cotentin Peninsular and east of the Orne]. The Army Group is trying to replace the panzer formations in action with infantry divisions as soon as possible, and to form mobile reserves with them.

In the next few days, the Army Group intends to remove the centre of its operations to the Carentan-Montebourg area, in order to annihilate the enemy there and to divert the danger threatening Cherbourg. Only when this has been successfully accomplished can the enemy between the Orne and the Vire be attacked. Unfortunately, this operation can no longer be supported by our fighter formations, as there are no longer any airfields near the front at our disposal.

Our operations in Normandy will be rendered exceptionally difficult, and even partially impossible, by the following conditions:

(a) the extraordinarily strong, and in some respects overwhelming superiority of the enemy Air Force.

As I personally and officers of my staff have repeatedly proved, and as unit commanders, especially *Obergruppenfürher* Sepp Dietrich, report, the enemy has complete control of the air over the battle area and up to 100km. behind the front. Almost all transport on roads, byroads and on open country is prevented by day by strong fighter-bomber and bomber formations. Movements of our troops in the battle area by day are almost completely prevented, while the enemy can operate freely. In rear areas all confined areas are continually exposed to attacks, and it is very difficult to bring up the necessary supplies of ammunition and fuel to the troops.

Even the movements of smaller formations, artillery taking up position, deployment of tanks and so on, are immediately bombarded from the air with annihilating effect. Troops and staffs are forced to hide in terrain which provides cover during the day, in order to escape these continual attacks from the air.

On June 9 in the battle area of the SS Corps, numerous enemy fighter bomber formations circled uninterruptedly over the battlefield and strong bomber formations bombarded troops, villages, bridges, and road junctions as heavily as possible without consideration for the population. Neither our flak nor the Luftwaffe seems to be in a position to check this crippling and destructive operation of the enemy Air Force (27,000 sorties in one day). The army and SS troops are defending themselves as well as they can with the means at their disposal, but ammunition is scarce and can be replaced only under the most difficult conditions.

(b) The effect of heavy naval artillery.

Up to 640 heavy calibre guns were used. The effect is so strong that operation with infantry or panzer formations in the area commanded by this

Feldmarshall Rommel with *Obergruppenführer* Sepp Dietrich, the commander of I SS Panzer Corps, who took over the defence of Caen on D+1.

quick-firing artillery is not possible. In spite of this heavy fire garrisons on the coast and the troops sent to counter-attack in the area of Montebourg have held their positions with the utmost tenacity. It must be expected, however, that the enemy warships will intervene further in the fighting on land, especially in the Cotentin Peninsula, if the Luftwaffe and our navy do not succeed in destroying them.

(c) The material equipment of the Anglo-Americans with numerous new weapons and war materials is far superior to the equipment of our divisions. As *Obergruppenfürher* Sepp Dietrich informed me, enemy armoured formations carry on the battle at a range of up to 3,500 meters with maximum expenditure of ammunition and splendidly supported by the enemy Air Force. This was also the case at Alamein. Furthermore, their great superiority in artillery and extremely large supplies of ammunition are increasingly apparent.

(d) Parachute and airborne troops are used in such large numbers and so effectively, that the troops attacked have a difficult task in defending themselves. If enemy airborne forces land in a territory unoccupied by us, they immediately make themselves ready for defence and can be defeated only with difficulty by infantry attacks with artillery support. Further operations of this type, especially in areas not occupied by our troops, must be expected. The Luftwaffe has unfortunately not been able to take action against these formations as was originally planned. Since the enemy can cripple our mobile formations with his Air Force by day, while he operates with fast moving forces and airborne troops, our position is becoming extraordinarily difficult.

I request that the Führer be informed of this.

Rommel
June 12, 1944

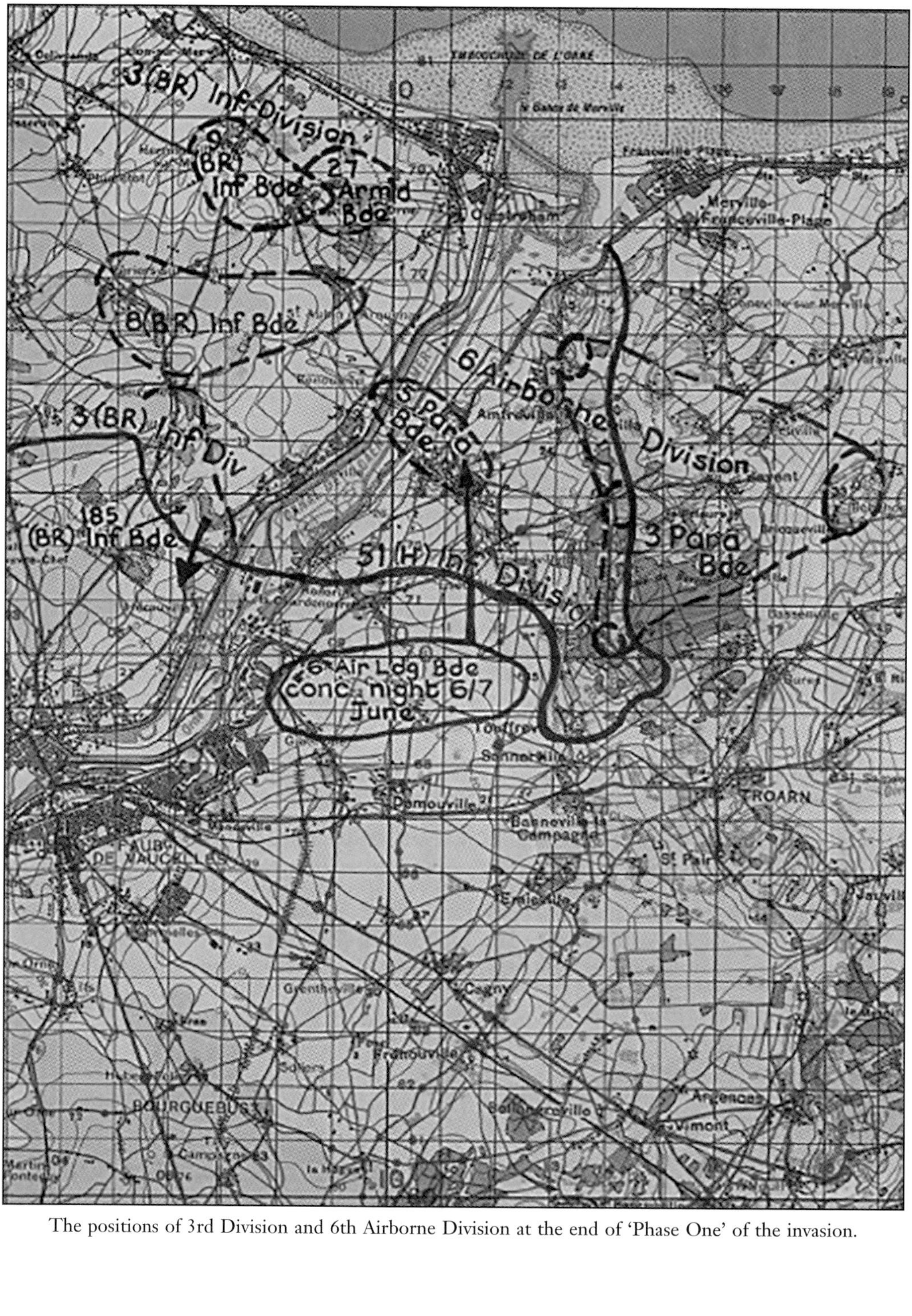

The positions of 3rd Division and 6th Airborne Division at the end of 'Phase One' of the invasion.

Notes

Introduction

1. TNA CAB 44/246.
2. Ingersoll, Ralph. *Top Secret* (Harcourt Brace & Co, New York, 1946).

Chapter 1: Caen and the Development of the 'Master Plan'

1. Morgan, Lt Gen Sir Fredrick, *Overture to Overlord* (Hodder & Stoughton Ltd, London, 1950).
2. Quoted by Eisenhower in *The Struggle for Europe* (Collins, London, 1952).
3. Ibid.
4. Ibid. Eisenhower noted in that 'it was an uphill battle. The shadow of Dunkirk, Norway and Greece still hung over the army ... and few of its senior officers believed that any cross-Channel invasion could succeed except at a ghastly price.' Churchill, believing that 'Overlord should be thrown overboard', advocated an invasion via the Aegean up to the Tehran Conference during the autumn of 1943.
5. Montgomery of El Alamein, *Memoirs* (Collins, London, 1948).
6. Every star has its tail! Despite military secretaries' best efforts commanders still like to have their familiar, tried and tested subordinates follow them.
7. de Guingand, Major General Sir Francis, *Operation Victory* (Hodder & Stoughton, London, 1947).
8. The list of Combined Ops beaches was comprehensive, ranging from small patches of sand below a cleft to the expanse of 6,000-yard Omaha Beach (313).
9. The two Armies chose names for their respective landing areas. Brigadier Belchem wrote in *All in the Day's March* that 'The British beaches were named GOLD, JUNO and SWORD, three words which I picked from an old Army manual which gave short words that were easily pronounced and understood on the phone or radio, for example a Glaswegian talking to a Texan'.
10. The Corps originally consisted of 3rd and 49th British divisions, but politics again prevailed, and 3rd Canadian Division was inserted to land on JUNO Beach instead of the 49th.
11. For discussion on provision of landing craft and shipping see Wilmot, *The Struggle for Europe* (Collins, London, 1952).
12. All commanders, past and present, should start a campaign with a clear plan to defeat the enemy and on which to base logistic estimates, etc. The issue is whether they are able to follow it.
13. For some of the various Allied commanders in attendance to have denied the basic concept of the master plan was disingenuous. Belchem wrote: 'There has been much speculation about when the master plan for operations up to the River Seine was made: indeed, even the fact that it was made in London before D-Day has been challenged. This question can readily be resolved. But it has also been declared that the original master plan was altered or modified during the course of operations between D-Day and the time that the Allies closed up to the River Seine. This was not the case, but I well understand how certain timings and important events which occurred during the battle led to misunderstandings even among responsible senior officers – American and British – and, more recently, among competent historians.' Presentations of plans to a variety of audiences were made on 21 Jan, a briefing and mapex (Ex THUNDERCLAP) on 7–8 Apr, 17 April, 7 May and 15 May.
14. Belchem became BGS (Ops) once the campaign began.
15. Belchem, Major General David, *Victory in Normandy* (Chatto & Windus, London 1981).

16. I Corps monograph, *The Liberation Campaign North West Europe 1944–1945, OVERLORD, D Day 6 June 1944, Book Two* (MLRS/TMA facsimile reprint, 2005).
17. Belchem, *op. cit.*
18. Illing, H.C., *No Better Soldier* (RRF Museum, Warwick, 2021).
19. Second Army Op O No. 1 reproduced in *An Account of the Operations of Second Army in Europe, Vol. 1* (HQ Second Army, August 1945). Beach obstacles started to appear on the Normandy beaches in February 1944.
20. Ibid. NEPTUNE, BIGOT, TOP SECRET, Op O No. 1, dated 21 April 1944.
21. RAF Besson in Oxfordshire was the home of the RAF Photo Reconnaissance Unit (PRU). Interpretation of the photographs was carried out 14 miles away at Danesfield House, Medmenham, Buckinghamshire.
22. TNA WO 171/258.
23. *I Corps, Liberation Campaign North-West Europe 1944–1915 – OVERLORD – D-Day 6 June 1944*, Book 2. (Reprint by MLRS Books).

Chapter 2: The Defenders of Caen

1. Wilhlemsmeyer, *From Invasion to Breakout, Part 1. BAR Special Report – Normandy Campaign, Vol 1* (British Army Review).
2. *Notes on the Operations of 21 Army Group 6 June 1944–5 May 1945.*
3. Overy, Richard, *Why the Allies Won* (Pimlico, London, 2006).
4. Albert Speer, the Reichsminister for Armaments and War Production, ordered the formation of Baukommando Becker. It was based in three French factories around Paris: Matford, Talbot and Hotchkiss.
5. *Schnelle* brigades were conceived as highly mobile formations based in France as a rapid reaction force. Entirely motorized, they were intended to cover ground quickly to reach the scene of an invasion.
6. Feuchtinger was a Nazi party organizer of events such as the Nuremberg Rallies and is widely believed to have gained his appointment on the back of these organizational skills and party interest, rather than military experience.
7. Contrary to received wisdom that there were no or few replacement panzers sent during the battles for Normandy, the 21st received thirty-four Panzer IVs at this time.
8. Wilhelmsmeyer, *From Invasion to Breakout, Part 1. BAR Special Report – Normandy Campaign, Vol. 1* (British Army Review).

Chapter 3: Preparation for Battle

1. In the same way that 2nd Canadian Division had been nominated for the Dieppe Raid ahead of a British division, with the other Empire formation fighting in the Mediterranean there was considerable political pressure from Ottawa for a Canadian division to be committed to battle. Similar political imperatives also dictated that 3rd Canadian Division joined I Corps for the invasion.
2. Quoted in Wright, *Mettle and Pasture* (Hellion & Co, Solihull, 2015).
3. Elison, V.C., *Europe Revisited; The East Riding Yeomanry in the Liberation of Europe* (privately published).
4. UTAH beach, 'being considered to some extent a separate operation' by VII US Corps, called for a separate rehearsal. This was the ill-fated Exercise TIGER held between 22 and 30 April.
5. Slapton Sands in Devon was already cleared, having been used extensively by US Army units since their arrival in the West Country during the autumn of 1943.
6. *Sussex World Today*. Units had been told that they need not respect property in the normal way during this exercise that sought to be as realistic as possible.
7. Amongst those divisions broken up was the 54th East Anglian Division (First Line TA) in December 1943. Its headquarters became the basis of HQ Lines of Communications, 21st Army Group. The division's artillery HQ became HQ8 AGRA, and HQ RE was re-rolled as the RE

HQ of 6th Airborne. 61st Division (War Raised) had already been relegated to Home Service and was also broken up in December 1943 to provide Build Up Control Organisation (BUCO). Twenty-eight battalions or regiments were required to provide hotel service and security.

8. Other nicknames for objectives used in orders, for example COD and HILLMAN, remain in common use.
9. Most accounts refer to 'Portsmouth', but as the naval base facilities there were needed for the Royal Navy, most embarkation in Area A took place at the adjacent beaches, hards and piers of Gosport, Stokes Bay and Southsea.
10. Eisenhower, Dwight D., *Crusade in Europe* (Heinemann Ltd, London, 1948).
11. Bletchley Park was able to decode German weather reports, but this period happened to coincide with one of the regular changes in cipher which took some time to break and resulted in the denial of German met reports from around the coast of France.

Chapter 4: Invasion

1. The Royal Navy had no tidal data for the coast of the Baie de Seine. Therefore, estimates for the landing beaches had to be extrapolated by the Liverpool Tidal Institute and the RN Hydrographic Department at Bath from tidal harmonics they held for Le Havre and Cherbourg. The average tidal range was a substantial at six metres, and the individual beach profiles would determine how quickly the sands were covered. The poor weather also played a marginal role in affecting tidal heights.
2. As with the Allied meteorologists, there was disagreement; some got their forecast for 6 June correct, the majority did not.
3. The most recent false alarm had been on 4 June.
4. Richter, Wilhelm, *716th Infantry Division (1943–28 Jun. 1944)* (NARA Document B 1A35, 1947).
5. Meyer, Hubert, *The History of the 12.SS-Panzerdivision 'Hitlerjugend'* (J.J. Fedorwicz, Winnipeg, 1994).
6. Translation: *Telephone Log of the German 7th Army 6 June – 30 June 1944* (Air Historical Branch, June 1948).
7. BHTV Interview, Assault on Normandy SWORD Beach, (Battlefield History TV/Pen & Sword, 2009).
8. Neave, Airey, *The War Diaries of Julius Neave* (privately published, 1994).
9. G (Ops) (Records), *The Operations of 21 Army Group 6 June 1944–5 May 1945; notes for report writers* (HQ BAOR, 1 September 1945).
10. Before civil twilight is the point before dawn when stars are still visible but it was light enough for the bombardment force to discern the coastline.
11. S3 contained the DDs, Priests and the assault troops of 8 Infantry Brigade.
12. Edwards, Commander Kenneth, *Operation Neptune* (Collins, St James' Place, London, 1946).
13. CMHQ report No. 128.
14. TNA WO 223/4, *50 Div: The Artillery Story, 1943–1944.*
15. Ibid.
16. CMHQ report No. 147.
17. Sources differ between 30 and 35 minutes, as the three regiments of artillery were sailing in a V formation and some came in range before others. The final rounds were to have burst before the first assault troops reached 'danger close' range.
18. The 3rd Division and 3rd Canadian Division fighting on the flanks of the armoured advance 'consumed prodigious amounts of artillery ammunition'.

Chapter 5: The Landing of the Assault Brigade

1. Account given to the author during an anniversary battlefield tour in 2000.
2. One of the tasks of COPPs in their clandestine recces of the beaches and their approaches was to estimate the tidal flow. This was inexact and only valid for a particular day in the tidal cycle. Therefore, estimations were made for other days.

3. Wormald, Major Derick, *The Record of Events – The Assault Landings with 3rd British Infantry Division* (The Pegasus Archive, recovered 09/23).
4. No DDs were sunk by rocket fire, but Lieutenant Burges, standing on his tank turret to con the DD, was mortally wounded by a fragment.
5. National Archives DEFE 2/436.
6. All timings for touchdown are somewhat suspect. Suffice it to say that they were on the beach more or less at the same time.
7. To add a layer of confusion, the *Wiederstandsneste* were renumbered on at least one occasion, when defences were thickened up. This author uses the WN numbers as on a map recovered from a German headquarters on D Day.
8. The Le Hamel bunker in WN-37 is perhaps the most notorious, with eight separate claims to have knocked it out!
9. TNA WO 171/1807.
10. It appears probable that with SWORD Beach's late inclusion in the assault, there was less data on its beach profile, etc., and the miscalculation that put the furthest obstacle in 4′ 6″ of sea water at H Hour was consequently greater than on the other beaches.
11. TNA, *Defences Queen Sector* (21 Army Group RE, DEFE 2/490).
12. CANLOAN, the Canada Loan program of 1944, saw officers lent to British Army units to supplement the by now much-diminished British officer corps and to 'provide alternate avenues for Canadian Army officers to see active service'. A total of 673 Canadian junior officers served with the British Army in North-West Europe.

Chapter 6: MORRIS and HILLMAN

1. TNA, WO 171/1332.
2. Confusingly, the actual Point 61 is 500 yards to the south-west on the Hermanville–Beuville road.
3. Miller, Major General Charles, *History of the 13th/18th Royal Hussars (Queen Mary's Own), 1922–1947* (Chisman, Bradshaw Ltd, London, 1946).
4. Nicholson, Colonel W.N., *The History of the Suffolk Regiment 1927–46* (N&M reprint of 1948 original, 2002).
5. Lovat, Lord, *March Past* (Weidenfeld & Nicholson, 1978).
6. In their memoirs the commandos have ubiquitously been uncomplimentary about 3rd Division soldiers remaining on the beach digging 'themselves into what amounted to a death trap'. While there will always be some faint hearts, the vast majority of those digging in would have been engineers and leading landing serials of the Beach Group whose jobs required them to remain on the beach.
7. Mills-Roberts, Brigadier Derek, *A Commando Chronicle – Clash by Night* (William Kimber, London, 1956).
8. Miller, Major General Charles, *History of the 13th/18th Royal Hussars (Queen Mary's Own) 1922–1947* (Bradshaw, London, 1949).
9. Lummis, Eric, The *1st Battalion The Suffolk Regiment and D Day* (Association Les Amis du Suffolk Regiment, 2002).
10. Lummis explains: 'This problem of communication with the smaller sets was a common one throughout the day. It was partly due to the very great number of sets working in a fairly small area but also because they had been netted several days previously before embarkation and some sets had come slightly off net.'
11. For those visiting HILLMAN, the 'sunken track' should not be confused with the 'sunken road' leading south from Colleville.
12. The barrel of the 17-pounder Firefly was too long for the DD equipment. Consequently, the 13/13 H's Fireflies were concentrated in C Squadron, which temporarily had a higher than usual proportion of 17-pounders.
13. Anon., *The Story of C Squadron – 13th/18th Royal Hussars (QMO)* (The Light Dragoons History Downloads).

14. The figures for the Norfolks' casualties on D-Day have been misreported over the years, and the whole incident has been the subject of much controversy, particularly between them and the Suffolks. The battalion suffered 150 killed and wounded.
15. While the Shermans came under fire from the direction of St Aubin d'Arquenay, during the early evening General Rennie drove through the village and reported it unoccupied.
16. Meyer, Kurt, *Grenadiers* (Fedorowicz, Manitoba, Canada, 2001).

Chapter 7: The Intermediate Brigade and the Drive on Caen

1. Interview with the author, 2004. The 'many colours' is a reference to the rings painted on helmets identifying an individual's role.
2. JAB, *The Story of 33rd Field Regiment RA from D-Day to VE Day* (typed ms, Höxter, June 1945).
3. This is the main body, recce and advance parties of F Beach Commando RN and 5 King's which had been landing since H+20.
4. Hastings Max, *Overlord: D-Day and the Battle for Normandy* (Michael Joseph, 1984).
5. TNA WO 171/702.
6. The information on tanks was from the air forces that were reporting armoured movement north to Caen and in a northerly direction around the city. The 'anti-tank obstacle' was a steep-sided valley running east-west across much of the line of advance.
7. Kortenhaus states that this German infantry was from III/736, but it could equally have been 10/192 *Panzergrenadiers*.
8. TNA CAB 106 3rd Division Narratives D-Day and D+1.
9. TNA CAB/106/999 3rd Division Narratives D-Day and D+1.
10. Gale, R.N., *With the 6th Airborne Division in Normandy* (London, Sampson and Low, 1948).
11. TNA CAB/44, *Liberation Campaign. North West Europe 1944–1945, OVERLORD, D Day 6 June 1944, Book 2* (War Office, 1947).
12. Captain Lummis in his widely circulated article roundly condemns Brigadier Smith for ordering 2 Warwicks to the left, but the orders and the presence of the enemy on the right speak for themselves.
13. TNA WO 171/863.
14. Operating on a narrow front, to maximize the availability of timely artillery support to the infantry the usual practice of a field regiment being allocated to a specific brigade was put aside in favour of distributing FOOs across all three infantry brigades and 27 Armoured Brigade.
15. Littlar, Bob, *BBC Peoples War*, April 2004.
16. https://queensregimentalassociation.org/middlesex-journals/volume-7.html.
17. Author's interview with Lt Oberst Krug, son of Oberst Krug, 2008.
18. https://warchronicle.com/.
19. TNA WO171/1341.
20. https://www.soldiersofshropshire.co.uk/.
21. Ibid.
22. Murray, Leonard, *The Wellingtonian* (Wellington Grammar School, 1945).
23. Kortenhaus, Werner, *The Combat History of the 21 Panzer Division* (Helion, Solihull, 2014)
24. Interview by Peter John, England, November 1999.
25. The effective range of the KwK 40, L/48 7.5-cm main armament of the Panzer IV was superior to the standard 75mm and 6-pounder guns but not to the 17-pounder or 3-inch guns of the Firefly and M10. The real German disadvantage was that the British were essentially static, probably in hull-down positions, while the panzers were moving and firing in the open.
26. 'Jockeying forward' or appearing on the ridge line until no longer in the enemy's arc of fire.
27. As the 1:25,000 map shows, Lebisey Wood was half orchard and half woodland.

Chapter 8: The Reserve Brigade

1. TNA WO 171/1384.
2. Across the assault divisions of the Second British Army, numerous bicycles had been issued, with at least one rifle company being so mounted to deliver the planned exploitation. The Commando

cycle troops were the first to arrive at Objective RUGGER, but most bicycles were abandoned on D-Day. However, 8 DLI 151 Bde (GOLD) were recorded attempting to use their bikes in a night move across country to Point 103 on D+3, after which they too abandoned them.
3. The target areas on SWORD Beach were nicknamed EMDEN, FÜSSEN and FREIBURG.
4. TNA WO 171/616.
5. Farrell, Trooper Jack, *BBC People's War*, 2005.
6. The source of the ordnance that hit brigade HQ is disputed. The Luftwaffe launched over 300 sorties against the assault area. Most were low-level tip-and-run strikes. The number of Allied sorties was more than ten times this number. The particular raid that hit 9 Brigade may have been carried out by six or eight JU-88 aircraft.
7. Quoted in Mace, *Forrard: The story of the East Riding Yeomanry* (Pen & Sword, Barnsley, 2001).
8. On D-Day even the Shermans that were to be delivered by LSTs and Rhino ferries were waterproofed as they were likely to have to wade to some extent.
9. Kortenhaus, Werner, *The Combat History of the 21.Panzer Division* (Helion & Co, Solihull, 2014).
10. TNA WO 171/863
11. Schulmann, Milton, *Defeat in the West* (Secker & Warburg, London 1947).
12. Scarffe, Norman, *Assault Division* (Collins, London, 1947).
13. Post-war interview quoted by CMHQ.
14. Zetterling, Niklas, *Normandy 1944: German Military Organization* (Fedorowicz Publishing Inc, Winnipeg, 2000).

Chapter 9: Lebisey – 185 Infantry Brigade's Battle

1. Author's interview, 2006, with Hubert Meyer 1A (Chief of Staff) of 12th *Hitlerjugend* SS Panzer Division.
2. Air attack on soft-skinned vehicles did have an indirect effect on panzer losses by depriving them of fuel and spares.
3. All the timings quoted in paragraphs 66–69 above are suspect. The War Diaries of 2 Warwick, 7 Field Regimental Headquarters and 185 British Infantry Brigade all vary widely.
4. Illing, H.C., *No Better Soldier* (RRF Museum, Warwick, 2001).
5. TNA WO 171/1387.
6. TNA CAB 44/247.
7. *The Battalion:The History of the 1st Battalion The Royal Norfolk Regiment during the World War, 1939–45* (Jarrold & Sons, Norwich, 1947).
8. TNA WO 171/1387.

Chapter 10: Cambes-en-Plaine – 9 Infantry Brigade's Battle

1. Wilson, Revd W.I.G., *Short History, 1st Bn KOSB* (privately published, 1945).
2. Elliston, V.C., *Europe Revisited: the East Riding Yeomanry in the Liberation of Europe* (privately published).
3. Quoted in Meyer, *The History of the 12.SS-Panzerdivision Hitlerjugend* (Fedorwicz, Winnipeg, 1994). *Oberleutnant* Fusen was one of the non-SS commanders, his qualification to serve in the division being his role as a leader in the Hitler Youth movement.
4. Meyer, Hubert, *The History of the 12.SS-Panzerdivision Hitlerjugend* (Fedorowicz, Winnipeg, 1994).
5. TNA Cab 44/247.
6. 3rd Division had yet to comply with the pre-invasion instruction that emanated from SHAEF to adopt the American 'H Hour' and use the traditional British red for enemy forces and blue for 'own forces' when marking maps.
7. Mace, Paul, *Forrard: the Story of the East Riding Yeomanry* (Pen & Sword, Barnsley, 2001).
8. Such were the levels of casualties that 21st Army Group had to introduce a third staff casualty planning figure beyond 'normal' and 'intense' – 'double intense'.

Chapter 11: 'The End of the First Phase'

1. de Guingand, Major General Sir Francis, *Operation Victory* (Hodder & Stoughton, London, 1947).
2. TNA CAB 44/247.
3. Administrative History of 21 Army Group, 6 June 1944–8 May 1945 (HQ BAOR, GERMANY, November 1945).
4. TNA CAB 44/247

Appendix I: Extracts from 3rd Infantry Divisions Op O No. 1

1. TNA WO 171/411

A tank crew of the 13/18 Hussars rest and write home at the end of the first phase of the battle of Normandy.

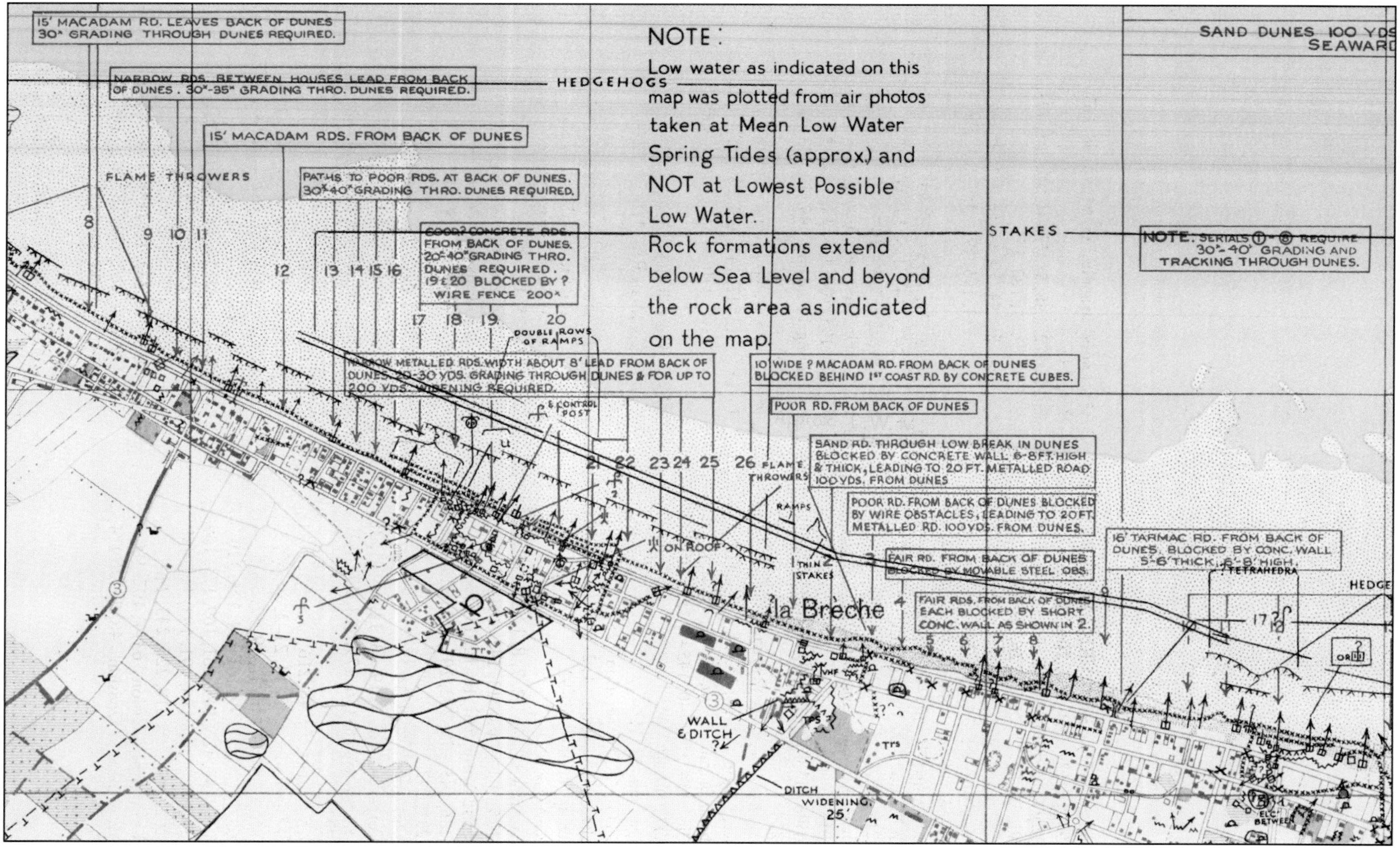

A section of the 1:12,500-GSGS-4490 Ouistreham sheet showing detail of the defences on SWORD Beach.

Index